Academic Mobility Programs and Engagement:
Emerging Research and Opportunities

Donna M Velliaris
Independent Researcher, Singapore

A volume in the Advances in Higher Education and Professional Development (AHEPD) Book Series

Published in the United States of America by
    IGI Global
    Information Science Reference (an imprint of IGI Global)
    701 E. Chocolate Avenue
    Hershey PA, USA 17033
    Tel: 717-533-8845
    Fax: 717-533-8661
    E-mail: cust@igi-global.com
    Web site: http://www.igi-global.com

Copyright © 2020 by IGI Global. All rights reserved. No part of this publication may be reproduced, stored or distributed in any form or by any means, electronic or mechanical, including photocopying, without written permission from the publisher.
Product or company names used in this set are for identification purposes only. Inclusion of the names of the products or companies does not indicate a claim of ownership by IGI Global of the trademark or registered trademark.

Library of Congress Cataloging-in-Publication Data

Names: Velliaris, Donna M., 1971- editor.
Title: Academic mobility programs and engagement : emerging research and
  opportunities / Donna M. Velliaris, editor.
Description: Hershey, PA : Information Science Reference, 2020. | Includes
  bibliographical references and index. | Summary: ""This book examines
  international and study abroad programs and their effect on students and
  student preparation"--Provided by publisher"-- Provided by publisher.
Identifiers: LCCN 2019031657 (print) | LCCN 2019031658 (ebook) | ISBN
  9781799816072 (hardcover) | ISBN 9781799816089 (paperback) | ISBN
  9781799816096 (ebook)
Subjects: LCSH: Foreign study. | Student mobility. | Education and
  globalization.
Classification: LCC LB2375 .A33 2020 (print) | LCC LB2375 (ebook) | DDC
  370.116--dc23
LC record available at https://lccn.loc.gov/2019031657
LC ebook record available at https://lccn.loc.gov/2019031658

This book is published in the IGI Global book series Advances in Higher Education and Professional Development (AHEPD) (ISSN: 2327-6983; eISSN: 2327-6991)

British Cataloguing in Publication Data
A Cataloguing in Publication record for this book is available from the British Library.

All work contributed to this book is new, previously-unpublished material.
The views expressed in this book are those of the authors, but not necessarily of the publisher.

For electronic access to this publication, please contact: eresources@igi-global.com.

Advances in Higher Education and Professional Development (AHEPD) Book Series

ISSN:2327-6983
EISSN:2327-6991

Editor-in-Chief: Jared Keengwe, University of North Dakota, USA

MISSION

As world economies continue to shift and change in response to global financial situations, job markets have begun to demand a more highly-skilled workforce. In many industries a college degree is the minimum requirement and further educational development is expected to advance. With these current trends in mind, the **Advances in Higher Education & Professional Development (AHEPD) Book Series** provides an outlet for researchers and academics to publish their research in these areas and to distribute these works to practitioners and other researchers.

AHEPD encompasses all research dealing with higher education pedagogy, development, and curriculum design, as well as all areas of professional development, regardless of focus.

COVERAGE

- Adult Education
- Assessment in Higher Education
- Career Training
- Coaching and Mentoring
- Continuing Professional Development
- Governance in Higher Education
- Higher Education Policy
- Pedagogy of Teaching Higher Education
- Vocational Education

IGI Global is currently accepting manuscripts for publication within this series. To submit a proposal for a volume in this series, please contact our Acquisition Editors at Acquisitions@igi-global.com or visit: http://www.igi-global.com/publish/.

The Advances in Higher Education and Professional Development (AHEPD) Book Series (ISSN 2327-6983) is published by IGI Global, 701 E. Chocolate Avenue, Hershey, PA 17033-1240, USA, www.igi-global.com. This series is composed of titles available for purchase individually; each title is edited to be contextually exclusive from any other title within the series. For pricing and ordering information please visit http://www.igi-global.com/book-series/advances-higher-education-professional-development/73681. Postmaster: Send all address changes to above address. ©© 2020 IGI Global. All rights, including translation in other languages reserved by the publisher. No part of this series may be reproduced or used in any form or by any means – graphics, electronic, or mechanical, including photocopying, recording, taping, or information and retrieval systems – without written permission from the publisher, except for non commercial, educational use, including classroom teaching purposes. The views expressed in this series are those of the authors, but not necessarily of IGI Global.

Titles in this Series

For a list of additional titles in this series, please visit:
https://www.igi-global.com/book-series/advances-higher-education-professional-development/73681

Technology-Enhanced Formative Assessment Practices in Higher Education
Christopher Ewart Dann (University of Southern Queensland, Australia) and Shirley O'Neill (University of Southern Queensland, Australia)
Information Science Reference • ©2020 • 348pp • H/C (ISBN: 9781799804260) • US $195.00

Handbook of Research on Innovative Pedagogies and Best Practices in Teacher Education
Jared Keengwe (University of North Dakota, USA)
Information Science Reference • ©2020 • 422pp • H/C (ISBN: 9781522592327) • US $260.00

The Formation of Intellectual Capital and Its Ability to Transform Higher Education Institutions and the Knowledge Society
Edgar Oliver Cardoso Espinosa (Instituto Politécnico Nacional, Mexico)
Information Science Reference • ©2019 • 312pp • H/C (ISBN: 9781522584612) • US $195.00

Engaging Teacher Candidates and Language Learners With Authentic Practice
Chesla Ann Lenkaitis (Binghamton University, USA) and Shannon M. Hilliker (Binghamton University, USA)
Information Science Reference • ©2019 • 368pp • H/C (ISBN: 9781522585435) • US $195.00

Case Study Methodology in Higher Education
Annette Baron (William Paterson University, USA) and Kelly McNeal (William Paterson University, USA)
Information Science Reference • ©2019 • 393pp • H/C (ISBN: 9781522594291) • US $195.00

Workforce Education at Oil and Gas Companies in the Permian Basin Emerging Research and Opportunities
Julie Neal (Dearing Sales, USA) and Brittany Lee Neal (Axip Energy Services, USA)
Business Science Reference • ©2019 • 131pp • H/C (ISBN: 9781522584643) • US $160.00

For an entire list of titles in this series, please visit:
https://www.igi-global.com/book-series/advances-higher-education-professional-development/73681

701 East Chocolate Avenue, Hershey, PA 17033, USA
Tel: 717-533-8845 x100 • Fax: 717-533-8661
E-Mail: cust@igi-global.com • www.igi-global.com

For Sofia & Leonardo

Table of Contents

Preface viii

Acknowledgment xvi

Chapter 1
To Study Abroad: A Complex Matrix of Influences 1
    Donna M. Velliaris, Independent Researcher, Singapore

Chapter 2
Intercultural Awareness and Short-Term Study Abroad Programs: An
Invitation to Liminality 31
    David Starr-Glass, SUNY Empire State College, USA

Chapter 3
Designing Short-Term, Faculty-Led Study Abroad Programs: A Value Co-
Creation Framework 57
    Sven Tuzovic, Queensland University of Technology, Australia

Chapter 4
The Academic Second Language (L2) Socialization and Acculturation of
International Exchange Students 80
    Jane Jackson, The Chinese University of Hong Kong, Hong Kong

Chapter 5
Facilitating International Healthcare Experiences: A Guide for Faculty,
Administrators, and Healthcare Providers 111
    Jon P. Wietholter, West Virginia University, USA
    Renier Coetzee, University of the Western Cape, South Africa
    Beth Nardella, West Virginia University, USA
    Douglas Slain, West Virginia University, USA

Chapter 6
Towards a Culturally Reflective Practitioner: Pre-Service Student Teachers in
Teaching Practicums Abroad 143
    Karin Vogt, University of Education Heidelberg, Germany

Chapter 7
Development of an Enhanced Study Abroad Curriculum in Teacher
Education 198
    Yasemin Kırkgöz, Cukurova University, Turkey

Appendix.. 225

Glossary 231

Related Readings... 243

About the Contributors 258

Index.. 262

Preface

Bienvenido, Bonjour, Geia, Guten Tag, Hei, Hej, Helo, Hola, Jambo, Konnichiwa, Namasté, Shalóm... The world contains billions of people in thousands of unique and distinct cultures. It is likely that one will never have enough time to experience them all, but with a study abroad program, one can have the opportunity to gain a greater understanding of our shared humanity and how it transcends borders.

Throughout this volume, the terms exchange student, foreign exchange student, foreign pupil, foreign student, international student, and/or overseas student are synonymous. And, 'Study Abroad' is the term given to a program that allows a student to live in a foreign country and attend a foreign university. In many cases, two universities have an arrangement, which allows them to exchange students so that these students can learn about a foreign culture and broaden their horizons. The chosen program may grant credit for courses taken at the foreign institution and some also arrange for a work-study or internship agreement. Principally, there needs to be an 'educative' connection between 'home' and 'host' destinations/organizations for advancing HE teaching and learning opportunities (Velliaris, 2016b, p. xxviii). That is, the more relevant the international experience is to the overall educational objectives of the degree program/specific course, the more students will benefit.

The internationalization of HE contributes to students' attainment of global career-readiness competencies desirable in a global economy—a mass of skills to prepare them to be members of a global workforce upon graduation. Proponents stress a number of 'positive' academic, career, intercultural, personal, and social benefits or key competencies for students undertaking a study abroad venture, including marketable skills such as: accepting international values and beliefs; adapting to unfamiliar situations; boosting one's sense of adventure; building confidence and increasing self-awareness; communicating across cultural and linguistic boundaries; deepening learning and inspiring rigor; detecting ethnocentrism; encouraging solidarity; engaging in active observation; enhancing civic-mindedness; facilitating intellectual growth; fostering empathy; practicing reflexive understanding; preventing stereotypes and prejudice; showing cultural humility; tolerating ambiguity; and

Preface

viewing situations from unique perspectives (see Crossman & Clarke, 2010; Hadis, 2005; Stebleton, Soria, & Cherney, 2013; Tarrant, Rubin, & Stoner, 2013; Velliaris, 2018b).

Traditionally, the standard reason to study abroad was the opportunity to increase second language (L2) proficiency. Many students study abroad to enhance language skills that will make them more competitive in the job market. When students are immersed in a culture where a L2 is primarily spoken, they make monumental gains in the acquisition of that language that could not take place inside a classroom. Language-focused HE study abroad programs offer chronological repetition of the TL. In intensive L2 learning, the shortened cycles between classes may equip participants with the benefits of a truly holistic educational experience (Campbell, 2016). Relatedly, students may live with host families, volunteer with local organizations, and explore the language through real-life and enriching excursions (see Velliaris, 2018a).

Significantly, learning a foreign language also has its own intrinsic value apart from the monetary bonus. One will learn so much about the way language and communication work in general, and speaking the local language allows interaction with other cultures on a deeper level. Plus, while learning another language is challenging, it is incredibly gratifying when one can finally express themself in a way that locals understand. And, wherever one goes, local life is different—from social greetings to going to the grocery store, from making friends to riding the bus—living abroad is both exciting and challenging. In essence, the community becomes an extended classroom that fosters L2 fluency while heightening one's perception of another culture and its people.

Some students may think that traveling abroad will hamper their studies when in fact it is quite the opposite. When done in a way that advances one's skills and knowledge, an international experience is incredibly desirable in the current globalized job market. Global encounters can facilitate a clearer sense of personal and professional purpose i.e., vision and ambition that may otherwise have been overlooked by staying domestic. Nevertheless, the decision to lead (*faculty*) and/ or participate (*student*) in study abroad is not always straightforward. Study abroad can be stressful and extremely tiring, both physically and mentally. The amount of work that is required should reflect this reality. This does not mean that the courses are less rigorous or that the students are learning less. They are actually learning more, but in varied ways. Certainly, academic engagement and student success do not automatically occur and are dependent on specific factors that shape the study abroad experience.

***

Learn traditional and non-traditional fine arts on the Greek island of Paros. Acquire new skills in textiles and find inspiration that can be applied to fabric, accessories, and furnishings in Accra, Ghana. Do a 4-week program on International Luxury Brand Marketing and International Business Management in one of the world's most vibrant cities, Paris. The ACICIS Creative Arts and Design Professional Practicum involves students collaborating with Indonesian peers and creative practitioners to produce work including, but not limited to animations, blogs, online installations, short films, social media apps, sound and video art, and websites. What about a 6-week Shanghai Summer Program taught entirely in English that offers an excellent introduction to contemporary China. It also provides a first-hand initiation into the essential aspects of doing business in China and its interaction with other important regions in the world.

Study 'Culture and Psychopathology'—mental health in a cross-cultural perspective—at the University of Bergen, Norway, where the crux of this course is to examine mental illness, their manifestations, diagnosis, and treatment in different cultural societies. Live aboard a catamaran sailboat in the British Virgin Islands, while being immersed in marine science and mastering practical skills that are needed for the toolbox of any aspiring aquatic biologist. Partake in a short-term sustainable development project in Ecuador, where students converge on a biodynamic grassroots farm in rural South America to learn about permaculture, biodiversity, and conservation. Or, get hands-on in all facets of wildlife capture and procedures on a 3-week course, managed by local wildlife veterinarians in South Africa.

Consider a program for midwifery, nutrition and pharmacy students with a unique work-integrated learning opportunity in Tonga, as well as in Samoa, where students can study health and wellness in the South Pacific. In Shanghai, step back in time with visits to traditional water towns like Wuzhen and Zhujiajiao, lined with narrow cobbled lanes, stone bridges, and rich history. Or visit the Pokhara Valley in rural Nepal to help rebuild, educate, and assist the children within the Nepali community. In Vienna, take courses in Music History, Music Theory, and Performance Studies, in a city full of music culture. Study in the same city that Mozart and Beethoven became household names and conduct your own way toward musical mastery with the support of knowledgeable professors and friends.

Travel to Bhutan to study animal ecology and the biogeography of the Eastern Himalayas. The Real-Life Applications of Intelligent Designs program in Latvia, provides students with hands-on and practical experiences such as Computer and Robotic System Design, Technical Graphics, Artificial Intelligence, Robot Systems Modelling and Microprocessor Controllers. This program takes a multidisciplinary approach with incorporated teamwork, so that students can successfully and efficiently reach their end goal, which is to create a functional robot. The University of La

Preface

Salle in Mexico has tremendous linkages with community organizations working in some of the poorer areas of Mexico City. This allows participants to get a feel for the 'front line' of dealing with health issues in a developing country.

International Human Rights Law in Argentina aims to provide students with a rich understanding of the history of 'Human Rights' abuse in Argentina over the last 40-years. This program gives students an understanding of the history of Human Rights abuse in Argentina over the past 4-decades, covering topics such as police abuse, specifically use of excessive force, and prison conditions. Tel Aviv is at the heart of the global startup movement, and experience with young businesses there allows students to gather intelligence on the latest trends and enhance their own innovative capabilities. Selected student entrepreneurs will spend 4-weeks based at some of Israel's most influential technology startups. Working alongside energetic and experienced innovators, students will learn first-hand the process of founding, investing and growing an early stage business in a global startup ecosystem.

International Relations and Threats to Global Security 3-week program in the Czech Republic covers topics such as cyber security, energy security, extremism, and terrorism. This intensive and dynamic program involves academic classes, active group work, guest presentations and visits to organizations such as the UN, OPEC, Radio Free Europe and others. The Maastricht University International Student Guesthouse is located within walking distance from downtown Maastricht behind the Court of Justice. Study Forensic Psychology encompassing the main themes of cognitive biases in the legal context, eyewitness memory, interviewing and interrogation, and the association of mental illness and crime. Or consider an exciting 4-week heritage-focused internship project, combined with an introduction to Chinese language and culture. This project is set amongst UNESCO recognized sites of historical importance in Kaiping in Guangdong province, China.

***

Based on the literature, it is difficult for anyone to deny the benefits of students participating in study abroad programs. Students returning from studying abroad usually describe the experience as "life changing". Yet, while these programs should be 'enjoyable', they should not be promoted or viewed as an 'easy study option' or 'time-off'. Studying abroad is not a vacation, and a vacation is not synonymous to study abroad (Perry, Stoner, & Tarrant, 2012). The legitimacy of study abroad is linked with fulfilling major/minor and/or elective requirements that students would take even if they had remained at their 'home' institution. Some students experience culture shock, homesickness, attachment, and/or mental health issues. Others will have disciplinary problems such as alcohol abuse, drug use, or cheating. Since the happenings of such programs are changeable—not always comfortable or even

Preface

positive—there are many 'Push-Pull' variables to contemplate from commonality of language; geographic location; healthcare facilities; ideological affinity; political interests; racial tolerance; reputation; safety; security; and social atmosphere (e.g., A. B. Ahmad, Hassan, & Al-Ahmedi, 2017; S. Z. Ahmad & Buchanan, 2017; Bodycott, 2009; Fang & Wang, 2014; Li & Bray, 2007; Li & Zhang, 2011; Mazzarol, 1998; Mazzarol & Soutar, 2002; Ming, 2010; Velliaris, 2016a).

This book presents *seven* chapters spanning various topics as presented by educators across the globe; *seven* different cultural contexts. The thread that binds these chapters together is the underlying notion that study abroad experiences, if implemented well, are fundamentally inspiring, enriching, and transformative. As with the first volume associated with this book, this volume was conceived with the following objectives (adapted Velliaris, 2016b, pp. xxviii-xxix):

- To broaden pedagogical expertise through connecting, informing and leading empirically-based and rigorous research activities associated with study abroad at the HE-level. The information may enrich existing programs/ courses, or create new ones by improving offerings and raising standards so that study abroad opportunities align with best practices, and successfully meet global challenges;
- To engage in intellectual exchange and present research that brings together concepts, strategies and approaches for internationalization, exchange, and study abroad issues surrounding outbound staff and students, and the cross-border delivery of HE across many parts of the world; and
- To facilitate deep(er) discussion into current and future research priorities with respect to theoretical, conceptual and practical aspects of internationalization via study abroad. This includes the motivations for, and the obstacles facing, regional, national and institutional policies, procedures, and methods related to the delivery of HE abroad.

The chapter contributors offer a variety of programs/initiatives related to international student mobility, cross cultural competency, recruitment marketplace, and study abroad programs. In order, the chapters are presented as:

Chapter 1—*To Study Abroad: A Complex Matrix of Influences*; Chapter 2—*Intercultural Awareness and Short-Term Study Abroad Programs: An Invitation to Liminality*; Chapter 3—*Designing Short-Term, Faculty-Led Study Abroad Programs: A Value Co-Creation Framework*; Chapter 4—*The Academic Second Language (L2) Socialization and Acculturation of International Exchange Students*; Chapter 5—*Facilitating International Healthcare Experiences: A Guide for Faculty, Administrators, and Healthcare Providers*; Chapter 6—*Towards a Culturally*

xii

Preface

Reflective Practitioner: Pre-Service Teachers in Teaching Practicums Abroad; and Chapter 7—*Development of an Enhanced Study Abroad Curriculum in Teacher Education.*

I trust this book will be a useful resource for those who wish to develop and strengthen existing and/or new programs in their HEIs as it is no longer sufficient that educators explore intercultural and global learning in the abstract—from the confines of their campus or classroom—we must foster programs that offer direct learning experiences around the globe. The wide range of programs currently available makes study abroad more flexible, affordable and accessible than ever before. While not everyone can go abroad for a full year, we hope you will agree after reading this book that there are study abroad options for everyone. Thus, I invite readers to discuss, share, and expand upon their own teachings, learnings and findings in the area of study abroad as there is much room for continued investment in this worthy endeavor.

***

From participants whose lifelong dreams come true, to those who use their experience to impact their research, to a change of attitude towards traveling abroad, to camaraderie that blossomed, and to a deep and profound impact that occurred, indeed, study abroad evokes a myriad of emotions. *Happy. Sad. Excited. Homesick. Independent. Lonely. Inspired. Exhausted. Energized. Shocked. Thrilled. Ill. Lost. Confused. Entertained. Bored. Accepted. Rejected. Annoyed. Content. Frustrated. Tired. Embarrassed. Overwhelmed. Free. Happy. Sad...*

Donna M. Velliaris
Independent Researcher, Singapore

REFERENCES

Ahmad, A. B., Hassan, H. A., & Al-Ahmedi, M. W. A. (2017). Motivations of government-sponsored Kurdish students for pursuing postgraduate studies abroad: An exploratory study. *Journal of Studies in International Education, 21*(2), 105–119. doi:10.1177/1028315316662982

Ahmad, S. Z., & Buchanan, F. R. (2017). Motivation factors in students decision to study at international branch campuses in Malaysia. *Studies in Higher Education, 42*(4), 651–668. doi:10.1080/03075079.2015.1067604

Bodycott, P. (2009). Choosing a higher education study abroad destination: What mainland Chinese parents and students rate as important. *Journal of Research in International Education, 8*(3), 349–373. doi:10.1177/1475240909345818

Campbell, R. (2016). Language learners' social interaction during study abroad: Opportunities, satisfaction, and benefits. In D. M. Velliaris & D. Coleman-George (Eds.), *Handbook of research on study abroad programs and outbound mobility* (pp. 722–754). Hershey, PA: IGI Global. doi:10.4018/978-1-5225-0169-5.ch029

Crossman, J. E., & Clarke, M. (2010). International experience and graduate employability: Stakeholder perceptions on the connection. *Higher Education, 59*(5), 599–613. doi:10.100710734-009-9268-z

Fang, W., & Wang, S. (2014). Chinese students' choice of transnational higher education in a globalized higher education market: A case study of W university. *Journal of Studies in International Education, 18*(5), 475–494. doi:10.1177/1028315314523989

Hadis, B. F. (2005). Why are they better students when they come back? Determinants of academic focusing gains in the study abroad experience. *Frontiers: The Interdisciplinary Journal of Study Abroad, 11*, 57–70.

Li, M., & Bray, M. (2007). Cross-border flows of students for higher education: Push–pull factors and motivations of mainland Chinese students in Hong Kong and Macau. *Higher Education, 53*(6), 791–818. doi:10.100710734-005-5423-3

Li, M., & Zhang, Y. (2011). Two-way flows of higher education students in mainland China in a global market: Trends, characteristics and problems. In S. Marginson (Ed.), *Higher education in the Asia-Pacific* (pp. 309–327). Springer. doi:10.1007/978-94-007-1500-4_16

Mazzarol, T. (1998). Critical success factors for international education marketing. *International Journal of Educational Management, 12*(4), 163–175. doi:10.1108/09513549810220623

Mazzarol, T., & Soutar, G. N. (2002). 'Push-pull' factors influencing international student destination choice. *International Journal of Educational Management, 16*(2), 82–90. doi:10.1108/09513540210418403

Ming, J. S. K. (2010). Institutional factors influencing students' college choice decision in Malaysia: A conceptual framework. *International Journal of Business and Social Science, 1*(3), 53–58.

Perry, L., Stoner, L., & Tarrant, M. (2012). More than a vacation: Short-term study abroad as a critically reflective, transformative learning experience. *Creative Education, 3*(5), 679–683. doi:10.4236/ce.2012.35101

Preface

Stebleton, M. J., Soria, K. M., & Cherney, B. (2013). The high impact of education abroad: College students' engagement in international experiences and the development of intercultural competencies. *Frontiers: The Interdisciplinary Journal of Study Abroad, 22*, 1–24.

Tarrant, M. A., Rubin, D. L., & Stoner, L. (2013). The added value of study abroad fostering a global citizenry. *Journal of Studies in International Education, 18*(2), 141–161. doi:10.1177/1028315313497589

Velliaris, D. M. (2016a). Choosing the right pathway: A matrix of influences related to selection of higher education destination abroad. In K. Bista & C. Foster (Eds.), *Global perspectives and local challenges surrounding international student mobility* (pp. 179–200). Hershey, PA: IGI Global. doi:10.4018/978-1-4666-9746-1.ch010

Velliaris, D. M. (2016b). Preface. In D. M. Velliaris & D. Coleman-George (Eds.), *Handbook of research on study abroad programs and outbound mobility* (pp. xxvii–xxxviii). Hershey, PA: IGI Global. doi:10.4018/978-1-5225-0169-5

Velliaris, D. M. (2018a). Preface. In D. M. Velliaris (Ed.), *Study abroad contexts for enhanced foreign language learning* (pp. xvi–xix). Hershey, PA: IGI Global. doi:10.4018/978-1-5225-3814-1

Velliaris, D. M. (2018b, December). Study abroad: Not all classrooms have four walls. *IGI Global Online Newsroom.* Retrieved from https://www.igi-global.com/newsroom/archive/study-abroad-not-all-classrooms/4017/

Acknowledgment

Foremost, I would like to thank each author for their contribution; heartfelt time and expertise shared and without whose support this book would not have become a reality. I feel honored to be able to share their vision and innovative thinking with educators around the world.

Traveling: it leaves you speechless then turns you into a storyteller. – Ibm Battuta

I am immensely thankful to my family and friends for encouraging me to publish this research work. It was indeed their love, sacrifice and support that helped me to concentrate and persevere in this direction. Their confidence in me helped me overcome an otherwise difficult academic year.

I would rather own a little and see the world, than own the world and see a little. – Alexander Sattler

I hope this book will promote an increased interest in and appreciation for cross cultural studies, its applications *in* and implications *for* our world, and the mission of HEIs to promote the development of all students as global citizens.

Travel is still the most intense mode of learning. – Kevin Kelly

Donna M. Velliaris
Independent Researcher, Singapore

Chapter 1
To Study Abroad:
A Complex Matrix of Influences

Donna M. Velliaris
Independent Researcher, Singapore

ABSTRACT

Universities globally are increasingly seeking to improve the international mobility of their students. There are several latent benefits that accrue to a university whose faculty and/or students actively participate in international exchange programs. Essentially, this can lead to an increase in the capacity to develop international relationships, greater diversity in the student population with all the benefits that stem from diversity, opportunities for benchmarking against best practices, and the university's international reputation spreading on a global scale. Drawing on extant literature, this descriptive chapter reviews many and varied scholarly works to elicit a comprehensive range of 'Push-Pull' factors or 'a complex matrix of influences' that play a role in tertiary-level students' decision-making in relation to study abroad.

DOI: 10.4018/978-1-7998-1607-2.ch001

Copyright © 2020, IGI Global. Copying or distributing in print or electronic forms without written permission of IGI Global is prohibited.

INTRODUCTION

Study abroad offers an invaluable chance to discover a diverse culture through a personal, professional, and educationally enriching experience. School choice, however, is not susceptible to 'one' definitive analysis. Different kinds of analysis bring out and highlight different aspects of and patterns of educational choice. The decision to facilitate (*faculty*) and/or undertake (*student*) a study abroad experience is not always a simple or straightforward one. Principally, there needs to be an 'educative' connection between the 'home' and 'host' destination/organization for advancing HE teaching and learning opportunities (Velliaris, 2018). Undoubtedly, the more relevant the international experience is to the overall educational objectives of the program/course, the more participants will benefit. Though there may be a plethora of recurring themes and patterns, attempts to reduce choice-making to one simple formula or metaphor will lead to dangerous over-simplification and misrepresentation.

BACKGROUND

The Push-Pull Model of International Student Choice

The 'Push-Pull' model was originally developed to explain the factors influencing the movement of people for migration (E. S. Lee, 1966), but it has since become the most common tool used by educational researchers to aid the examination and explanation of international student motivations and decisions. The model has been used to understand international student flows, the decision or motivation to study abroad, and international students' choice of country and higher education institution (HEI). Although the basic 'Push-Pull' model of international student choice is valuable as an explanatory mechanism, it does have limitations (Li & Bray, 2007).

Both 'Push-Pull' factors are forces that impact on students' behaviors and choices, but the individual preferences and personal characteristics of students are largely unaccounted for. Individual students may react to different 'Push-Pull' factors in different ways. Various researchers have built upon this model to develop other sophisticated conceptual models of international student choice (see Velliaris & Coleman-George, 2016). Relatedly, Mazzarol and Soutar (2002) recognized that the decision process through which an international/foreign student moves when selecting a final study destination, appears to involve at least *three* distinct stages (pp. 85-86):

- **Stage One:** The student must decide to study internationally, rather than locally. This can be influenced by a series of 'push' factors within the home country. Once the decision to study abroad has been made the next decision is the selection of a host country.
- **Stage Two:** Certain 'pull' factors become important, making one host country relatively more attractive than another.
- **Stage Three:** The student selects a HEI. A variety of additional 'pull' factors make a HEI more attractive than its competitors. Such factors include alliances or coalitions, an institution's reputation for quality, degree of innovation, market profile, offshore teaching programs, promotion and marketing efforts e.g., the use of agents and advertising, range of courses, resources, size of the alumni base, staff expertise, and use of information technology.

At any one time, a student may hold multiple—positive and negative—images of a HEI and these images are likely to change over time as the student gains new information or has new experiences or thoughts. A university cannot easily be conceptualized in a single image because each campus, each department, and each professor occupies their own image(s). Stakeholders can also hold different and multiple images simultaneously, because each uses different criteria when assessing a HEI.

Complex Matrix of Influences

The overall increase in study abroad participation may well be attributable to the availability of shorter programs, as campuses move beyond a one-size-fits-all approach to one that provides opportunities through flexibility. Short-term programs cost less, and so may be accessible to more students; therein acting as a springboard for potential future travels (Tarrant, Rubin, & Stoner, 2013) and other transformative learning experiences (Perry, Stoner, & Tarrant, 2012). Nevertheless, in their study of selection of HE abroad, Ready, David and Ball (2001) noted that students confront a 'complex matrix' of influences that can be effectively represented by overlapping spheres of influence i.e., the individual, family, friends and the HEI. As added by Salisbury, Ubac, Paulsen and Pascrell (2009, p. 124), 'each decision shapes the plausibility of potential options in subsequent decisions'. Indeed, the relative weight of these spheres may shift and change over time and generate different degrees of overlap.

Irrespective of the program length, studies show that study abroad is related to an increase in academic performance, appreciation for cultural differences, disciplinary learning, graduation rates, practical travel skills, self-knowledge, and sensitivity to cultural contexts. It also enhances job prospects, because employers desire graduates who have experiences that reflect their ability to adapt to unfamiliar situations, interact with a variety of cultures, and exhibit intercultural understanding.

LITERATURE REVIEW

Chronology of Push and Pull Factors

In the literature pertaining specifically to the cross-border mobility of students, the 'Push-Pull' model is a widely accepted analytical framework. Neice and Braun (1977) explained that: (a) the 'push' factors have strength in the initial reasons for studying abroad; (b) while the 'pull' factors dominate the choices, especially the appeal of program availability. In essence, the motivations and flow of international students are a function of the combined 'Push-Pull' factors as influenced by intervening obstacles (Sirowy & Inkeles, 1984, p. 65)

'Push' Factors: Operate within a source 'home' country to initiate a student's decision to study overseas and include for example: (a) a lack of HE opportunities; (b) government policies; (c) poor quality local educational facilities; (d) scholarships favorable to mobility; (e) the low-level of internationalization of education; and (f) the perceived and actual comparative advantage of the value of a foreign degree in the job markets both home and abroad.

'Pull' Factors: Operate in the receiving 'host' country to make that country desirable as a place to live and study, and include for example: (a) advanced research conditions; (b) better employment opportunities and career prospects; (c) higher quality education; (d) scholarships; and (e) superiority of the social and economic environment.

Tracing the literature pertaining specifically to the cross-border mobility of students, the following discussion captures the criteria/factors of 'Push-Pull' influence across different nations, different disciplines, and different student cohorts from 20+ studies since 1990.

In the 1990s…

According to Madams (1990), in general terms, school choice was differentiated by four criteria: (1) educational; (2) compositional; (3) structural; and (4) reputational diversity (p. 275). Cummins (1993) recorded that the major reasons for overseas study fell into three categories: (1) lack of domestic facilities, especially in certain

To Study Abroad

subject areas, prompted many students/governments to seek education in other countries; (2) commercial value of a foreign degree encouraged individuals to seek HE abroad; and (3) knowing and gaining experience in another country and culture inspired many to seek education in foreign countries.

Harvey (1996) presented the seven Ps for satisfied school clients based on where they want to go i.e., product, place, promotion and price, and in relation to the people, process and physical evidence (p. 30). They share how historically the teaching profession has resisted the implications of the 'commercial' or 'price' aspects of education, preferring to implement what it perceives as educationally desirable practices, regardless of cost. In other words, 'It is thought to be unprofessional, if not unethical, for professional carers to try to attract custom when their implicit professional codes emphasize looking after people altruistically' (p. 31).Yet, educational marketing requires the identification of student and community needs and a commitment to meeting those needs with a high quality product.

Mazzarol et al. (1996) reported that Australia's comparative advantage in the supply of education to the Asian region stemmed from four primary factors: (1) close proximity to the region; (2) sound quality of its product; (3) competitive fees and cost of living; and (4) safe and comfortable environment. In the same report, examination of the existing literature coupled with their own research, uncovered 15 factors as being likely to influence student choice of study destination (1996, pp. 29-30). Those factors included: availability of scholarships or work; climate in host country; cost/fees; ease of visa processing and visa cost; family and friends in host country; geographic proximity of host country; historical or economic links between host country and home country; lifestyle in host country; overall value for money; plans for immigration; recognition of qualifications; reputation of the host HEI; safety e.g., crime rate; specific teaching programs e.g., science and technology; and international standing of the host country.

Gorard's (1999, pp. 31-33) study provided a 'classification model' comprising five overarching categories. In order, they incorporated: (1) *academic*—belief that a student will fare better academically at a particular type of school; (2) *organizational*—reputation, ethos, atmosphere, class size and the physical environment are important; (3) *security*—belief that discipline, teaching of moral values and respect for others, as well as an avoidance of bullying and, therefore, the happiness of a student is important; (4) *selective*—gender, religion and other certain social background(s) are desirable; and (5) *situational*—convenience in terms of location and ease of travel/commutation.

In the 2000s...

Joseph and Joseph (2000) found five dominant selection criteria from 200 Indonesian students seeking tertiary studies abroad. The criteria encompassed, in rank order of importance, included: (1) course and career information; (2) physical aspects and facilities; (3) cost of education; (4) degree i.e., content and structure; and (5) value of education (p. 42). Bradshaw, Espinoza and Hausman (2001) also identified five chief factors considered by students in selecting a college, namely: (1) economic considerations i.e., location of campus and work opportunities; (2) quality and responsiveness of personnel i.e., helpfulness and accessibility; (3) research activities; (4) size of the HEI; and (5) social opportunities i.e., athletic programs and social life. In the same year, Mazzarol and Soutar (2001) carried out investigations in China, India, Indonesia, and Taiwan concerning the determinant factors that affected students' choices of education abroad. They found that the four most important '*push*' factors were: (1) a desire to gain better understanding of the West; (2) a perception that an overseas course of study is better than a local one; (3) an intention to migrate after graduation; and/or (4) students' (in)ability to gain entry to programs in their own country.

Mazzarol and Soutar (2002) continued their studies and observed six factors central to students' choice: (1) cost; (2) environment; (3) geographic proximity; (4) knowledge and awareness; (5) recommendation(s); and (6) social links. Arpan, Raney and Zivnuska (2003) reduced that number and identified three main factors: (1) academic rating; (2) athletic rating; and (3) news coverage. Chen's (2006) research findings underpinning East Asian students' reasons for pursuing graduate studies in Canada revealed the following characteristics: a positive country image i.e., a peaceful country, a diverse and tolerant society; a straightforward visa process and reasonable ease of obtaining a student visa; a good reputation for a quality education and research capability; a wide variety of program specialties, research projects, and strong faculty; and relatively low tuition fees and living expenses (p. 95). Further, Chen (2006) also recorded that many students, especially those from China, chose Canada because of difficulties in obtaining a US visa i.e., a strong negative *pushing* factor from the US and a strong *pulling* factor for Canada, which benefits from its geographic proximity (p. 101).

Li and Bray (2007, p. 795) categorized the 'motives' of students into four (potentially) overlapping groups: (1) *academic motives*—pursuit of qualifications and professional development; (2) *economic motives*—access to scholarships, estimated economic returns from study, and prospects for employment; (3) *political motives*—commitment to society and enhancement of political status and power;

To Study Abroad

and (4) *social and cultural motives*—desire to obtain experience and understanding of other societies. A study published by Yang (2007, p. 7) focused on why Chinese students had chosen Western HE, uncovered a plethora of reasons that included: being better prepared for their career in the future; difficult to gain entry in China; family's financial background; future migration opportunity after graduation; to gain Western experience; to have broader perspective on life; high quality of education; improve English; independence; international exposure; learn Western culture; overseas education is of higher quality; travel opportunities; and wide(r) range of programs to choose from. Verbik and Lasanowski (2007) stressed, however, how the usually high value of certain currencies—the UK pound (£) and US dollar ($) most prominent amongst them—could arguably dissuade students even further from going to high-cost nations, since unfavorable exchange rates exacerbate the already considerable financial concerns of foreign students, especially those from Africa and Southeast Asia (p. 8).

Varghese (2008) listed eight factors influencing student flow in cross-border education, which included: (1) acquisition of foreign language and culture; (2) cost of education; (3) easy visa formalities; (4) employment opportunities; (5) ideological affinity; (6) increasing income levels in the countries of origin; (7) language proficiency; and (8) perceived academic superiority of the HEI in the host country (pp. 22-25). In a study conducted by Sung and Yang (2008), university image attractiveness was measured through three variables: (1) university personality e.g., friendly, stable, practical, warm; (2) external prestige e.g., looked upon as a prestigious school in society overall, acquaintances think highly, high rankings, positive media coverage; and (3) university reputation e.g., student care top priority, strong prospects for future growth, well-managed, socially responsible, financially sound.

Bodycott (2009) examined what 100 Mainland Chinese students rated as most important when considering study abroad and uncovered eight key indicators, namely: (1) onsite accommodation; (2) range of programs available; (3) English-speaking environment; (4) language and academic support services; (5) general facilities i.e., buildings and grounds; (6) international education experiences during courses; (7) relatives or friends studying in the area; (8) social and emotional support services (p. 365). Salisbury, Umbach, Paulsen and Pascarella (2009, p. 123) believed that the process of deciding whether or not to study abroad was almost identical to *College Choice Theory*. That is, there are three decision-making stages that follow in sequential order, namely: (1) the development of the predisposition or intent to study abroad; (2) the search for an appropriate study abroad program; and (3) the selection *of* and departure *for* a particular location and program.

In the 2010s…

Padlee, Kamaruddin and Baharun (2010) examined the selection criteria by international students of private HEIs in Malaysia. They focused on factors that private international students considered important in their decision to choose Malaysia as their educational destination. Through factor analysis, seven dimensions were revealed in explaining the decision criteria of international students, namely: (1) cost; (2) customer focus; (3) facilities; (4) influencers; (5) location; (6) quality of learning environment; and (7) socialization (p. 206).

Macready and Tucker (2011, pp. 21-25) summarized 'motivation' categories derived from factors that influence international education as being: (1) exploring cultural heritage; (2) experience of living abroad; (3) willingness to travel; (4) better academic offerings; and (5) professional career boost. Macready and Tucker (2011) presented eight pull factors in international student mobility, namely: (1) high-quality study opportunities; (2) specialize study opportunities; (3) language; (4) traditional links and diasporas; (5) affordable cost; (6) international recognized qualifications; (7) good prospects of successful graduation within a predictable time; and (8) effective marketing/country support/visa arrangements. Further, Li and Zhang (2011, p. 313) found several concerns affecting Chinese students' choices of destination countries that embraced: cultural, economic, historical, and political relations between/among China and the destination countries; the development of education and the advantages offered by the destination countries; educational costs and funding, such as tuition and scholarship policies; the language environment and the medium of instruction e.g., English-speaking countries have firm advantages; enrolment; and visa and immigration polic(ies).

Lee and Morrish's (2012) preliminary research highlighted the importance of continuing research into three key values in Chinese family decision-making with regards to international HE, namely: (1) traditional values rooted in Confucianism; (2) child-centeredness; and (3) modern Western values (p. 63). In her study, Foster (2013) learned the key pull factors or benefits of study abroad for Brazilian students to the UK as: (1) improving English; (2) having an experience of study abroad; and (3) research opportunities for postgraduate students. Language issues were particularly important as English language proficiency for Brazilian students was a prime benefit of study abroad (p. 197). Nachatar Singh, Schapper, and Jack (2014) performed a case study at a Malaysian University. More significant than the attributes of any HEI, they discovered that international students had chosen Malaysia for its key social and cultural pull factors, which included: (1) Malaysia as a safe environment; (2) shared cultural values with the students' own background; (3) financial benefits

To Study Abroad

derived from low tuition fees and low cost of living; (4) proximity to the students' home country; as well as (5) access to culturally important items such as halal and other dietary requirements (p. 463).

Fang and Wang (2014) noted the major pull factors of 'transnational' HE in their study as including: (1) advanced foreign knowledge and concepts; (2) chances to study abroad; (3) cultivation of an international person; (4) degrees of Chinese partner HEIs; (5) degrees of foreign partner HEIs; (6) foreign culture and foreign teaching methods; (7) improvement of foreign language ability and cross-culture communication ability; and (8) location of programs. Other pull factors include: easy access; family background of attending students; labor market-oriented majors; and preparation for further study abroad (p. 483). In addition, Fang and Wang (2014) noted the major push factors of domestic HE in their study as including: (1) family influence; (2) lack of access to satisfying domestic HEIs; (3) lack of access to satisfying major fields; (4) low internationalization levels; and (5) low language training capacity of domestic HEIs. Other push factors included: lack of access to domestic HEIs; lack of suitable major fields; low competitiveness of degrees in job markets; and low education quality (p. 483). Fang and Wang (2014) noted the major push factors of overseas HE as including: (1) high costs; and (2) high requirements on one's language ability. Other push factors included: negative views on employment prospects of degrees gained abroad; difficulty in acquiring advanced degrees in foreign countries; difficulty in obtaining visas; distance from home; family influence; lack of access to satisfying foreign HEIs; and worry over one's ability to live and adapt to a new society (p. 483).

In the same year, Agrey and Lampadan (2014) uncovered five factors emerged as being those that significantly influenced decision-making on which HEI to attend. These included: (1) support systems, both physical i.e., bookstore, guidance/ counselling office, and non-physical i.e., scholarships, credit transferability, spiritual programming; (2) learning environment i.e., modern learning environment and facilities, reputation, beautiful campus, library and computer lab, and job prospects i.e., high rate of graduates being employed; (3) having good sporting facilities; (4) a strong student life program i.e., health care services, residential accommodation, and activities i.e., wide range of extracurricular activities; and finally (5) a safe and friendly environment i.e., safe campus as well as supporting faculty (p. 391).

In 2015, Gong and Huybers conveyed in their article three major factors influencing the education destination choices of Chinese students, namely: (1) the safety conditions in the destination country; (2) the global university rankings of the destination university combined with the overall education quality of the destination country; and (3) students' expected annual expenditure (2015, p. 214). Özoğlu, Gür, and Coşkun (2015) told how pull factors such as cultural, historical, religious and ethnic affinities seemed to be very influential in international students' choice of

HE in Turkey. Given that at least one-quarter of all international students in Turkey receive scholarships, funding opportunities are certainly a primary pull factor. In addition to these social and political pull factors, there were also academic and economic pull factors such as the quality of education and the comparatively low cost of education and living in Turkey that were persuasive (p. 235).

Velliaris (2016) described three themes that captured the reasons underpinning international students choosing a tertiary-level pathway HEI in Australia as: Theme 1—*physical environment* i.e., the attractiveness of Australia's physical environment and easy relaxed lifestyle has been used as a promotional tool in international education advertising. Australia has an image of being sunny and warm); Theme 2—*reputation for educational quality* i.e., the overall image is the sum of opinions, ideas, and impressions that prospective students have of the HEI; formed from word-of-mouth, past experience, and marketing activities; and Theme 3—*social networks and word-of-mouth referrals* i.e., parents and relatives who have graduated from a particular HEI and enjoyed the experience are likely to recommend it to their children, other family members and/or friends. Recruitment agents who have graduated from a particular HEI also make strong advocates.

Jiani's (2016) research centered on how Mainland China is commonly perceived as a major 'sending' nation of international students, but it is also an important 'receiving' nation of international students (p. 563). It was found that rather than the '…reputation and perceived high quality of institutions… the strong economic growth of China is a major factor that encourages international students to seek higher education opportunities in China' (p. 577). Ahmad, Hassan and Al-Ahmedi's (2017) main research objective was to identify the influential factors that motivated government-sponsored Kurdish students to undertake postgraduate studies abroad and their choice of study abroad destination. They found that students were pushed by a desire for enhancing their 'future career advancement' followed by the 'high quality of overseas education' (p. 115).

Nicholls' (2018) survey investigation into the reasons for international HE students choosing to study in the US, found that about 35% of the respondents identified the 'quality' as their most prevalent choice. Nghia's (2019) study identified 12 factors that motivated Vietnamese students to pursue international education abroad. The six pull factors were: (1) avoidance of bad practices in Vietnamese education; (2) being asked to study abroad by family; (3) competitive entry into Vietnamese universities; (4) establishing relationships with international friends; (5) experiencing foreign cultures; and (6) improving chances of employment internationally. The six push factors were: (1) improving foreign language competence; (2) obtaining international experience; (3) poor educational quality in Vietnam; (4) pursuing foreign educational values; (5) pursuit of immigration opportunities; and (6) unavailability of a desired program.

To Study Abroad

Insights Gained and Lessons Learned

The lists below collate both 'Push-Pull' factors taken from the associated literature (e.g., S. Z. Ahmad & Buchanan, 2017; Bodycott, 2009; Bodycott & Lai, 2012; L-H Chen, 2007; Cubillo, Sánchez, & Cerviño, 2006; Fang & Wang, 2014; Gorard, 1999; C. K. C. Lee & Morrish, 2012; MacKenzie, 2010; Mazzarol, 1998; Mazzarol, et al., 1996; Mazzarol & Soutar, 2002; Ming, 2010; Oliveira & Soares, 2016; Price, Matzdorf, Smith, & Agahi, 2003; Reay, Davies, David, & Ball, 2001; Velliaris, 2014; Velliaris & Willis, 2013, 2014; Zhou, 1998).

Agent

- Brand reputation
- Market profile
- Offshore recruitment offices
- Promotional efforts
- Quality reputation/recommendation(s)

Affordability

- Commutation/transportation
- Cost effectiveness
- Costs associated with computer use, phone use, internet access & email
- Coverage for medical evacuation & repatriation
- Currency exchange
- Extra-curricular activities
- International airfares
- Medical exams, vaccinations, prescriptions, & other medical expenses for the duration of the program
- Off campus conveniences
- Overall value for money
- Refund policies and late payment penalties
- Standards of living/accommodation
- Student visa costs
- Textbooks and other amenities
- Travel independent of the program
- Tuition fees

Campus Environment

- Aesthetics/attractiveness
- Ample resources e.g., computer rooms
- Campus visits/open days
- Childcare facilities
- Class discrimination
- Cleanliness
- Counselling service/social emotional support services
- Cross-cultural/intercultural/transnational student mix
- Ethnic minorities
- Events on campus
- Gender (im)balance
- Location in relation to city center
- Low racial discrimination/ inclusive
- Multiculturality
- On-campus housing
- Quiet self-study areas e.g., library
- Range of services e.g., counselling, medical
- Ratio of local to overseas students
- Rumor and reputation
- Safety and security
- Science and/or technology-based programs
- Size/spaciousness
- Social atmosphere/facilities
- Social mix/social mixing
- Sporting facilities
- Student-friendly attitude
- Studious cohort
- Transportation to and from
- University-owned accommodation

Faculty

- Admission to graduate school
- Availability of academic staff
- Cross-cultural diversity/multiculturality
- Earning prospects/higher status
- Faculty-led study abroad programs
- Faculty-student ratio

To Study Abroad

Graduate Attributes

- Active observation/listening skills
- Civic-mindedness
- Cultural humility
- Empathy and reflexive understanding
- Increased self-awareness
- International contacts
- International links
- International values
- Internationally-minded/experienced
- Open-mindedness
- Sense of adventure
- Tolerance of ambiguity

Institutional Features

- Admissions process/speed of acceptance
- Affiliations
- Athletic ranking
- Entrance examinations
- Examination results
- Family background of attending students
- Global perspective
- Growth in overseas student enrolments
- High-quality image/reputation
- International cooperative activities
- International strategic alliances and coalitions
- International strategic alliances and coalitions
- Language and academic support services
- Lecture theatre facilities
- Library facilities e.g., availability of books
- Links/alliances with other institutions
- Modern/up-to-date facilities
- Multi-modal platforms
- Offshore teaching programs
- Prominent academic staff e.g., professors
- Public or private system
- Quality and responsiveness of personnel
- Range of student clubs & societies

- Ranking position/prestige
- Religious affiliation
- Strength of national/international alumni
- Technically superior
- Tuition policies
- Website presentation

Locale

- City/town/rural or remote
- Comfortable climate
- Commonality of language
- Country image
- Cultural aspirations
- Cultural diversity & religious freedom
- Dietary restrictions
- Economic linkages between home-host
- English language proficiency
- Financially stability of host country
- Friendliness/social activities
- Friends/relatives live and/or study there
- Geographic proximity of home-host countries
- Historical links between home-host countries
- Ideological affinity
- Other foreign language proficiency
- Political interests via foreign assistance
- Quality of life
- Racial discrimination
- Reputation of town/city
- Transportation/parking
- Visa processing/restrictions

Study Programs

- (In)compatibility academic calendar
- Academic facilities
- Attractive course content
- Blended learning
- Brochures & handbook
- Career preparation

To Study Abroad

- Core courses/mandatory component
- Curriculum
- Duration of course/program
- Ease of travel between home & host
- Elective courses
- Evaluation & assessment procedures
- Family and friends' recommendations
- Flexible entry e.g., semester intakes
- Flexible study mode
- Government promotion agencies
- Home country student advisors
- International links
- Internships/mentorships
- Language policy
- Language support services
- Limited opportunities/lack of choice
- Links with industry
- Marriage
- Medical conditions
- Mental health issues
- Military service
- Morals and values
- Natural/manmade disaster
- News coverage
- Offshore/online/distance teaching programs
- Online learning

Other

- Current and future wages
- Opportunities to travel
- Parental support
- Poor academic performance
- Practicum placements
- Pregnancy
- Prior credit status
- Private recruitment agencies
- Reciprocal exchange programs
- Recognition of foreign degree
- Related work experience

- Scholarship opportunities
- Specific &/or range of specializations
- Sponsorships/scholarships
- Timing
- Willingness to recognize prior qualifications
- Word-of-mouth referrals
- Work-integrated learning (wil) component(s)
- Work-study balance

Increasingly, the emergence of new types of providers, forms of educational delivery, and collaborative partnerships, along with traditional private and public HEIs, has seen face-to-face and/or virtual modes of HE delivery through articulation, franchising, twinning, validation, and joint or double degree arrangements (Agrey & Lampadan, 2014). Some HEIs also seek to establish a physical presence through branch campuses, independent HEIs, teaching and testing centers, and acquisitions or mergers (Altbach & Knight, 2007, p. 195). In other words, students' 'Push-Pull' influencers may continue to propagate as the global HE market becomes inundated with even more nations, locations, echelons and categories available for consideration/contemplation.

LIMITATIONS, RECOMMENDATIONS AND FUTURE DIRECTIONS

The growing number and diversification of players in the international HE student market partly explains why countries are seeking innovative strategies to attract higher numbers of students. Unquestionably, HEIs across the globe are experiencing increased competition to attract foreign students. There is clearly a need for (more) explicit knowledge about what underpins their decision to study abroad and the location they have selected. For HEIs to be successful in attracting students, institutional enrolment management needs to intelligibly understand the factors that impact student choice and tailor recruitment efforts and other organizational marketing procedures to increase the chances of students selecting their HEI as their first choice (refer to Appendices A and B). Ideally, more students will take advantage of well-designed cross-cultural educational opportunities and, as greater numbers of students seek out opportunities for education abroad, it is imperative to learn about their experiences.

To Study Abroad

The following questions categorized under four main themes—personal, professional, academic, and environment—can help steer potential candidates in their decision-making. These guiding questions are certainly not exhaustive.

Personal

1. *Can I live away from family and friends for a while? How long do study abroad programs take? Would I enjoy this type of experience? Am I emotionally ready for the experience?*
2. *Do I have to speak a second language to study abroad? Do I want fluency in another language?*
3. *Do I want to explore my identity e.g., personal cultural heritage?*
4. *Do I want to increase my self-confidence and self-advocacy skills?*
5. *Does my personal situation conform with my study abroad aspirations?*
6. *How much does it cost to study abroad? Can I afford it? Can I get financial aid? Where can I find study abroad scholarships? What is the total cost?*
7. *What do I personally want to get out of a study abroad experience?*
8. *When can I start applying for study abroad programs? How do I get started?*
9. *Why study abroad? Where in the world should I study? How long can I realistically plan to be abroad e.g., quarter, semester, year, summer etc.?*
10. *Will the study abroad program align with my values?*

Professional

1. *Are there language, cultural, or other area studies courses available that would enhance my study abroad experience?*
2. *Do I want to incorporate service or experiential learning? Internships or work? Build my network?*
3. *How will I build upon my education to date?*
4. *Is there a geographic region or program structure that would lend itself well to enhancing my area of study and/or contribute to my professional goals?*
5. *Is there an area of interest that I may be able to purse while abroad that is perhaps not offered at home?*
6. *What are my life goals and aspirations?*
7. *What are the entry requirements for study abroad programs?*
8. *What skills do I want to gain abroad that will help me after graduation?*
9. *Will this program get me where I want to be in life?*
10. *Would engaging in an internship, research, or service-learning opportunity abroad help me to meet my professional aspirations?*

To Study Abroad

Academic

1. *Academically, when is the best time academically for me to study abroad? Would it make more sense to go abroad in the 1st, 2nd or 3rd Year of my degree program?*
2. *Are there any considerations or restrictions in my department around receiving credit from abroad? How many credits can I bring back towards my major/minor?*
3. *Are there milestone courses e.g., prerequisites, or other required classes/opportunities on campus that I may miss if absent for a particular semester? Could a required class be taken abroad?*
4. *Are there support resources I will need while abroad e.g., tutoring etc.?*
5. *At the end of the program, am I transferring credits or actual grades back to my home university? Can I take elective credits, or do I need to meet specific degree requirements while abroad?*
6. *Does the host institution have a reciprocal arrangement with my home university to validate each other's degrees? Are both countries part of a multi-country accord or protocol that can validate and provide equivalence of my degree?*
7. *Is the institution or university prestigious and globally recognized for its quality of education?*
8. *What academic goals do I have for study abroad e.g., language, regional experience, etc.?*
9. *What type of coursework do I need in a study abroad program for it to make sense for my degree? Do I need to take specific class(es) while abroad in order to graduate on time?*
10. *What will I achieve studying abroad that I cannot in my home country?*

Environment

1. *Are there particular health concerns for the area(s) where I would like to study?*
2. *Are there safety/security concerns I should be aware of in the region(s) where I would like to study?*
3. *Do I prefer a small or large city, or perhaps something off the beaten path? Do I prefer a traditional study abroad location or something more exotic?*
4. *Does the visa allow me to work and study at the same time? Will I be able to find part-time employment while studying abroad?*
5. *What are the important cultural norms and expectations in the host country?*
6. *What extracurricular hobbies or activities can I pursue overseas?*
7. *Where will I live during my study abroad program?*

To Study Abroad

8. *Will I be able to meet any specific needs that I have in my day-to-day life? Food shopping, healthcare, dentistry?*
9. *Will I feel safe enough to concentrate on my studies?*
10. *Will I need to modify my dress and/or behavior in order to comply with cultural norms and local laws?*

The current generation of 'savvy student customers' are knowledgeable about the opportunities available in certain countries. For example, visa schemes and immigration procedures will play an increasingly important role in the decision-making process, with students not only seeking employment upon graduation, but perhaps (at least temporary) residency in their country of choice. Countries that facilitate the arrival and integration of overseas students through employment and immigration initiatives are likely to be more competitive in the market.

In summary, this chapter reinforces the need for policy-makers, institutional leaders and recruiters to understand motivations to pursue overseas studies and to ensure push, pull, and structural factors are aligned for successful foreign student recruitment outcomes (J.-M. & Dongkoo, 2017). As the global HE market continues to grow, so too has/will competition to attract international students amongst governments and educational providers. In order to capitalize on this continued growth, the onus is on HEIs to develop and implement programs to facilitate the social and educational needs of international students. Selection criteria—as presented in Table 1—provides implications for stakeholders to deploy their educational resources, as well as develop effective promotional and marketing strategies for promoting their 'home' HEI internationally.

CONCLUSION

HE choice abroad is more complicated than in one's 'home' context as satisfying cultural and linguistic preferences for example, as well as fulfilling many and varied admissions criteria, may restrict the range of HEIs from which students feel that they can make a high-quality choice. Thus, managing and understanding students' underpinning motivations will be ever more significant as demand for HE continues to grow—nationally and internationally—and HE delivery continues to evolve and expand into online, open access, on-campus and distance modes of study. Thereafter, HE may not be the same experience for all and may not offer the same rewards for all (Reay, Davies, et al., 2001, p. 872).

This descriptive chapter was designed to share conceptual and empirical understanding(s) for the ways that certain 'factors' affect students' destination for study abroad. This work reveals a range of issues influencing intent to study abroad, involving students' (and their parents') social, cultural and educational discernments. And, as the HE student population continues to grow more diverse, it is incumbent upon the community to (re)consider the contexts from which students come and recognize that their pre-enrolment capital will shape how they engage with the educational opportunities available to them. If HEIs are to succeed in the long-term, they must understand the need for identifying the attributes that potential overseas students consider important/imperative when choosing an overseas HEI for pursuing tertiary-level studies.

REFERENCES

Agrey, L., & Lampadan, N. (2014). Determinant factors contributing to student choice in selecting a university. *Journal of Education and Human Development*, *3*(2), 391–404.

Ahmad, A. B., Hassan, H. A., & Al-Ahmedi, M. W. A. (2017). Motivations of government-sponsored Kurdish students for pursuing postgraduate studies abroad: An exploratory study. *Journal of Studies in International Education*, *21*(2), 105–119. doi:10.1177/1028315316662982

Ahmad, S. Z., & Buchanan, F. R. (2017). Motivation factors in students decision to study at international branch campuses in Malaysia. *Studies in Higher Education*, *42*(4), 651–668. doi:10.1080/03075079.2015.1067604

Altbach, P. G., & Knight, J. (2007). The internationalization of higher education: Motivations and realities. *Journal of Studies in International Education*, *11*(3-4), 290–305. doi:10.1177/1028315307303542

Arpan, L. M., Raney, A. A., & Zivnuska, S. (2003). A cognitive approach to understanding university image. *Corporate Communications*, *8*(2), 97–113. doi:10.1108/1356328031047535

Bodycott, P. (2009). Choosing a higher education study abroad destination: What mainland Chinese parents and students rate as important. *Journal of Research in International Education*, *8*(3), 349–373. doi:10.1177/1475240909345818

Bodycott, P., & Lai, A. (2012). The influence and implications of Chinese culture in the decision to undertake cross-border higher education. *Journal of Studies in International Education*, *16*(3), 252–270. doi:10.1177/1028315311418517

Bradshaw, G. S., Espinoza, S., & Hausman, S. (2001). The college decision-making of high achieving students. *College and University*, *77*(2), 15–22.

Chen, L.-H. (2006). Attracting East Asian students to Canadian graduate schools. *Canadian Journal of Higher Education, 36*(2), 77–105.

Chen, L.-H. (2007). East-Asian students' choice of Canadian graduate schools. *International Journal of Educational Advancement, 7*(4), 271–306. doi:10.1057/palgrave.ijea.2150071

Cubillo, J. M., Sánchez, J., & Cerviño, J. (2006). International students' decision-making process. *International Journal of Educational Management, 20*(2), 101–115. doi:10.1108/09513540610646091

Cummins, W. K. (1993). Global trends in overseas study. In C. D. Godwin (Ed.), *International investment in human capital: overseas education for development* (pp. 31–46). New York, NY: Institute of International Education.

Fang, W., & Wang, S. (2014). Chinese students' choice of transnational higher education in a globalized higher education market: A case study of W university. *Journal of Studies in International Education, 18*(5), 475–494. doi:10.1177/1028315314523989

Foster, M. (2013). Student destination choices in international education: Exploring Brazilian students' attitudes to study abroad. *Practice and Evidence of Scholarship of Teaching and Learning in Higher Education, 8*(3), 176–202.

Gong, X., & Huybers, T. (2015). Chinese students and higher education destinations: Findings from a choice experiment. *Australian Journal of Education, 59*(2), 196–218. doi:10.1177/0004944115584482

Gorard, S. (1999). 'Well. That about wraps it up for school choice research': A state of the art review. *School Leadership & Management, 19*(1), 25–47. doi:10.1080/13632439969320

Harvey, J. A. (1996). Marketing schools and consumer choice. *International Journal of Educational Management, 10*(4), 26–32. doi:10.1108/09513549610122165

Hulstrand, J. (2006). Education abroad: On the fast track. In NAFSA: Association of International Educators (Ed.), International Educator (pp. 46-55). Academic Press.

James-MacEachern, M., & Yun, D. (2017). Exploring factors influencing international students' decision to choose a higher education institution. *International Journal of Educational Management, 31*(3), 343–363. doi:10.1108/IJEM-11-2015-0158

Jiani, M. A. (2016). Why and how international students choose Mainland China as a higher education study abroad destination. *Higher Education, 74*(4), 563–579. doi:10.100710734-016-0066-0

Joseph, M., & Joseph, B. (2000). Indonesian students' perceptions of choice criteria in the selection of a tertiary institution: Strategic implications. *International Journal of Educational Management, 14*(4), 40–44. doi:10.1108/09513540010310396

Lee, C. K. C., & Morrish, S. C. (2012). Cultural values and higher education choices: Chinese families. *Australasian Marketing Journal, 20*(1), 59–64. doi:10.1016/j.ausmj.2011.10.015

Lee, E. S. (1966). A theory of migration. *Demography, 3*(1), 47–57. doi:10.2307/2060063

Li, M., & Bray, M. (2007). Cross-border flows of students for higher education: Push–pull factors and motivations of mainland Chinese students in Hong Kong and Macau. *Higher Education, 53*(6), 791–818. doi:10.100710734-005-5423-3

Li, M., & Zhang, Y. (2011). Two-way flows of higher education students in mainland China in a global market: Trends, characteristics and problems. In S. Marginson (Ed.), *Higher education in the Asia-Pacific* (pp. 309–327). Springer. doi:10.1007/978-94-007-1500-4_16

MacKenzie, P. (2010). School choice in an international context. *Journal of Research in International Education, 9*(2), 107–123. doi:10.1177/1475240910370813

Macready, C., & Tucker, C. (2011). *Who goes where and why? An overview and analysis of global educational mobility*. New York, NY: Institute of International Education.

Maddaus, J. (1990). Parental choice of school: What parents think and do. *Review of Research in Education, 16*, 267–295.

Mazzarol, T. (1998). Critical success factors for international education marketing. *International Journal of Educational Management, 12*(4), 163–175. doi:10.1108/09513549810220623

Mazzarol, T., Savery, L. K., & Kemp, S. (1996). *International students who choose not to study in Australia: An examination of Taiwan and Indonesia*. Perth, Australia: Curtin Business School, Curtin University of Technology.

Mazzarol, T., & Soutar, G. N. (2001). *The global market for higher education: Sustainable competitive strategies for the new millennium*. Cheltenham, UK: Edward Elgar.

Mazzarol, T., & Soutar, G. N. (2002). 'Push-pull' factors influencing international student destination choice. *International Journal of Educational Management, 16*(2), 82–90. doi:10.1108/09513540210418403

Ming, J. S. K. (2010). Institutional factors influencing students' college choice decision in Malaysia: A conceptual framework. *International Journal of Business and Social Science, 1*(3), 53–58.

Nachatar Singh, J. K., Schapper, J., & Jack, G. (2014). The importance of place for international students' choice of university: A case study at a Malaysian university. *Journal of Studies in International Education, 18*(5), 463–474. doi:10.1177/1028315314523990

Neice, D. C., & Braun, P. H. (1977). *Patron for the world*. Ottawa, Canada: Canadian Bureau for International Education.

Nghia, T. L. H. (2019). Motivations for studying abroad and immigration intentions: The case of Vietnamese students. *Journal of International Students*, 1-19. doi:10.32674/jis.v0i0.731

Nicholls, S. (2018). Influences on international student choice of study destination: Evidence from the United States. *Journal of International Students, 8*(2), 597–622. doi:10.32674/jis.v8i2.94

Oliveira, D. B., & Soares, A. M. (2016). Studying abroad: Developing a model for the decision process of international students. *Journal of Higher Education Policy and Management, 38*(2), 126–139. doi:10.1080/1360080X.2016.1150234

Özoğlu, M., Gür, B. S., & Coşkun, İ. (2015). Factors influencing international students' choice to study in Turkey and challenges they experience in Turkey. *Research in Comparative and International Education, 10*(2), 223–237. doi:10.1177/1745499915571718

Padlee, S. F., Kamaruddin, A. R., & Baharun, R. (2010). International students' choice behavior for higher education at Malaysian private universities. *International Journal of Marketing Studies, 2*(2), 202–211. doi:10.5539/ijms.v2n2p202

Perry, L., Stoner, L., & Tarrant, M. (2012). More than a vacation: Short-term study abroad as a critically reflective, transformative learning experience. *Creative Education, 3*(5), 679–683. doi:10.4236/ce.2012.35101

Price, I. F., Matzdorf, F., Smith, L., & Agahi, H. (2003). The impact of facilities on student choice of university. *Facilities, 21*(10), 212–222. doi:10.1108/02632770310493580

Reay, D., David, M., & Ball, S. J. (2001). Making a difference?: Institutional habituses and higher education choice. *Sociological Research Online, 5*(4), 1–12. doi:10.5153ro.548

Reay, D., Davies, J., David, M., & Ball, S. J. (2001). Choices of degree or degrees of choice? Class, race and the higher education choice process. *Sociology, 35*(4), 855–874.

Salisbury, M. H., Umbach, P. D., Paulsen, M. B., & Pascarella, E. T. (2009). Going global: Understanding the choice process of the intent to study abroad. *Research in Higher Education, 50*(2), 119–143. doi:10.100711162-008-9111-x

Sirowy, L., & Inkeles, A. (1984). University-level student exchanges: The US role in global perspective. In E. G. Barber (Ed.), Foreign student flows: Their significance for American higher education (pp. 31-85). Wayzata, MN: Institute of International Education.

Sung, M., & Yang, S. (2008). Toward the model of university image: The influence of brand personality, external prestige, and reputation. *Journal of Public Relations Research, 20*(4), 357–376. doi:10.1080/10627260802153207

Tarrant, M. A., Rubin, D. L., & Stoner, L. (2013). The added value of study abroad fostering a global citizenry. *Journal of Studies in International Education, 18*(2), 141–161. doi:10.1177/1028315313497589

The Forum on Education Abroad (Producer). (2011). *Standards of good practice for education abroad.* Retrieved from http://www.mobility.unimelb.edu.au/resources/readings/ForumEA-StandardsGoodPractice2011-4thEdition.pdf

Varghese, N. V. (2008). *Globalization of higher education and cross-border student mobility.* Retrieved from http://unesco.atlasproject.eu/unesco/file/efee962c-24ce-408a-8e2c-f4e19ae1c717/c8c7fe00-c770-11e1-9b21-0800200c9a66/157989e.pdf

Velliaris, D. M. (2014). *Foreign parents in Tokyo and their school choice preferences.* Paper presented at the West East Institute (WEI): International Academic Conference, Bali, Indonesia.

Velliaris, D. M. (2016). Choosing the right pathway: A matrix of influences related to selection of higher education destination abroad. In K. Bista & C. Foster (Eds.), *Global perspectives and local challenges surrounding international student mobility* (pp. 179–200). Hershey, PA: IGI Global. doi:10.4018/978-1-4666-9746-1.ch010

Velliaris, D. M. (2018, December). Study abroad: Not all classrooms have four walls. *IGI Global Online Newsroom.* Retrieved from https://www.igi-global.com/newsroom/archive/study-abroad-not-all-classrooms/4017/

Velliaris, D. M., & Coleman-George, D. (Eds.). (2016). *Handbook of research on study abroad programs and outbound mobility*. Hershey, PA: IGI Global. doi:10.4018/978-1-5225-0169-5

Velliaris, D. M., & Willis, C. R. (2013). School choice for transnational parents in Tokyo. *Journal of Research in International Education, 12*(3), 228–238. doi:10.1177/1475240913511583

Velliaris, D. M., & Willis, C. R. (2014). International family profiles and parental school choice in Tokyo. *Journal of Research in International Education, 13*(3), 235–247. doi:10.1177/1475240914556204

Verbik, L., & Lasanowski, V. (2007). International student mobility: Patterns and trends. *World Education News and Reviews, 20*(10), 1–16.

Yang, M. (2007). What attracts mainland Chinese students to Australian higher education. *Studies in Learning. Evaluation Innovation and Development, 4*(2), 1–12.

Zhou, M. (1998). 'Parachute kids' in Southern California: The educational experience of Chinese children in transnational families. *Educational Policy, 12*(6), 682–704. doi:10.1177/0895904898012006005

To Study Abroad

APPENDIX A

Key Elements for a Successful Study Abroad Program (adapted Hulstrand, 2006, p. 50)
Key elements to create and maintain successful, high-quality, short-term education abroad programs:

1. A safe and secure environment
2. Affordable program design
3. Balance in program activities
4. Competent, experienced staff
5. Delivering what you promise i.e., meeting student expectations
6. Faculty buy-in and participation
7. Good predeparture orientation and preparation
8. Incorporation of local language
9. Integration into the curriculum
10. Interaction with the host community
11. Maintenance of a strong, healthy group dynamic
12. Opportunities for cultural enrichment, and a faculty leader trained to provide on-site interpretation and support
13. Opportunities for debriefing, reflection, reintegration upon return to the campus
14. Opportunities for guided reflection
15. Unassailable academic integrity

APPENDIX B

The Standards of Good Practice for Education Abroad (adapted The Forum on Education Abroad, 2011, pp. 10-12)

1. **Mission**
The organization, with respect to education abroad, has a formally adopted mission statement for its overall operations and for its individual programs that is known to and accepted by its faculty and staff.

- **Assessment of Mission Achievement:** The organization regularly analyzes the degree to which it is achieving its overall mission and its mission statements for each program and utilizes these findings to assure continuous improvement.

To Study Abroad

- **Mission and Commitment:** The organization has mission statements appropriate for each program.

2. **Student Learning and Development**

The organization has stated educational objectives that foster student learning and development; has an established process for regularly collecting and analyzing data to assess the degree to which it is accomplishing each; and utilizes these findings to monitor, maintain, support, and continuously improve student success.

- **Academic Growth:** The program provides academic learning opportunities appropriate to the program's mission.
- **Intercultural Understanding:** The organization fosters inter-cultural understanding.
- **Language and Communication:** The organization encourages the development of language and/or inter-cultural communication skills.
- **Student Development:** The program provides opportunities that encourage student development e.g., leadership skills, service orientation, maturity, tolerance for ambiguity.

3. **Academic Framework**

The organization maintains clearly stated and publicly available policies on academic matters related to education abroad; regularly reviews them for relevance and effectiveness; and implements appropriate changes as needed.

- **Academic Coursework:** The organization provides an academically challenging program of study.
- **Academic Credit:** The organization has clearly stated and publicly available policies on the awarding of academic credit.
- **Academic Integration:** The organization fosters the integration of student learning abroad with requirements and learning at the home institution and regularly evaluates its success in this area.
- **Academic Planning:** The home institution encourages students to make education abroad decisions with reference to degree progress, in consultation with their academic adviser and has an ongoing process in place to measure its success and continuously improve in this area.
- **Career Planning:** The home institution has a process in place to stay abreast of changes to academic and co-curricular offerings on programs abroad and provides program selection advising that takes into account students' career goals and interests.

- **Internships and Field Research:** When offered for credit, internships and field opportunities have appropriate academic and field supervision.
- **On-Site Advising:** The program advises students on academic matters in cooperation with home institution advising and regularly evaluates its success in doing so.

4. Student Preparation for the Learning Environment Abroad

The organization has processes in place to assess student needs, provides advising and orientation support to address these needs that is consistent with the program's mission and regularly assesses the quality of this support, and utilizes its findings to continuously monitor, maintain, support, and improve its advising and orientation processes.

- **Pre- and Post-Departure Advising and Orientation:** The program uses past experiences, student and staff evaluations, current research, and ongoing communication with students to assess students' needs and provide appropriate orientation and advising support to meet these needs as they evolve throughout the term of education abroad and regularly evaluates the effectiveness of its orientation and advising support.
- **Returning Student Support:** The organization and program staff have processes in place to assess their students' re-entry needs, provide support for students returning from abroad that addresses these needs, and regularly evaluate the effectiveness of this support.

5. Student Selection and Code of Conduct

The organization maintains, and makes publicly accessible, its commitment to fair and appropriate policies regarding student selection and code of conduct.

- **Code of Conduct:** The organization makes explicit its student code of conduct and its disciplinary processes.
- **Student Selection:** The recruitment and selection processes are transparent and fair.

6. Policies and Procedures

The organization has in place policies and procedures that govern its education abroad programs and practices and regularly reviews these policies to assure their effectiveness and appropriateness.

- **Advising:** The organization is committed to and implements an advising model appropriate to students' curricular, intellectual, and personal development.

To Study Abroad

- **Affordability and Financial Assistance:** The organization provides proactive assistance to students and families concerning the provision of internal and/or external financial aid.
- **Communications:** The organization is committed to and practices open, accurate, and honest communications.
- **Marketing:** The organization follows accepted ethical practices in marketing.
- **Personnel:** The organization has defined policies with respect to personnel.
- **Policies:** The organization has adequate and published policies that govern its education abroad programs.
- **Program Assessment:** The organization has established, and regularly utilizes formal review and evaluation processes of its policies and procedures and applies the results to continuously improve them.

7. **Organizational and Program Resources**

The organization provides adequate financial and personnel resources to support its programs.

- **Academic Personnel:** Program faculty members have the qualifications, knowledge, and appropriate level of engagement to support the curriculum and the learning environment of students inside and outside the classroom.
- **Administrative and Support Personnel:** Program staff members have the qualifications, knowledge, and appropriate level of engagement to administer the program effectively and to assure the well-being of students.
- **Assessment:** Results are linked to the institution's ongoing planning and resource allocation processes.
- **Financial Resources:** The organization devotes adequate financial resources to each program.
- **Learning and Academic Support Facilities:** Each program has facilities adequate to realize program mission, recognizing that amenities might vary according to the host environment and culture.
- **Student Housing:** Students are provided with or assisted in securing appropriate housing.

8. **Health, Safety, Security and Risk Management**

The organization assures continuous attention to the health, safety, and security of its students, faculty, and staff, from program development stages through program implementation, by way of established policies, procedures, student orientation, and faculty and staff training.

To Study Abroad

- Risk assessments are conducted as part of the development process for new programs to evaluate and mitigate potential risks prior to the commencement of the activity.
- The organization considers health, safety, security and risk management in program development.
- The organization ensures continuous attention to the safety of students, faculty and staff at all locations, with particular attention to safety issues in more dangerous locations.
- The organization focuses continuous attention on health issues for program students, faculty and staff.
- The organization is knowledgeable about and complies with applicable laws and regulations.
- The organization maintains adequate insurance coverage and conducts regular risk-management review involving appropriate training and personnel.

9. **Ethics and Integrity**

The organization educates its employees in and adheres to its own code of ethics and/or to the ethical principles of the Forum's Code of Ethics for Education Abroad.

- **Intercultural Relations:** The organization is considerate and respectful of the cultures and values of the countries in which it operates or sponsors programs and from which it draws students.
- **Operations:** The organization operates its programs in accordance with ethical principles.
- **Student Life:** The organization conducts its activities and advises students in an ethically responsible manner.

Chapter 2

Intercultural Awareness and Short–Term Study Abroad Programs:
An Invitation to Liminality

David Starr-Glass
iD https://orcid.org/0000-0003-4769-0558
SUNY Empire State College, USA

ABSTRACT

One of the desired and anticipated outcomes of study abroad is that participants, who are exposed to difference, will develop a deeper appreciation of intercultural awareness. For students about to graduate and function in an increasingly globalized world, intercultural awareness is a fundamental requirement and a valued asset. Although greater intercultural awareness is associated with longer study abroad experiences, the historical and current reality is that students predominantly chose shorter stays. To optimize intercultural awareness gains for students and their faculty, and to provide greater benefits for the internationalization of their colleges and universities, it is suggested that short-term study abroad programs focus on the inherent liminality of the experience. This chapter explores liminality and the opportunities and challenges associated with the liminally-centered study abroad program.

DOI: 10.4018/978-1-7998-1607-2.ch002

Copyright © 2020, IGI Global. Copying or distributing in print or electronic forms without written permission of IGI Global is prohibited.

INTRODUCTION

Many of those involved with them—students, program organizers, and faculty—attest to the potential transformative impact of study abroad programs, even programs that have a short duration. For example, Milstein (2005), who considered study abroad programs from the perspective of learner self-efficacy, noted that many returning students 'describe a transformation in their very sense of self, both in how they experience their own cultures and in how they view their life paths…. an increased sense of empowerment, an enriched sense of belief in their own capabilities' (p. 218). Similar comments are reflected in other research on study abroad, particularly in those that center on second language (L2) proficiency (Cubillos & Ilvento, 2013; Kim & Cha, 2017; Perry, Stoner, & Tarrant, 2012).

For example, Salisbury (2011) concluded that 'studying abroad significantly affects the positive development of intercultural competence' and adds that this positive development was noticeable, in varying degrees, for all study abroad participants irrespective of their 'gender, race, SES [socioeconomic status], institutional type, pre-college tested academic preparation, [intercultural competence] pretest score, or college experiences' (p. 92). Other researchers and scholars have reported that study abroad programs often provide participants with both personal benefits and valuable marketplace skills. At the level of personal development, study abroad can promote the 'acceptance of difference in others, tolerance of ambiguity, self-awareness, confidence in meeting new people, and greater independence and self-confidence' (American Institute for Foreign Study, 2013, p. 13). From a vocational and career perspective, these programs can 'develop several important employment-related skills (e.g., intercultural competence, global awareness, foreign language skills) to which they [students] may have been less exposed [before travel]' (Di Pietro, 2013, p. 18).

Research indicates that study abroad programs provide students with multiple benefits that may not be available on their domestic campuses. These include: (a) increased and developing intercultural awareness, understanding, and sensitivity (Czerwionka, Artamonova, & Barbosa, 2015; Jackson 2018); (b) a stronger and more appreciative understanding of both cultural diversity and multiculturalism (Wooldridge, Peet, & Meyer, 2018); and, (c) higher levels of intercultural competency (Hermond, Vairez, &Tanner, 2018; Nichols, 2011; Yarosha, Lukic, & Santibáñez-Gruber, 2018). As noted previously, study abroad programs even of a relatively short duration (4-5 weeks) also appear to contribute positively and significantly to the student's sense of self-confidence and self-efficacy (Czerwionka et al., 2015; Lee & Negrelli, 2018; Nguyen, Jefferies, & Rojas. 2018).

Intercultural Awareness and Short-Term Study Abroad Programs

One recurring variable associated with study abroad outcomes is the duration of the program. In general, programs of short duration (4-7 weeks) may actually *reduce* levels of intercultural awareness and intercultural competency: they may produce and reinforce insulating bubbles of familiarity for those experiencing the shock and difference of new cultures. On the other hand, longer periods of study abroad (8-12 weeks) usually result in increased levels of intercultural awareness, sensitivity, and competence even although these increases may be relatively modest. Some researchers have argued that the optimal development of intercultural competency is associated with programs in which students learn for a full semester—i.e., 13-18 weeks—in their target country (Vande Berg, Connor-Litton, & Paige, 2009). It is perhaps of significance to note that while this particular research work included measures of intercultural competency it centered primarily on the acquisition of foreign language skills. Although a robust positive correlation between study abroad duration and intercultural competency has not been established, it seems probable that the *quality* of the stay—in terms of interaction with the local community, intercultural friendships and shared experiences, etc.—and its length, are both significant.

This chapter reconsiders the short-term study abroad experience with a focus the development of intercultural awareness. In particular, this chapter considers such experiences as offering learners an invitation into the liminality that accompanies study abroad. It considers the elements of study abroad, explores the dimension of intercultural awareness, and reviews the nature and power of liminality.

BACKGROUND

Study abroad programs are energetically encouraged at the institution level and also, in many cases, promoted as national policy. So far as the higher education (HE) community is concerned, study abroad is regarded as providing exceptional value in terms of cognitive opportunities, competency development, and experiential enrichment for individual students, their accompanying faculty, and the institution at large. For students and faculty, the key issues are often seen as the development of intercultural awareness, increased cross-cultural communication skills, and the growing ability to connect and relate across cultural divides. Institutionally, study abroad programs enhance the college's reputation, advance its internationalization agenda, and contribute—sometimes subtly and sometimes obliquely—to a growing atmosphere of diversity and to the accumulation of cultural capital on the home campus (King, Findlay, & Ahrens, 2010).

Study Abroad: Perceived and Projected Value

Many national governments recognize the value of study abroad and have instituted policies or funding opportunities that encourage such experiences. At a national level, study abroad is frequently associated with increasing competitive advantage in international markets and with contributing to a more globally attuned labor force. Government and HE perspectives are often perceived as complementary and mutually supportive and this is perhaps most evidently in the European Union, where study abroad and increased international student mobility—conspicuously in the form of the *Erasmus+ Program*—are seen as providing benefit and added value for program participants, their colleges, and the sponsoring countries.

Significantly, in the *Erasmus+ Program*, study abroad has been understood as an important *rite of passage* for European undergraduates (Murphy-Lejeune, 2002). This attitude to study abroad is mirrored in a recent review of the impact of the *Erasmus+ Program* which recognizes that international student mobility turns those who participate 'into different people, defining a maturing process full of opportunities and challenges, and most likely for many constituting a rite of passage to greater independence' (European Commission, 2014, p. 92).

In the United States, there is little direct federal endorsement of, or support for, study abroad. This is somewhat surprising since the US is still the number one destination for inward-bound international student immigration, even although these numbers peaked in 2016 and seem to be declining. In passing, it might be of interest to note that some commentators attribute this recent decline to emerging complexities in the US such as: (a) the underlying historical ambivalence of US attitudes towards internationalized education; (b) the present political climate in which isolationism, xenophobia, and anti-immigrant sentiments have proliferated; or simply (c) to what Hans De Wit and Altbach (2018) characterized as the 'dramatic instability in international education' in their article of the same name. Attitudes and perspectives regarding in-bound international student mobility may color student and institutional attitudes towards study abroad and it will be interesting to note future US trends in in-bound and out-bound student migration.

It is indeed surprising that no comprehensive or coordinated US national policy on international education and study abroad has materialized. It was only in 2012 that the US Department of Education formulated a 'first-ever, fully articulated international strategy'. This document identified two broad goals for internationalizing education: 'strengthening US education and advancing our nation's international priorities' (USDE, 2012, p. 1). These national goals were to be advanced through five specific initiatives within HE: (a) providing world-class education for all US students; (b) ensuring that all US students acquire global competencies; (c) introducing international

Intercultural Awareness and Short-Term Study Abroad Programs

standards and benchmarking; (d) applying lessons learned about globalization from other countries; and (e) advancing US education diplomacy and engagement with other countries. Although this landmark document made no direct mention of study abroad programs, it did affirm 'the Department's commitment to preparing today's youth, and our country more broadly, for a globalized world, and to engaging with the international community to improve education' (p. 1).

Despite a rather belated and tentative interest in the advantages of international education and study abroad at the national level, US HE has generally embraced the opportunities that such experiences provide. Braskamp, Braskamp, and Merrill (2009) acknowledged that educational experiences abroad have become 'an increasingly important educational program (experience) in global learning and development, intercultural competence, intercultural maturity, and intercultural sensitivity of students.... a powerful influence on student's attitudes, intercultural skills, learning within a discipline, and views of an education abroad experience' (pp. 101-102). Considerable thought and careful planning are required to provide optimal learning abroad experiences; however, prioritizing learner transformation and incorporating this 'into the core objectives of study abroad courses may encourage faculty (and institutions) to acknowledge the added value of study abroad beyond the classroom' (Tarrant, Rubin, & Stoner, 2014, p. 156).

Study Abroad: US Student Participation

The appreciation, at the institutional and student level, of this 'powerful influence' and its 'added value' seems to be reflected in the growing number of US students who participate in study abroad. In the academic year 2016/17, as many as 332,727 students received academic credit for study abroad experiences. This represents a 2.3% increase over the prior year; more importantly, it is double what it was at the beginning of the millennium. Those venturing abroad are predominantly female (67.3%). They are also predominantly White (70.8%), although Whites as a percentage of the total has steadily declined over the last ten years (it was 81.9% in 2006/07) as other ethnic groups have increased their levels of participation. For example, Hispanic or Latino/a students now account for 10.2% of the total (6.0% in 2006/07); Asian and Pacific Islanders students make up 8.2% (6.7% in 2006/07); and Black or African-American students constitute 6.1% of all US students studying abroad (3.8% in 2006/07) (Institute of International Education 2018).

US students currently opting for studying abroad travel to 25 countries, with 40% of them heading for the six most favored study abroad destinations: the United Kingdom, Italy, Spain, France, Germany, and China (in order of popularity). In addition to those involved in short-, medium-, and long-term study abroad programs,

35

a further 36,975 participated in foreign non-credit work, research projects, internships or volunteering situations in 2016/17 (Institute of International Education 2018).

Undergraduate attitudes towards study abroad are generally positive and the comments of those returning from such experiences are often exceptionally favorable. However, despite this—and despite the high institutional status afforded to study abroad—participation rates and lengths of stay are modest. In total, it is estimated that in the academic year 2016/17 about 16% of those enrolled in US baccalaureate degree programs participated in study abroad. Likewise, two-thirds of these students (65%) remained in their destination country for less than eight weeks, while almost all of the remainder (33%) stayed for a full semester. Only a few (2%) remained in their target country for a complete academic or calendar year (Institute of International Education, 2018).

Study Abroad: The Decision to Participate

In order to explore the gap between positive perceptions but low participation it may be useful to explore the student decision-making process associated with study abroad. Examining the decisions that students make to participate, or not to participate, in study abroad experiences Salisbury, Umbach, Paulsen, and Pascarella (2009) concluded that the decision-making framework employed was 'virtually identical' to the one that students used in deciding to go to college—that is, *college choice theory* (Cabrera & La Nasa, 2000; Moogan, Baron, & Harris, 1999; St. John, Paulsen, & Carter, 2005).

College choice theory recognizes three phases in the decision-making process and an appreciation of these sequential phases may shed light on decisions to engage in study abroad:

- **Phase One:** The initial development of an aspiration, consideration, predisposition, or desire to enroll in college, or to participate in a study abroad program. For study abroad this probably occurs in the student's first two years in the undergraduate program.
- **Phase Two:** The student-directed search for a college (or study abroad program) that will satisfy perceived needs, expectations, and preferences. For study abroad programs, this suggest that the institution should have a clear understanding of what students look for in these programs and the expectations they are trying to fulfill. The needs and expectations of the student population are not a matter of conjecture: they can only be understood through carefully designed and proactive institutional research.

- **Phase Three:** The final selection and departure for the chosen study abroad destination. The decision-making process utilizes the student's awareness of the target country and also his or her perception of the nature and amount of capital—that is, human, financial, social, and cultural capital—that are believed to be presently available to the student and which are anticipated to accrue as a result of the study abroad experience (Perna, 2006).

In their extensive study of students considering study abroad options, Salisbury et al. (2009) found that one of the strongest inhibitors to considering study abroad was the student's perceived lack of financial capital or available funding. Financial capital, however, is only *one* of the forms of capital that is evaluated in making decisions in complex social situations. In the past, study abroad has often been considered the prerogative of those of higher socioeconomic status. This historic association still clouds the perception and consideration of many students who come from lower socioeconomic, from ethnic minority families, or who are the first in their families to engage in HE. Salisbury et al. (2009) confirmed that lower income students, even those eligible for federal financial aid, 'are less likely to plan to study abroad than higher income students…. [those receiving] federal financial aid are 11 percentage points less likely to intend to study abroad than are those not getting federal aid' (p. 134).

The other gains and losses that seem to be considered by those contemplating study abroad are connected with social and cultural capital. These include: (a) the level of social and cultural capital that the student *brings* to college from high school, prior employment, military service etc.; and (b) the social and cultural capital that he or she *accumulates* during the period of the college stay. The social and cultural capital acquired before college, coupled with the socioeconomic status of the student's family, tends to determine whether study abroad will be contemplated. For example, it has been estimated that for students considering study abroad: (a) 48% will eventually participate if they have low socioeconomic status, low pre-college capital, but *high* college-accumulated capital; (b) the participation rate is 75% for students with an average socioeconomic status, average pre-college capital, and *high* college-accumulated capital; and, (c) participation is highest (85%) for those with high socioeconomic status, high pre-college capital, and *high* college-accumulated capital (Salisbury et al., 2009, p. 138). In other words, a high level of *college-accumulated* social and cultural capital seems to be a positive predictor of study abroad participation irrespective of the student's socioeconomic status or pre-college capital. This would seem to have significant implications for HEs and their policies to encourage participation in study abroad experiences.

Students in college can acquire social and cultural capital in a number of ways: (a) by adjusting well to college life; (b) by performing satisfactorily in their coursework; and/ or (c) by developing a supportive and influential network of social connection (Tan, 2017; Wells, 2008). Nevertheless, even for students with high college-accumulated capital the decision to participate in a study abroad experience is significantly and negative moderated by lower measures of their socioeconomic status and pre-college capital. It would seem that self-imposed limits and reservations (based on these two metrics) are generated even *before* the student enters college and even before he or she considers study abroad. These self-imposed limits seem to impact both the decision to participate in study abroad and the length the stay in the target country.

Increased study abroad participation, especially for ethnic minorities, may ultimately be an issue of student choice. Similarly, extended duration of the study abroad experience may also be a matter of personal choice and preference. Nevertheless, there is a strong case for institutionally-driven involvement, encouragement, and promotion of these programs. Such promotion would undoubtedly challenge 'policy makers and administrators [to] develop innovative strategies to effectively use scarce resources, offer quality programs that meet students' academic needs, and expand the availability of study abroad to a diverse range of students' (Blumenthal & Gutierrez, 2009, p. 4). Further, if the decision to participate in study abroad is moderated by student perceptions of college-accumulated capital then colleges may advance and promote these programs by encouraging students to evaluate their *current* social and cultural capital more positively and to better appreciate the *anticipated* capital gains from study abroad participation, rather than focus on claims regarding the inherent *present value* of study abroad experiences.

Study Abroad: Introduction to Intercultural Awareness

Cultural awareness has been defined as 'an ability to evaluate critically and on the basis of explicit criteria perspectives, practices and products in one's own and other cultures and countries' (Byram, 1997, p. 53). Cultural awareness is inevitably 'intercultural' awareness, since the critical exploration of any 'other' culture suggests and initiates a consideration of the individual's own culture. Frequently, this consideration has never been previously undertaken because we are so embedded in our own cultural world that its assumptions, beliefs, and values are taken for granted, barely recognized, and rarely if ever questioned. As Lo Bianco (2003) pointed out, we constantly see *our* world through *our* given cultural lens, thus making the 'the viewpoint and behavioral norms of the observer *invisible,* rendering it as a natural or normal point from which others are scrutinized… [making] the practices, lifestyles and values of the observed, *overtly visible*' (p. 17, emphasis in original).

Intercultural Awareness and Short-Term Study Abroad Programs

Cultural awareness has been conceptualized as having three levels:

1. At a primary (or basic) level, cultural difference is realized but cannot be fully articulated or associated with any systematic analysis of the new culture; indeed, the very construct of 'culture' may not enter into the recognition or explanation of difference. At this level there is usually a slowly developing ability to compare and contrast the difference that is encountered with one's own particular cultural reference. Even although difference is discernable it is generally perceived as something that is unique, contextual, and explainable in terms of generalization, inconsistencies, and stereotypes (Baker, 2012).

2. At a secondary (or intermediate) level, cultural difference is recognized as a product of reference, with the manifestation and behavior of the 'other' attributed to an inherent system or pattern of difference that is accepted but only partially understood. This level is more nuanced than the first and is usually paralleled by an attempt to develop more specific knowledge about the second culture, to systematically explore and better understand it, and to try to function within it (Baker, 2012).

3. At a tertiary (or advanced) level, the second culture is more comprehensively appreciated. It is not regarded as essentially differenced, self-contained, and impermeable. Rather, it is understood to be a social and cultural system that is dynamic and fluid—a separate system that is nevertheless nested in a broader international context and shaped (to some degree at least) by these external forces and influences (Baker, 2011, 2012). At this level of intercultural awareness, we begin to appreciate the other culture as a source of evolving newness, not as a simply a repository of difference. There is an appreciation that the second culture is a system within which we are presently living, or within which we could reasonably consider living.

This tripartite hierarchy of cultural awareness comes into place when an individual explores another culture, internalizes a response to it, and ultimately develops an intercultural competency when interacting with or in that culture. *Intercultural competency* has been used extensively in considering cultural and yet there is still no definitive agreement among scholars regarding the elements that comprise it or the relative importance of those elements (Chiu, Lonner, Matsumoto, & Ward, 2013):

- Byram and Fleming (1998) suggested that a person possessing intercultural competency has 'knowledge of one, or, preferably, more cultures and social identities and… [possesses] the capacity to discover and relate to new people from other contexts for which they have not been prepared directly' (p. 9).

- Deardorff (2006) understood intercultural competency as 'the ability to communicate effectively and appropriately in intercultural situations based on one's intercultural knowledge, skills, and attitudes' (pp. 247-248).
- Wilson, Ward, and Fischer (2013) defined intercultural competency as the 'culture-specific skills required to (a) function effectively within a new cultural context and/or (b) interact effectively with people from different cultural backgrounds' (p. 901).

Intercultural awareness—and certainly intercultural competence—is a critical capacity for those in HE, especially for students who will have to deal with an increasingly inter-connected, inter-related, and globalized world in their futures. The connection between initiating and accelerating intercultural awareness through study abroad has been clearly demonstrated in multiple research projects (Deardorff, 2009; Medina-López-Portillo, 2004; Rexeisen, Anderson, Lawton, & Hubbard, 2008; Vande Berg et al., 2009). However, it is far from obvious that simple exposure to different cultures inevitably produces intercultural awareness or enhances intercultural competence. It seems that much hinges on the way in which the study abroad program is structured, on how learners are encouraged in their explorations of cultural difference, and the degree to which participants are supported in recognizing and coping with the difference they encounter (Bennett, 2010).

LIMINALITY: THE SPACE OF OPPORTUNITY

Looking at international educational experiences, the Lincoln Commission (2005) characterized study abroad as one of the 'signs of a well-educated graduate' (p. 6). If current US graduates predominantly do not exhibit such signs, it may be that they have not been challenged by their colleges to grasp the opportunity of what is undoubtedly a *disruptive experience* that forces them to reconsider, re-evaluate, and re-form their prior notions of learning and education. In a very real sense, those who embark on study abroad experiences find themselves in a '*betwixt and between*' situation.

In social transitions, individuals move from one set of socially-constructed predictabilities, roles, and status to another. In these transitions there is a tripartite structure: 'before', 'betwixt and between', and 'after'. The intermediate 'betwixt and between' is recognized by those passing through it as an integral part of a transition process. It can be thought of an unstructured space that allows for reflection, growth, and anticipated change. It is more commonly known as the liminal phase.

Intercultural Awareness and Short-Term Study Abroad Programs

The *liminal* phase provides a constructive space for pausing, reconstructing, and reflecting. It is a resilient space that resists the encroachment of the oppositional duality of what has come before and what will follow. The liminal phase is usually recognized as a part of a transition, as a phase in a progression, and as part of a movement from one social role to another. Liminal periods are often brief and transient but sometimes they can be more extended: the prolonged betwixt and between of undergraduate life is such an example. Undergraduate life is that ambiguous time bounded by two socially constructed rites of passage—graduating from high school and graduating from college. Between these two events there is no clear marker of social progression, transition, or status change. Lacking these markers, undergraduate life is all too readily experienced as a static place—as a 'stuck place' (Meyer & Land, 2005, p. 373).

In his seminal work, van Gennep (1960) observed that an individual's life 'in any society is a series of passages from one age to another and from one occupation to another... a man's life comes to be made up of a succession of stages with similar ends and beginnings' (pp. 2-3). The different phases of the individual's life are entered via socially recognized ceremonies rites of passage that again follow a tripartite structure or sequence: (a) a break or discontinuity with the person's prior role or status (the 'before', or the pre-liminal); (b) an intermediate phase of disassociation (the liminal or 'betwixt and between' phase); and (c) a final phase in which the person re-enters social life with his or her newly acquired role or status (the 'after', or post-liminal).

Transitions in life are inevitable, but they can cause concern or even be profoundly disruptive. Rites of passage are socially and communally recognized events that ease the individual's changing responsibilities, roles, and status. Rites of passage allow participants the opportunity to appreciate that the transformation is both recognized and anticipated. They provide participants with an understanding of the nature of the change, and with the means of creating a new sense of meaning in their lives. Rites of passage offer powerful signals and provide landmarks by which individuals can plan and define their life progression.

At the heart of the rite of passage—literally the central space that must be passed through in the journey—is liminality. Liminal spaces are evident in undergraduate life, in the study abroad experience, and in 'the learner's transformation from the state of unconscious incompetence toward a more conscious incompetence, and then onward to a conscious cognitive competence' (Szkudlarek, McNett, & Romani, 2013, p. 489).

- **Space for Transition:** Liminality (Latin, *limen* = a threshold) is a sensed ambiguity which provides the threshold that must be crossed to reach a new status or sense of being. The liminal phase is transitional, anticipated, of limited duration, and belongs to neither the 'before' nor the 'after' of the transition. Turner (1969) portrayed liminality as 'a moment in and out of time… [when] a generalized social bond that has ceased to be and has simultaneously yet to be fragmented into a multiplicity of structural ties' (p. 96). Those in liminal states are 'neither here nor there; they are betwixt and between the positions assigned and arrayed by law, custom, convention and ceremonial' (p. 95). Liminality, he observed, is 'a cultural realm that has few or none of the attributes of the past or coming state' (p. 94). Others have viewed liminality as 'a state of being neither here nor there—neither completely inside nor outside a given situation, structure or mindset' (Madison, 2005, p. 158).

- **Space for Questioning:** Liminality affords an open and unstructured space for pausing, reflecting, and bridging past and future. Liminality does not 'simply reproduce traditional power dynamics, social practices, modes of participation, and fixed senses of self, but rather create spaces within which to question these' (Cook-Sather, 2006, p. 122). Liminal spaces are bounded by certainties, limited in duration, and an integral part of transitions. The liminal space is characterized by 'its lack of fixity or permanence; it is not and cannot be a fixed space, a fixed point or a fixed set of processes because things are liminal with respect to other things, primarily the center' (Conroy & Ruyter, 2009, p. 5, emphasis in original). Liminal spaces allow 'transformed way of understanding, or interpreting, or viewing something, without which the learner cannot progress, and results in a reformulation of the learners' frame of meaning…. a transformed internal view of subject matter, subject landscape, or even world view' (Meyer, Land, & Baillie, 2010, p. ix).

- **Space for Struggling with Identity:** If rites of passages are not provided, there is no social or cognitive space in which to question. There is only the nebulous void of perplexity, doubt, and uncertainty. Arnett (2004), who considered adulthood and the process of becoming an adult, observed that many emerging adults are suspended in the transition as though they were 'like an age in-between, neither adolescent nor adult, on the way to adulthood but not there yet…. asked whether they feel they have reached adulthood, their responses are often ambiguous, with one foot in yes and the other in no' (p. 15, emphasis in original). These are the emerging adults that we encounter in the classrooms and on college campuses. Their struggles to make sense of a social identity parallel their struggle to make sense of what they are studying, which in turn may parallel their attempts to come to an understanding of intercultural difference. Superficially, these may seem like personal cognitive struggles, but they are not. Fundamentally, they are *affective* struggles and struggles to comprehend and affirm realities about which students may be deeply uncertain and about which they have little or no experience.

SOLUTIONS AND RECOMMENDATIONS

Maximizing the impact and value of study abroad can potentially be accomplished by refocusing it as a significant and transformative event in the trajectory of undergraduate life. As such, study abroad may better be understood by institutions and students as *a rite of passage*—a rite of passage that acknowledges and celebrates the liminal core that is at its center (Grabowski, Wearing, Lyons, Tarrant, & Landon, 2017; Starr-Glass, 2016a, 2016b).

Perry, Stoner, and Tarrant (2012) suggested that 'within study abroad experiences, exposure to new places, cultures, and learning environments where a students' preconceived and established notions and beliefs are tested, may act as the catalyst or impetus for bring forth a transformative experience' (p. 682). In his seminal work on overseas youth expeditions, Beames (2004) noted that a crucial part of the rite of passage involves integrating participants back into their community with their new and recognized status. On the outward expedition, while there was a 'focus on what people were gaining from their experience, there appeared to be little attention paid to discussing how a young person could return to be a contributor to their community rather than being a drain on its resources' (p. 35).

In advancing study abroad, colleges may be well advised to pay particular attention to reintegration participants into the learning community as changed and valued contributors. One of those aspects of change and gained value is the developing skill of intercultural awareness. The reorientation on the study abroad experience to a communally-recognized rite of passage will make it more visible, attractive, and desirable for students. It may move study abroad away from being an *optional* part of academic life to an *essential* part of demonstrated growth and development during the undergraduate years. This will require institutional intervention and structuring. It will require the academy to have a deeper understanding of the present obstacles and challenges that students attach to study abroad. It also requires them to have a deeper understanding of the social and cultural dynamics of rites of passage and of the core of all such transformations, liminality.

Study abroad has considerable intrinsic value for students, faculty, and their communities of learning. To optimize this inherent value, it is suggested that institutions of higher learning reposition study abroad as a college-recognized rite of passage. Study abroad should be presented and promoted as an integrated and comprehensive expression of institutional philosophy, mission, and strategic advancement. Critical in projecting study abroad as a rite of passage is the acceptance and appreciation of the liminality that accompanies it. In any attempt to reposition study abroad in the college and in the perception maps of students, the following questions—and more particularly their answers—may be particularly useful in ensuring the success and benefit of study abroad for both the student and the institution.

- **How do we understand our institutional climate?** Historically, small liberal arts colleges have had higher percentages of students engaged in study abroad programs; whereas, the larger state colleges have lower percentages in these programs, as do research universities, regional institutions, and community colleges (Hoffa, 2007; Salisbury et al., 2009). These differences may be traced back to the philosophical and educational outlooks of these institutions and the socioeconomic profile of their constituencies. Colleges wishing to advance study abroad need to examine their practices, expressed preferences, and projected sentiments concerning the value of these experiences. For example, a survey of predominantly four-year colleges indicated that financial barriers were the primary deterrent to students from participation. Other studies have revealed that a 'lack of staff and advisors to handle more study abroad students… [and] not enough interest on the part of faculty members' were more significant than lack of student interest (Blumenthal & Gutierrez, 2009, p. 14).

- **How do we, as an institution, understand comprehensive internationalization?** Comprehensive internationalization and high-impact educational practices—that is educational practices which focus on deep learning, student engagement, and knowledge retention, integration, and transferability (Kuh, 2008)—can be used as tactical enactments to realize the vision of the academy. And yet, tactical components can only be effective if they are part of an overarching, coordinated, and interlocking strategy. Institutions of higher education (HEIs) should not consider study abroad as isolated and supplemental: they should promote it as part of a broader and decisive strategy. Vision and mission statements are critical for creating institutional goals, but they often seem distant, inspirational, and rhetorical. Long-term educational strategies and interlocking short-term instructional tactics are the ways through which these goals are expressed and reached. Tactics alone are of little value unless they reflect the implementation of a focused strategy (Hudzik, 2011; Hudzik & McCarthy, 2012; Peterson & Helms, 2014).

- **Are our students prepared to participate in study abroad?** Study abroad programs provide cognitive and experiential opportunities for engaging with the realities of internationalization and globalization. They open up a constructive liminal space, where thoughts and feelings are accepted as lived experiences, not as textbook case studies. They provide participants with the opportunity to reflect on critical incidents, obtain different perspectives, and embark on explorations that can be unexpected and personally transformative. These opportunities are lost if, among other things, students are inadequately prepared to experience difference or to embrace liminality (Hoffer, 2010; VeLure Roholt & Fisher, 2013).

During the semester before study abroad, students should be provided with an extensive program that sets out expectations, promotes learning opportunities, provides guidance, and explores the reaction to difference and the central place of liminality (Starr-Glass, 2016a). In preparing for study abroad, it is crucial to emphasize the opportunities presented by travel in robust academic terms, pointing out the role of the transcultural observer, the ways in which we respond to difference, and the anticipated educational benefits. Often, however, these perspectives are never presented and in many cases these opportunities are never fully identified. All too often, anticipated outcomes and change are never discussed. For example, a study of the reflections of study abroad participants revealed what many study abroad proponents had already suspected: student self-reported learning experiences (mostly about fun, travel, and making friends) were 'in stark contrast to the lofty rhetoric of their home university' (Forsey, Broomhall, & Davis, 2012, p. 129).

- **Are our students sufficiently prepared to enter and engage with liminality?** Those who will participate in study abroad have undoubtedly experienced liminality in their lives; however, they may not be able to recognize or appreciate the liminal space. They may even find liminality challenging and counter-intuitive. McCabe (2013) understood that mediation between cultures requires continual movement across borders, interaction with 'others', making transient sense of the situation, and 'carrying out projects and communicating with people inhabiting different worlds of meaning' (p. 156). McCabe (2013) further noted that 'in this fluid space… [we] listen to multiple voices, gain insider views, and communicate across boundaries…. [we] live in a perennial space of liminality where meanings are grasped and often negotiated' (p. 160).

Ideally, this is the space that study abroad students should be invited to enter. For that to happen, the existence of this space—with its fluidity, openness, and potential uninhibited creativity—needs to be thoughtfully and realistically communicated to students. Study abroad participants should be sensitized to the role of liminality in the change process—a change process in which they themselves will be intimately involved. In the present author's experience with business students, an introduction to liminality can often be most effectively initiated by considering real-world experiences and case studies drawn from the organizational and management consulting literatures (Czarniawska & Mazza, 2003; Simpson, Sturges, & Weight, 2009; Szakolczai, 2014).

- **Are our students cognitively and emotionally supported while abroad?** Students need to be supported, encouraged, and guided during their study abroad program. They need to be aware of the disruptions and structural ambiguity of the liminal experience. They need guidance in the 'reconstruction of identity (in which the sense of self is disrupted) in such a way that the new identity is meaningful for the individual and their community' (Beech, 2010, pp. 296-297). They need to be supported in 'living in liminality'—supported in recognizing the shock of entering a new culture, in accepting ambiguity, and in trying to make sense of their feelings (Morgan, 2018; O'Reilly, 2018). It may be particularly valuable if students have a guide or mentor, who can support them confront liminality, deal with disruption and dislocation, reflect on encounters with the 'other', and support them in exploring intercultural awareness. Mentors need to have prior experience, sensitivity, and a genuine interest in helping. They may be faculty members who have gained an understanding of the study abroad process and the ways in which it impacts participants. Alternatively, they may profitably be recruited by the institution from faculty who have a good track record in supervising international postgraduate research students who face the same liminal issues as study abroad students (Manathunga, 2007, 2017).
- **How do we receive and treat our returning students?** The study abroad experience is not an isolated event: it is part of a process. Returning students need the opportunity to reflect on their experience and share them with their learning community. These students can sometimes—depending on the length of their stay abroad—experience doubts and apprehension about re-entering their personal and college-centered worlds. Return and readjustment are little researched areas and our appreciation of the process and its dynamics are, in the main, drawn from populations of expatriates who have often spent considerable times abroad. Nevertheless, return and reintegration are an integral part of the study abroad process and deserves attention.

There may be difficulty in readjusting to everyday living: an element of 'culture shock' and perhaps a heightened skepticism about US cultural and social norms (Szkudlarek, 2009; Wielkiewicz & Turkowsi, 2010). Rather than being considered a 'pathological' or adverse reaction, re-entry experiences can be more profitably understood as an extension of the disjunction of liminality. Re-entry can challenge the student to reflect on the study abroad experience, try to make more sense of it, consider what has been learned, and to appreciate personal change—especially in intercultural awareness and sensitivity. Wielkiewicz and Turkowsi (2010) suggested the use of focus groups for those returning from study abroad programs, groups in which 'students are invited to discuss their experiences after study abroad… [providing] a venue for exploring any reentry difficulties they may encounter, make valuable contributions to the knowledge base, and point toward topics that deserve deeper study' (p. 649).

FUTURE RESEARCH DIRECTIONS

Study abroad is often portrayed as a leisurely, fun-filled, and vacation-like visit to an exotic place. Yet, it is increasingly recognized that study abroad presents opportunities for personal transitions and has the power of 'opening a learner's metaphoric eyes and enlightening their perspectives' (Perry et al., 2012, p. 683). This suggests a number of avenues of inquiry that may be of value in the academy's attempt to advocate and support study abroad for its student population.

First, the central premise of this chapter is that study abroad is an explicit invitation to engage in liminality. In turn, it has been suggested that liminality is a necessary pre-requisite for personal transformation, specifically for the development of intercultural awareness. There exists a plethora of positive and supportive statements regarding these assumptions in the literature and in student journals. Nevertheless, more extensive and evidence-based research is required to explore and clarify the linkage between study abroad and the liminal state. Concluding his essay on *Liminality and Experience*, Szakolczai (2008) observed that 'liminality is among the most important conceptual tools that are at once innovative and deeply based on the most important historical and anthropological traditions of mankind' (p. 167). Further research into the constructive and empowering role that liminality plays in study abroad experiences may only serve to underscore that importance.

Second, research indicates that the length of the study abroad experience is important—longer stays are often associated with a deeper cultivation of intercultural awareness. However, historically and currently, students opt for shorter stays. There are many reasons for this preference: cost, extension of the undergraduate period, and concerns about timely graduation to mention but a few. Many scholars and educators consider that longer stays are preferable and should be promoted more vigorously (Haynes, 2011; Savicki, 2008). It has been suggested that 'if colleges and universities have as an objective student growth in global-mindedness, they should promote semester-long programs.… academic majors that consider such an experience crucial should consider making it a requirement of their particular degree plans' (Kehl & Morris, 2008, pp. 77-78). With this in mind, research is needed to clarify and quantify the relationship between length of stay and levels of student benefit. This research would start with the premise that optimum study abroad length depends on the nature of the anticipated outcome—whether that outcome is related to intercultural awareness, intercultural competence, or language and communication skills.

Third, study abroad experiences have been linked to institutional strategic realignment because it is understood that these experiences benefit all educational stakeholders in an increasingly competitive global world. Strategic initiatives are by definition emergent and ongoing. Research is required to: (a) better determine the profile of study abroad participants; (b) assess their learning and experiential gains; (c) establish the degree to which preparatory study abroad workshops and seminars are effective; (d) determine the relevancy and effectiveness of preparatory programs in changing study abroad participation rates and in enhancing the quality of the learning outcomes.

CONCLUSION

Institutions of higher learning that recognize significant shifts in their operational environments need to change their educational paradigms, their educational goals, and their strategic emphases. Critical and strategic changes are needed to successful adapt and to advance the wellbeing of students in a world that is being reshaped by the pressures, norms, and expectations of an increasingly globalized world. Contemplated institutional changes need to be real and convincing, not simply rhetorical. They need to center on those who are directly involved but who are all too often disregarded or sidelined: the student population. One suggested change is the way in which institutions recognize, promote, and celebrate the study abroad experience as a community-centered accomplishment in undergraduate life. Making study abroad the anticipated norm—rather than the desired exception—creates value in terms of social and cultural capital for the institution, for its campus-based faculty, and crucially for participating students. Making study abroad a rite of passage provides benefit for all parties (Starr-Glass, 2016a).

Rather than concentrate on the *extrinsic* value provided by elevating study abroad to a legitimate rite of passage, it may be even more important to consider the *intrinsic* value of the way in which study abroad actually *becomes* a rite of passage. It may be expedient for colleges and HEIs to focus on the social *process* at work in study abroad rather than on the learning *product* created through its completion. Study abroad can reinvigorate undergraduates by exposing them to exhilarating experiences that are new and fresh. It can lead to new considerations of what has been learned and of what remains to be learned. Study abroad is rooted in the experience of difference and that experience can trigger different ways of thinking, different levels of awareness, and different appreciations of what lies beyond the campus and beyond the familiar.

This shift in thinking, feeling, and appreciation certainly crystalizes once the study abroad experience has been undertaken; however, the possibility of such a shift becomes nascent during the unfettered 'betwixt and between' space that lies at the core of the experience itself. Reconceptualizing study abroad as a dynamic *social process*, rather than as a static *learning product*, may provide us with a deeper insight into the dynamics of study abroad and into how such experiences may be optimized to produce desired outcomes such as intercultural awareness, sensitivity, and competency.

Liminality has a potency and transformative potential, but it cannot be forced or imposed—it needs to materialize spontaneously within the study abroad experience. At best, all we can do is to extend an invitation to learners to recognize, accept, and explore the liminality that they encounter. With study abroad programs that last for only for a few weeks, program organizers may sense a need to carefully structure and choreograph the event to provide participants with maximum content and exposure. That engineered buzz of activity and excitement is obviously well-intentioned, but it probably inhibits, or postpones, the onset of liminality. Liminality is made available to those who participate in study abroad experiences that have a short duration. Nevertheless, encouraging participants to remain abroad for a longer period—ideally for a full semester—has a better chance of allowing liminality to materialize and of utilizing the transformative potential that it provides.

REFERENCES

American Institute for Foreign Study. (2013). *AIFS study abroad outcomes: A view from our alumni1990-2010*. Stamford, CT: Author. Retrieved from http://www.aifsabroad.com/advisors/pdf/AIFS_Study_Abroad_Outcomes.pdf

Arnett, J. J. (2004). *Emerging adulthood: The winding road from the late teens through the twenties*. Oxford, UK: Oxford University Press.

Baker, W. (2011). Intercultural awareness: Modelling an understanding of cultures in intercultural communication through English as a lingua franca. *Language and Intercultural Communication, 11*(3), 197–214. doi:10.1080/14708477.2011.577779

Baker, W. (2012). From cultural awareness to intercultural awareness: Culture in ELT. *ELT Journal, 66*(1), 62–70. doi:10.1093/elt/ccr017

Beames, S. (2004). Overseas youth expeditions with Raleigh International: A rite of passage? *Australian Journal of Outdoor Education, 8*(1), 29–36. doi:10.1007/BF03400793

Beech, N. (2011). Liminality and the practices of identity reconstruction. *Human Relations, 64*(2), 285–302. doi:10.1177/0018726710371235

Bennett, M. J. (2010). A short conceptual history of intercultural learning in study abroad. In W. W. Hoffa & S. C. DePaul (Eds.), *A history of US study abroad: 1965 to the present* (pp. 419–449). Lancaster, PA: Frontiers–The Interdisciplinary Journal of Study Abroad.

Blumenthal, P., & Gutierrez, R. (Eds.). (2009). *Expanding study abroad capacity at US colleges and universities: Meeting America's global education challenge.* White Paper on Expanding Capacity and Diversity in Study Abroad. Washington, DC: Institute of International Education.

Braskamp, L. A., Braskamp, D. C., & Merrill, K. C. (2009). Assessing progress in global learning and development of students with education abroad experiences. *Frontiers: The Interdisciplinary Journal of Study Abroad, 18*, 101–118.

Byram, M. (1997). *Teaching and assessing intercultural communicative competence.* Clevedon, UK: Multilingual Matters.

Byram, M., & Fleming, M. (Eds.). (1998). *Language learning an intercultural perspective.* Cambridge, UK: Cambridge University Press.

Cabrera, A. F., & La Nasa, S. M. (2000). Understanding the college-choice process. *New Directions for Institutional Research, 107*(107), 5–22. doi:10.1002/ir.10701

Chiu, C.-Y., Lonner, W. J., Matsumoto, D., & Ward, C. (2013). Cross-cultural competence: Theory, research, and application. *Journal of Cross-Cultural Psychology, 44*(6), 843–848. doi:10.1177/0022022113493716

Conroy, J., & Ruyter, D. (2009). Contest, contradiction, and security: The moral possibilities of liminal education. *Journal of Educational Change, 10*(1), 1–12. doi:10.100710833-008-9072-z

Cook-Sather, A. (2006). Newly betwixt and between: Revising liminality in the context of a teacher preparation program. *Anthropology & Education Quarterly, 37*(2), 110–127. doi:10.1525/aeq.2006.37.2.110

Intercultural Awareness and Short-Term Study Abroad Programs

Cubillos, J. H., & Ilvento, T. (2013). The impact of study abroad on students' self-efficacy perceptions. *Foreign Language Annals, 45*(4), 494–511. doi:10.1111/j.1944-9720.2013.12002.x

Czarniawska, B., & Mazza, C. (2003). Consulting as a liminal space. *Human Relations, 56*(3), 267–290. doi:10.1177/0018726703056003612

Czerwionka, L., Artamonova, T., & Barbosa, M. (2015). Intercultural knowledge development: Evidence from student interviews during short-term study abroad. *International Journal of Intercultural Relations, 49*, 80–99. doi:10.1016/j.ijintrel.2015.06.012

De Wit, H., & Altbach, P. G. (2018, August 11). Dramatic instability in higher education [Blog post]. Retrieved from http://www.insidehighered.com/blogs/worldview/dramatic-instability-international-higher-education

Deardorff, D. K. (2006). Identification and assessment of intercultural competence as a student outcome of internationalization. *Journal of Studies in International Education, 10*(3), 241–266. doi:10.1177/1028315306287002

Deardorff, D. K. (2009). Implementing intercultural competence assessment. In D. K. Deardorff (Ed.), *The SAGE handbook of intercultural competence* (pp. 477–491). Thousand Oaks, CA: Sage.

Di Pietro, G. (2013). *Do study abroad programs enhance the employability of graduates?* Discussion Paper #7675. Institute for the Study of Labor (Forschungsinstitut zur Zukunft der Arbeit). Bonn, Germany: IZA. Retrieved from http://ftp.iza.org/dp7675.pdf

European Commission. (2014). *The Erasmus impact study: Effects of mobility on the skills and employability of students and the internationalization of higher education institutions.* Luxembourg: Publications Office of the European Union. Retrieved from http://ec.europa.eu/education/library/study/2014/erasmus-impact_en.pdf

Forsey, M., Broomhall, S., & Davis, J. (2011). Broadening the mind? Australian student reflections on the experience of overseas study. *Journal of Studies in International Education, 16*(2), 128–139. doi:10.1177/1028315311407511

Grabowski, S., Wearing, S., Lyons, K., Tarrant, M., & Landon, A. (2017). A rite of passage? Exploring youth transformation and global citizenry in the study abroad experience. *Tourism Recreation Research, 42*(2), 139–149. doi:10.1080/0250828 1.2017.1292177

Haynes, C. (2011). Overcoming the study abroad hype. *Journal of the National Collegiate Honors Council, 12*(1), 17–24.

Hermond, D., Vairez, M. R., & Tanner, T. (2018). Enhancing the cultural competency of prospective leaders via a study abroad experience. *Administrative Issues Journal: Connecting Education, Practice, and Research, 8*(1), 18–27.

Hoffa, W. W. (2007). A history of US study abroad. Carlisle, PA: Frontiers–The Interdisciplinary Journal of Study Abroad/ The Forum on Education Abroad.

Hoffer, B. (2010). Personal epistemologies, learning and cultural context. In M. B. Baxter Magolda, E. G. Creamer, & P. S. Meszaro (Eds.), *Development and assessment of self-authorship: Exploring the concept across cultures* (pp. 133–150). Sterling, VA: Stylus.

Hudzik, J. K. (2011). Comprehensive internationalization: From concept to action. Washington, DC: NAFSA-Association of International Educators.

Hudzik, J. K., & McCarthy, J. S. (2012). *Leading comprehensive internationalization: Strategy and tactics for action*. Washington, DC: NAFSA.

Institute of International Education. (2018). *Open doors 2014 fast fact*. Retrieved from https://www.iie.org/Research-and-Insights/Open-Doors/Fact-Sheets-and-Infographics/Fast-Facts

Jackson, J. (2018). *Interculturality in international education*. New York, NY: Routledge. doi:10.4324/9780429490026

Kehl, K., & Morris, J. (2008). Differences in global-mindedness between short-term and semester-long study abroad participants at selected private universities. *Frontiers: The Interdisciplinary Journal of Study Abroad, 11*, 67–79.

Kim, H.-I., & Cha, K.-A. (2017). Effects of experience abroad and language proficiency on self-efficacy beliefs in language learning. *Psychological Reports, 120*(4), 670–694. doi:10.1177/0033294117697088 PMID:28558539

King, R., Findlay, A., & Ahrens, J. (2010). *International student mobility literature review*. Project Report. Bristol, UK: Higher Education Funding Council for England. Retrieved from http://sro.sussex.ac.uk/id/eprint/12011/1/KingFindlayAhrens_International_Student_Mobility_Literature_Review.pdf

Kuh, G. D. (2008). *High-impact educational practices: What they are, who has access to them, and why they matter*. Washington, DC: Association of American Colleges and Universities.

Intercultural Awareness and Short-Term Study Abroad Programs

Lee, J., & Negrelli, K. (2018). Cultural identification, acculturation, and academic experience abroad: A case of a joint faculty-led short-term study abroad program. *Journal of International Students, 8*(2), 1152–1172. doi:10.32674/jis.v8i2.138

Lincoln Commission. (2005). *Global competence and national needs: One million Americans studying abroad.* Washington, DC: Commission of the Abraham Lincoln Study Abroad Fellowship Program.

Lo Bianco, J. (2003). Culture: Visible, invisible and multiple. In J. Lo Bianco & C. Crozet (Eds.), *Teaching invisible culture: Classroom practice and theory* (pp. 11–35). Melbourne, Australia: Language Australia.

Madison, D. S. (2005). *Critical ethnography: Method, ethics, and performance.* Thousand Oaks, CA: Sage.

Manathunga, C. (2007). Intercultural postgraduate supervision: Ethnographic journeys of identity and power. In D. Palfreyman & D. L. McBride (Eds.), *Learning and teaching across cultures in higher education* (pp. 93–112). London, UK: Palgrave Macmillan. doi:10.1057/9780230590427_6

Manathunga, C. (2017). Intercultural doctoral supervision: The centrality of place, time and other forms of knowledge. *Arts and Humanities in Higher Education, 16*(1), 113–124. doi:10.1177/1474022215580119

McCabe, M. (2013). 360 on method. *Journal of Business Anthropology, 2*(2), 155–161. Retrieved from https://rauli.cbs.dk/index.php/jba/article/view/4957/5383

Medina-López-Portillo, A. (2004). Intercultural learning assessment: A link between program duration and the development of intercultural sensitivity. *Frontiers: The Interdisciplinary Journal of Study Abroad, 10*, 179–199.

Meyer, J. H. F., & Land, R. (2005). Threshold concepts and troublesome knowledge (2): Epistemological considerations and a conceptual framework for teaching and learning. *Higher Education, 49*(3), 373–388. doi:10.100710734-004-6779-5

Meyer, J. H. F., Land, R., & Baillie, C. (Eds.). (2010). *Threshold concepts and transformational learning.* Rotterdam, The Netherlands: Sense.

Milstein, T. (2005). Transformation abroad: Sojourning and the perceived enhancement of self-efficacy. *International Journal of Intercultural Relations, 29*(2), 217–238. doi:10.1016/j.ijintrel.2005.05.005

Moogan, Y. J., Baron, S., & Harris, K. (1999). Decision-making behavior of potential higher education students. *Higher Education Quarterly, 53*(3), 211–228. doi:10.1111/1468-2273.00127

Morgan, D. (2018). *Learning in liminality: A hermeneutic phenomenological investigation of student nurse learning during a study abroad journey* (Unpublished doctoral thesis). Northumbria University. Retrieved from http://nrl.northumbria.ac.uk/35991/

Murphy-Lejeune, E. (2002). *Student mobility and narrative in Europe: The new strangers.* London, UK: Routledge. doi:10.4324/9780203167038

Nguyen, A. D., Jefferies, J., & Rojas, B. (2018). Short-term, big impact? Changes in self-efficacy and cultural intelligence, and the adjustment of multicultural and monocultural students abroad. *International Journal of Intercultural Relations, 66,* 119–129. doi:10.1016/j.ijintrel.2018.08.001

Nichols, K. P. (2011). *Fostering intercultural competence through study abroad: A gender-based analysis of individual and program factors influencing development* (Doctoral dissertation). University of Minnesota. Retrieved from http://conservancy.umn.edu/bitstream/handle/11299/119984/?sequence=1

O'Reilly, Z. (2018). Living liminality: Everyday experiences of asylum seekers in the 'Direct Provision' system in Ireland. *Gender, Place and Culture, 25*(6), 821–842. doi:10.1080/0966369X.2018.1473345

Perna, L. W. (2006). Studying college access and choice: A proposed conceptual model. In J. C. Smart (Ed.), *Higher education: Handbook of theory and research* (Vol. 21, pp. 99–157). New York, NY: Springer. doi:10.1007/1-4020-4512-3_3

Perry, L., Stoner, L., & Tarrant, M. (2012). More than a vacation: Short-term study abroad as a critically reflective, transformative learning experience. *Creative Education, 3*(5), 679–683. doi:10.4236/ce.2012.35101

Peterson, P. M., & Helms, R. M. (2014). *Challenges and opportunities for the global engagement of higher education.* Washington, DC: American Council on Education. Retrieved from http://www.acenet.edu/news-room/Documents/CIGE-Insights-2014-Challenges-Opps-Global-Engagement.pdf

Rexeisen, R. J., Anderson, P. H., Lawton, L., & Hubbard, A. C. (2008). Study abroad and intercultural development: A longitudinal study. *Frontiers: The Interdisciplinary Journal of Study Abroad, 17,* 1–20.

Salisbury, M. H. (2011). *The effect of study abroad on intercultural competence among undergraduate college students* (Doctoral dissertation). University of Iowa. Retrieved from http://ir.uiowa.edu/cgi/viewcontent.cgi?article=2458&context=etd

Salisbury, M. H., Umbach, P. D., Paulsen, M. B., & Pascarella, E. T. (2009). Going global: Understanding the choice process of the intent to study abroad. *Research in Higher Education, 50*(2), 119–143. doi:10.100711162-008-9111-x

Savicki, V. (Ed.). (2008). *Developing intercultural competence and transformation: Theory, research and application in international education.* Sterling, VA: Stylus.

Simpson, R., Sturges, J., & Weight, P. (2009). Transient, unsettling and creative space: Experiences of liminality through the accounts of Chinese students on a UK-based MBA. *Management Learning, 41*(1), 53–70. doi:10.1177/1350507609350830

St. John, E. P., Paulsen, M. B., & Carter, D. (2005). Diversity, college costs, and postsecondary opportunity: An examination of the financial nexus between college choice and persistence for African Americans and Whites. *The Journal of Higher Education, 76*(5), 545–569. doi:10.1353/jhe.2005.0035

Starr-Glass, D. (2016a). Repositioning study abroad as a rite of passage: Impact, implications, and implementation. In D. Velliaris & D. Coleman-George (Eds.), *Handbook of research on study abroad programs and outbound mobility* (pp. 89–114). Hershey, PA: IGI Global. doi:10.4018/978-1-5225-0169-5.ch004

Starr-Glass, D. (2016b). Strategies for business educators planning study abroad programs: Making the connection. In J. A. Rhodes & T. M. Milby (Eds.), *Advancing teacher education and curriculum development through study abroad programs* (pp. 250–273). Hershey, PA: IGI Global. doi:10.4018/978-1-4666-9672-3.ch014

Szakolczai, A. (2009). Liminality and experience: Structuring transitory situations and transformative events. *International Political Anthropology, 2*(1), 141–172.

Szakolczai, A. (2014). Living permanent liminality: The recent transition experience in Ireland. *Irish Journal of Sociology, 22*(1), 28–50. doi:10.7227/IJS.22.1.3

Szkudlarek, B. (2009). Reentry: A review of the literature. *International Journal of Intercultural Relations, 34*(1), 1–21. doi:10.1016/j.ijintrel.2009.06.006

Szkudlarek, B., McNett, J., Romani, L., & Lane, H. (2013). The past, present, and future of cross-cultural management education: The educators' perspective. *Academy of Management Learning & Education, 12*(3), 477–493. doi:10.5465/amle.2012.0233

Tan, C. (2017). Examining cultural capital and student achievement: Results of a meta-analytic review. *The Alberta Journal of Educational Research, 63*, 139–159.

Tarrant, M. A., Rubin, D. L., & Stoner, L. (2014). The added value of study abroad: Fostering a global citizenry. *Journal of Studies in International Education, 18*(2), 141–161. doi:10.1177/1028315313497589

Turner, V. W. (1969). *The ritual process: Structure and anti-structure*. Chicago, IL: Aldine Publishing Company.

U.S. Department of Education. (2012). *Succeeding globally through international education and engagement— US Department of Education International Strategy 2012-16*. Washington, DC: U.S. Department of Education. Retrieved from http://www2.ed.gov/about/inits/ed/internationaled/international-strategy-2012-16.pdf

van Gennep, A. (1960). *The rites of passage*. Chicago, IL: University of Chicago Press.

Vande Berg, M., Connor-Linton, J., & Paige, R. M. (2009). The Georgetown Consortium Project: Interventions for study abroad learning. *Frontiers: The Interdisciplinary Journal of Study Abroad, 18*, 1–75.

VeLure Roholt, R., & Fisher, C. (2013). Expect the unexpected: International short-term study course pedagogies and practices. *Journal of Social Work Education, 49*(1), 48–65. doi:10.1080/10437797.2013.755416

Wells, R. (2008). Social and cultural capital, race and ethnicity, and college student retention. *Journal of College Student Retention, 10*(2), 103–128. doi:10.2190/CS.10.2.a

Wielkiewicz, R. M., & Turkowsi, L. W. (2010). Reentry issues upon returning from study abroad programs. *Journal of College Student Development, 51*(6), 649–664. doi:10.1353/csd.2010.0015

Wilson, J., Ward, C., & Fischer, R. (2013). Beyond culture learning theory: What can personality tell us about cultural competence. *Journal of Cross-Cultural Psychology, 44*(6), 900–927. doi:10.1177/0022022113492889

Wooldridge, D. G., Peet, S., & Meyer, L. L. (2018). Transforming professionals through short-term study-abroad experiences. *Delta Kappa Gamma Bulletin, 84*(4), 31–36.

Yarosha, M., Lukic, D., & Santibáñez-Gruber, R. (2018). Intercultural competence for students in international joint master programmes. *International Journal of Intercultural Relations, 66*, 52–72. doi:10.1016/j.ijintrel.2018.06.003

Chapter 3

Designing Short-Term, Faculty-Led Study Abroad Programs:
A Value Co-Creation Framework

Sven Tuzovic
iD https://orcid.org/0000-0002-4043-9275
Queensland University of Technology, Australia

ABSTRACT

Study abroad education has become an increasingly important educational program for teaching global learning and intercultural competence, maturity, and sensitivity of students. However, tuition costs of study abroad tours can be daunting. Thus, the question arises how value can be defined and, more importantly, how value is created. This chapter adopts the lens of service-dominant logic (SDL) and value co-creation to suggest that students should be engaged as an active co-creator of their study abroad experience. Based on focus groups and an analysis of student reflection papers, this chapter proposes that the value process of short-term, faculty-led study abroad tours consists of three stages: (1) value proposition and potential, (2) resource integration and value co-creation, and (3) assessment of value realization. The framework provides faculty with a way to understand, adapt, and manage the resource integration and influence students' perceptions of their study abroad experience.

DOI: 10.4018/978-1-7998-1607-2.ch003

Copyright © 2020, IGI Global. Copying or distributing in print or electronic forms without written permission of IGI Global is prohibited.

INTRODUCTION

Over the last decade, student mobility and study abroad programs have become an increasingly important topic in higher education (HE). Universities worldwide promote learning abroad as part of their internationalization agenda that aims to help students enhance personal growth, intercultural competence, global outlooks, and employability (Gribble & Tran, 2016). The annual 'Open Doors' survey finds that study abroad participation has steadily increased over the last decade (IIE, 2018). In 2016/17, over 332,000 US students studied abroad for academic credit (IIE, 2018), compared to 283,000 in 2011/12 (Redden, 2013). And according to the International Consultants for Education and Fairs (ICEF) approximately five million tertiary students were studying abroad in 2016, an increase of 67% since 2005 (International Research and Analysis Unit, 2016).

International student mobility can be divided broadly into two categories: (1) degree mobility, i.e., students seeking fully degrees in foreign countries and (2) intra-degree student mobility or learning abroad i.e., students include an international learning experience as part of their domestically delivered degree (Gribble & Tran, 2016). Furthermore, learning abroad can take different forms, from semester and year-long programs to short-term, two- to four-week intensive study tours. The focus in this chapter is limited only to short-term, faculty-led study abroad programs which are defined as one to eight-weeks in duration (Gaia, 2015). Semester-long programs do not involve necessarily an active learning component since students attend courses at another institution (Simpson & Pham, 2007), whereas short-term study abroad tours, as course components, provide educators with opportunities to achieve holistic education (Ritz, 2011).

Research shows that study abroad is related to students' development of global and intercultural competencies, self-knowledge and self-management, and increased academic performance and graduation rates (Gaia, 2015; Rowan-Kenyon & Niehaus, 2011; Stebleton et al., 2013). However, despite the growing popularity of shorter study abroad tours, little is known about how students make meaning of study abroad experiences (Rowan-Kenyon & Niehaus, 2011) and the mechanisms for enhancing their perceived value. Díaz-Méndez & Gummesson (2012) argue that 'value that students expect and actually obtain (…) is a result of the conjunction between lecturers' teaching quality and their learning capabilities' (p. 576). The authors further note that a student-lecturer relationship 'requires being approached from a value co-creation perspective' (p. 576).

In the context of studying abroad, students are often introduced to the host country both via side trips and through their own adventurousness (Gray et al., 2002; Simpson & Pham, 2006). Assuming that students immerse themselves physically, emotionally and mentally in their host culture they co-create their learning experience which has a direct influence on learning outcomes, program satisfaction and positive word of mouth (WOM). Viewing faculty-led study abroad programs through the lens of co-creation may have important implications for the design and management of these courses since the faculty member involved has to identify and organize value-creating activities.

Drawing on service-dominant logic (SDL) (Vargo & Lusch, 2004, 2006, 2008, 2016, 2017; Wilden et al., 2017) and value co-creation literature (Ordanini & Pasini, 2008; Prahalad, 2004; Prahalad & Ramaswamy, 2004; Ranjan & Read, 2016; Vargo et al., 2008), the purpose of this chapter is to develop a framework of how value is co-created before, during, and after faculty-led study-abroad programs and to identify roles and resources of study abroad participants during the stages of planning and preparation, cultural immersion and re-entry. This chapter aims to address the following research questions:

- *How does value co-creation take place in faculty-led study abroad programs?*
- *What are the roles of faculty leader and students within the value creation process?*

This chapter is organized as follows. The next section provides a brief discussion of literature associated with value co-creation, SDL, and study abroad in HE. Next, a qualitative study is described that involved: (a) focus group interviews with students who recently had completed an international study tour; and (b) the analysis of student reflection papers. Based on the data the author develops a conceptual framework of value co-creation in faculty-led short-term study abroad programs. Specifically, this chapter identifies how faculty and students act as resource integrator. Furthermore, the results suggest unique student and faculty roles during the value collaboration process. Finally, this chapter concludes with a discussion of limitations and future research opportunities.

LITERATURE REVIEW

Value Co-Creation

The concept of *value* has been extensively studied in literature in multiple disciplines including marketing, economics, sociology and psychology. Over the last decade, the topic of *value co-creation* (e.g., Payne et al., 2004; Prahalad, 2004; Prahalad & Ramaswamy, 2004) has gained widespread attention, in particular within the domain of SDL (e.g., Grönroos, 2008, Vargo & Lusch, 2004; 2008; Vargo et al., 2008). Value co-creation can be defined as the 'benefit realized from integration of resources through activities and interactions with collaborators in the customer's service network' (McColl-Kennedy et al., 2012, p. 375). A resource is anything an individual or firm can draw upon for support, either tangible or intangible (Greer et al., 2016). Literature distinguishes between operand and operant resources. While *operand* resources refer to physical goods, infrastructure, or geographical location, *operant* resources are the intangible resources including knowledge, skills, know-how, and/or experiences.

SDL initially focused on the roles of customers and suppliers in co-creation (Vargo & Lusch, 2004), however, the perspective has shifted more recently. Vargo and Lusch (2016) now argued that co-creation takes place far more widely in exchanges between generic actors. The broader conceptualization allows to consider academic and non-academic actors (Hughes & Vafeas, 2018). In HE, students become co-creator of their learning experiences. For example, students engage in university programs and activities in which they enhance their operant resources through acquiring new skills and building knowledge.

Value Co-Creation in Higher Education

Some scholars have addressed the principles of SDL and value co-creation in the context of HE (Baron & Harris, 2006; Díaz-Méndez & Gummesson, 2012; Dziewanowska, 2017; Dollinger et al., 2018; Fagerstrøm & Ghinea, 2013; Ford & Bowen, 2008). For example, Lusch and Wu (2012) argue that the 'product' of education is a co-created learning experience. Recent research argues that value co-creation in HE is a 'process whereby students' resources are integrated with organizational resources to facilitate a range of activities and experiences that encourage exchange and interaction which can lead to better practice and innovation' (Dollinger et al., 2018, p. 211).

One implication of value co-creation in HE is that 'the focus of learning should move towards an understanding of interactions and relationships from a consumer experience perspective, rather than from the perspective of a supplier' (Baron & Harris, 2006, p. 292), which implies greater collaboration with students while also learning from them as well as being adaptive to their individual and dynamic needs.

Experiential Learning and Short-Term Study Abroad Programs

Literature argues that short-term, study abroad programs can offer experiential and holistic learning opportunities when designed pedagogically (Ritz, 2011). Experiential learning (e.g., Gremler et al., 2000; Seaman et al., 2017) refers to an interactive teaching style with new roles for teacher and students. From a student perspective, such experiential methods or real-world projects are perceived as effective for their

Designing Short-Term, Faculty-Led Study Abroad Programs

learning (Karns, 2005). To achieve this potential, the instructor must design an environment in which students actively participate in the learning process (Bobbitt et al., 2000). Forms of experiential learning include e.g., real-world course projects, field trips, case studies, simulations, business audits and community-based service-learning (Andrews, 2007; Finsterwalder et al., 2010; Govekar & Rishi, 2007; Tuzovic & Kuppelwieser, 2014). From a student perspective, such experiential methods or authentic projects are perceived as effective for their learning (Karns, 2005).

Within the last decade, study abroad programs have become increasingly recognized as a further form of experiential learning (Gray et al., 2002; Ritz, 2011) and a method to improve cultural competency (Gaia, 2015; Koskinen & Tossavainen, 2004). Similar to field experiences and internships, these programs extend traditional active learning methods beyond the classroom (Hopkins, 1999; Katula & Threnhauser, 1999). Moreover, study tours 'take students beyond the familiar and the experience is turned into deep learning through a reflective assessment of the lessons learned' (Vandeveer & Menefee, 2006, p. 201).

Learning Outcomes of Study Abroad Programs

Study abroad is associated with a number of benefits and positive learning outcomes. Research had found that studying abroad is linked to academic performance, personal development, self-confidence, intercultural communication skills and cultural competency (e.g., Costello, 2015; Gaia, 2015; Rowan-Kenyon & Niehaus, 2011; Vandeveer & Menefee, 2006; Williams, 2005). Cubillos and Ilvento (2013) argued that international study experiences enhance self-efficacy beliefs among foreign language learners. According to Zimmermann and Neyer (2013), students showed improvements in five core traits compared to their peers: openness, conscientiousness, extraversion, agreeableness and emotional stability. Koskinen and Tossavainen (2004) found that gaining intercultural competence consists of different ethno-categories in three phases:

Orientation phase: Transition from one culture to another
- preparation
- dialogue between the participants

Study abroad phase: Adjustment to the difference
- language barrier
- tutoring and mentoring
- team membership

Re-entry phase: Gaining intercultural sensitivity
- recollecting past memories
- attitudes towards the difference
- meaning of study abroad

Besides learning outcomes, university administrators are particularly interested in surveying students upon their return with regard to their program satisfaction. Service marketing literature has identified perceived value as a driver of customer satisfaction. The challenge within HE and study abroad is, however, that students may not realize the value during their education, but only years after graduation (Chalcraft & Lynch, 2011).

EXPLORATORY RESEARCH STUDY

Research Design

In order to understand the value creation process of short-term, faculty-led study abroad programs the author first conducted a focus group study with undergraduate students who had participated in a study abroad program. The focus group methodology was used to better understand students' interpretations of their experiences. Focus groups are a popular technique for gathering qualitative data across a wide range of academic and applied research interests (Krueger & Casey, 2014) and have been applied previously in study abroad research (e.g., Lemmons, 2015; Pengelly, 2018). The technique involves the use of in-depth group discussion among participants chosen because they present a purposive, although not necessarily representative, sample of a specific population (Rabiee, 2004; Thomas et al., 1995). Participants express their own views and experiences in the language of their choice in guided conversation with the other participants.

In total, three focus groups were conducted with 19 undergraduate students who had been enrolled in eleven different study abroad programs across global destinations (Ecuador, Egypt,

England, Germany, Greece, Iceland, India, Italy, Martinique, Norway, South Africa, and Switzerland). Participants shared similar age-range and socio-characteristics. Interviews were semi-structured and lasted between 60-70 minutes. A discussion guide was developed that included questions of main topics reflecting the research objectives. This ensured to keep the discussion on track and to cover important themes for consistency. Questions included: *How did the faculty leader contribute to your study abroad experience before/during the trip? How did you*

Designing Short-Term, Faculty-Led Study Abroad Programs

contribute to your study-abroad experience before/during the trip? What are key factors that influenced your study abroad experience? What are the benefits that you see in study abroad programs?

In addition to focus groups, this research utilized reflective journals that were collected over several years from different (undergraduate and MBA) student cohorts. Following transformative learning theory (Mezirow, 1991), students had to submit a reflection paper upon return as part of the course requirements and explain what they had learned during their study abroad time.

Analysis

Focus groups were video-taped and audio-recorded and then transcribed to facilitate analysis, with each participant signing a consent form at the beginning of the focus group. While audio-recording is sufficient for data transcription, the additional videotaping allowed capture of non-verbal interactions and group dynamics, supplementing the oral text and enabling more meaningful analysis. Transcripts of the focus group interviews as well as the reflection papers were then subsequently imported into MAXQDA, a software package designed for coding qualitative data (www.maxqda.de).) Literature advocates the use of a computer-based approach since it allows the researcher to cut, paste, sort, arrange and re-arrange the data (Krueger & Casey, 2014). The data coding was conducted by the author.

The reliability of the results was enhanced by documenting the empirical research process thoroughly. The coding structure was developed in the context of critical discussion and reflection with colleagues involved in marketing research. External validity was enhanced by drawing analytical conclusions based on the literature review.

Framework of Study Abroad Value Co-Creation

Figure 1 presents the conceptual framework. The process of study abroad value co-creation can be distinguished in three main phases: (1) pre-travel study abroad value proposition; (2) on-travel resource integration and co-creation of value-in-host country context; and (3) post-travel value realization. The outcomes of the study abroad program include learning outcomes, students' program satisfaction and WOM.

1. Pre-Travel Value Proposition and Value Potential

The first stage refers to the value proposition and value potential provided by the faculty member. The faculty leader cannot deliver value on their own but only a value proposition that has potentially value to students who register for a study abroad program (Vargo & Lusch, 2004, 2016). For example, faculty members are

63

Figure 1. Conceptual framework

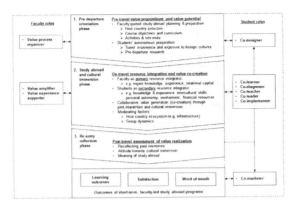

responsible for choosing the host country, setting the objectives of the study tour, developing the curriculum, selecting activities and site visits, establishing relationships with the hosts, organizing transportation and accommodation, advertising the study abroad program to recruit students, orienting the students to the course and travel requirements, and providing relevant information about the host country (e.g., country profile including politics, history, culture; language guides, mobile phone and Internet options, costs of living etc.). This 'before-the fact' or 'backstage' process requires considerable time and effort, typically several months before departure. Students commented on the preparation as they spoke about perceived value for their study abroad experience.

We did a lot of work last fall preparing for the trip and she really knew; she could tell us what we could expect and what we should be prepared for and then when we got there.
[FG1-4, Female, South Africa]

In preparation for the course we had a bunch of a reading we had to do. Just some articles and research, some of which was written by our professor, which was kind of cool and then some of which was written by other people.
[FG1-2, Female, India]

Thus, faculty inhibit the role as value process organizer during the pre-departure preparation phase (cf. Aarikka-Stenroos & Jaakkola, 2012). This role is critical as students may feel overwhelmed and underprepared for traveling to a foreign country. For example, MBA students made suggestions in their reflection papers of the necessity to provide more 'tools' such as short lists with basic language phrases or a basic overview of the public transportation system. As a result, faculty should

Designing Short-Term, Faculty-Led Study Abroad Programs

carefully consider students' backgrounds and previous exposure to foreign cultures for their potential influence on the study abroad experience. Some students may have had only minor international travel experience and exposure to foreign cultures (*'Besides Canada, this was my first trip outside of the US'*), while others may have traveled more extensively (*'I had traveled frequently with my family. [...] But I've also been to New Zealand, Australia, Japan, Canada, and Mexico'*).

2. On-Travel Resource Integration and Value Co-Creation Process

The second stage reflects the resource integration and co-creation process. According to Díaz-Méndez and Gummesson (2012), students and faculty play the two principal roles in university service value co-creation process. This becomes even more evident in faculty-led study tours.

Faculty as Primary Resource Integrator

During the cultural immersion phase in the host country, the faculty member's role changes from teacher to a more holistic role that includes being mentor, tour guide, translator, or plainly 'mom'. Faculty act as value amplifiers to boost and improve the students' study abroad experience by applying their specialist (cultural) knowledge, accumulated experience and professional objectivity in the host country (c.f. Aarikka-Stenroos & Jaakkola, 2012, p. 21). That includes pushing students' cultural immersion process and making them to step outside their 'comfort zone'.

You could not have asked for a better professor, guide, friend, mom, nurse. There were a lot of health issues on the trip just because the foods different there and the water's different, so we had a little bit of stomach problems. Everybody did. She kind of took care of us, and we every now and then kind of fell into calling her 'ama' which is just mom in Indian language. So, she was just awesome, I could not ask for anyone better. She was so knowledgeable, but at the same time took on the mom role when you weren't feeling well. So, she was everything in one. [...] She did an excellent job of really pushing us into living like Indians. We wore Indian clothing; we ate strictly Indian food. I mean so it was just nice for her to push us like that. Really far outside of our comfort zone, but we quickly felt a lot better because we were with her. I just think that there was none better to go with.
[FG1-2, Female, India]

In some cases, faculty take the 'extra mile' and contribute to students' learning experience by 'shared cultural interactions' e.g., inviting students to his/her family home in the host country or having personal friends joining students at restaurants or evening social activities. Students pointed out how much they enjoyed the interaction with their course leader throughout their host country visit i.e., getting to know the professor outside of the classroom. A study tour is not perceived as a regular class but rather a unique learning experience supported through social interactions with the instructor, separate from the academic program. This supports prior research which shows that educators can establish emotional and social connections with study abroad participants and therefore expand students' development beyond intellectual learning (Ritz, 2011). This role of faculty can be termed as value experience supporter (c.f. Aarikka-Stenroos & Jaakkola, 2012, p. 22).

Our professor is from India so we got to meet her mom and her sister and got to hang out in their homes and so that was really nice to have kind of like an 'in' on the culture. So, you weren't just really like walking around as this mindless tourist. You kind of got to see like behind the scenes, which was really nice.
[FG1-2, Female, India]

From a *resource perspective*, faculty leaders need to demonstrate three different types of capabilities: representational, cultural, and social. *Representational resources* reflect the image students have to the faculty member. This includes the instructor's reputation or a student's comfort in choosing this faculty member for the study abroad tour. *Cultural resources* relate to the instructor's knowledge, expertise, and experience in leading the short-term study tour. Finally, *social resources* reflect the interactions between students and faculty actors. This includes the instructor's friendliness and helpfulness as well as the social atmosphere.

Students as Secondary Resource Integrators

Previous research suggests that students 'should be engaged as an active co-producer of the university experience' (Bowden & D'Allessandro, 2011). This research identified seven roles of students in the context of study tours: co-learner, co-diagnoser, co-teacher, co-leader, co-implementor, co-marketer, and co-designer (see Aarikka-Stenroos & Jaakkola, 2012). Students may first act as *co-diagnoser* as they provide information about relevant issues. For example, study tour participants in Ecuador were taught by local teachers and the students complained to their faculty leader about the teaching style. The faculty leader then sat down with the students to solve the problem.

So, our professor […] who came with us was willing to sit down and talk with us and figure out what is it that we wanted to change. Then she had a dialogue with the director and with the professor. She was willing to work with us so that went pretty well I thought.
[FG3-2, Male, Ecuador]

Designing Short-Term, Faculty-Led Study Abroad Programs

Another important role of study abroad students is the role of *co-teacher* and/or *co-leader*. For example, several students mentioned that they were tasked with duties to become a group leader who is responsible for all logistics of that day. In other cases, students were actively involved in teaching parts of the curriculum.

We would appoint people for the day. Our professor would assign somebody. Like 'Today so and so is in charge or this, so that means here are the metro tickets, you're in charge of them, you're handing them out, you're finding out where we're going for the day'. Which I thought was good because it means that one person had to know their way around somewhere really well. And had to initiate and facilitate more discussions and things. Everyone had their chance to be more of a leader in navigating different places, which I thought was good.
[FG3-3, Female, Iceland and Norway]

Finally, students can also take on the role as *co-implementor,* which means that they act on their own behalf without any assistance from the faculty member. Such students feel confident enough to find their own solution. While faculty should encourage such behavior, the unique characteristics of the host country pose important constraints. For example, while one student studying abroad in Switzerland encouraged faculty to give students 'freedom' to explore, another student commented about security risks in India.

Enablers: I think it starts off with faculty. It's really important for the professors to help us get out of the shell or to break down those barriers. But then once we're out there, once we're established, then I think professors need to let go. Just like parents do almost. Professors just need to step back and let us run the show a little bit, let us work on those leadership roles.
[FG2-3, Male, Switzerland]

Prohibitors: Just speaking to South Africa in general, there was obviously a huge safety concern in South Africa. Sometimes we were frustrated just feeling like our hands were being held wherever we went. We didn't really have a lot of freedom to branch out and go out of sight of the bus or things like that.
[FG1-4, Female, South Africa]

Resource Integration of Study Abroad Participants

In the context of short-term study abroad programs, students co-create their learning experience through cultural immersion and the integration of resources (co-learner). Participants possess different operant resources (e.g., skills, knowledge), which they integrate with the resources provided by faculty to co-produce their study tour experiences (Baron & Harris, 2008; Chalcraft & Lynch, 2011; Vargo & Lusch, 2006, 2016, 2017). Results indicated several categories of participants' operant resources (Warnaby et al., 2009; see Figure 2).

- **Faculty Resources:** students articulated various types of faculty-possessed operant resources that can be grouped in three categories: representational, cultural, and social resources (Warnaby et al., 2009).
- **Representational Resources:** reflect the image students have to the faculty member. This includes the instructor's reputation or a student's comfort in choosing this faculty member for the study abroad program.
- **Cultural (Host Country) Resources:** relate to the instructor's knowledge, expertise, and experience in leading the study tour.
- **Social Resources:** reflect the interactions between students and faculty actors. This includes the instructor's friendliness and helpfulness as well as the social atmosphere.
- **Student Resources:** the student role in value co-creation is likely to vary depending on the student's *operand* resource (i.e., financial situation), together with *physical*, *intercultural* and *social resources*, in particular the individual's personality and willingness of risk taking, classified as *operant* resources.

Moderating Factors

Furthermore, the *ecosystem of the host country* (actors, infrastructure, etc.) can have positive or negative moderating effects. For example, the results indicate differences based on the program structure and the host country. In countries such as South

Figure 2. Operant resources of study abroad participants

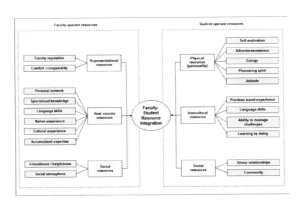

Designing Short-Term, Faculty-Led Study Abroad Programs

Africa, India and Egypt, students did not venture out on their own as compared to those in countries like Switzerland, Norway or Germany. From a value creation perspective, faculty leaders should recognize supportive and stimulating as well as restrictive and limiting host country factors that can positively or negatively influence study abroad students' value-in-use.

I think that it kind of depends on where you are as far as how much freedom you were given. I know in India we were given very little free time, and we did very few activities without Videa. Which I think in India was appropriate because the culture is so different and what's expected of you and the safety issues. I really appreciate being with her almost all the time, but there were certain instances, like there was this little store probably like 3 blocks from where we were staying and so we would walk as groups to that store. But even then, just to that store and back we were followed by beggar for almost the full walk. It was extremely uncomfortable. We ended up almost running back to our hotel. [...] I think if I was maybe in Italy or somewhere where it's a little safer, I really would have appreciated like a weekend free to do something, but in our situation, I really appreciated being with Videa or with someone who could speak the language and understand the culture just because you needed that in order to be safe there. I think it depends on where you are. [FG1-2, Female, India]

Yet, students appreciated to have the opportunity to discover the host country in small groups or, if possible, on their own. Students perceived the cultural immersion as valuable for their overall experience, including their personal development.

3. Post-Travel Value Realization

Faculty leaders have to understand that from a service-centered viewpoint the value of a short-term study abroad program is always uniquely determined by students as the beneficiaries (Vargo & Lusch, 2006, 2016, 2017). The discussion with participants illustrates that value is not equal to the price (i.e., costs) of the study tour. Instead, students agreed that the benefit is far greater than the costs associated with the program. The following comment exemplifies this view.

I thought I got more out of the trip than the price was, because I got to meet new people that I didn't really know before. And I got great friendships from it, and I got to experience a completely different place. I've never been to Europe, so it was completely new to me. Now I have a bigger world view so it made me a better person and a better student overall because I can see how different people handle stuff. [FG2-2, Male, Switzerland]

In many cases, students are required to submit a reflection paper after they have returned to campus. As part of this assignment, journaling is often mandatory and includes a record of experiences, reflection on those experiences, and an evaluation. The *post-travel reflection* may reinforce a student's perceived value. In addition, faculty leaders may organize regular *debriefing* sessions, an act that allows for review and reflection, during the travels in the host country. Although debriefing most commonly occurs following the international experience, time to reflect can be quite valuable during the study tour experience itself, and for which some faculty have found daily sessions helpful. It represents an evaluation, summarization, sharing and recounting of learning opportunities for individuals or a team.

We had meetings pretty regularly in the evening where we could decompress, talk about what we saw, how we felt, how things may have surprised us. So, it was really great.
[FG1-5, Male, South Africa]

At the end of each day we would actually debrief about what happened like you guys said. So, a couple days were really emotional for us because we were in a poor school, like the poorest school you can be in, and it was really difficult because in the next day we were in the richest school, the nicest school you can be in. We were just so emotionally conflicted, and so those debriefings at night had to do with what happened that day and what did we think, were really helpful.
[FG1-2, Female, India]

4. Outcomes of Short-Term, Faculty-Led, Study Abroad Programs

The outcomes of short-term study abroad programs can be addressed in three categories: (1) learning outcomes; (2) program satisfaction; and (3) WOM. Participants demonstrate higher levels of confidence, independence, and maturity that come from dealing successfully with challenges in the host country (e.g., communication in a foreign language, getting lost on public transportation). As a result of their study abroad experience, students 'overwhelmingly feel as if they have grown' (Vandeveer & Menefee, 2006, p. 205). In addition, students improved their understanding and awareness about other cultures and languages (Gaia, 2015).

Many students express their appreciation in their reflection papers and in subsequent encounters on campus (Simpson & Pham, 2007). Collectively they set the stage for positive WOM and endorsements to other students contemplating future international learning opportunities. As such, participants of study abroad tours exhibit the role as co-marketer, promoting the course, the host country, and/ or the faculty leader.

Designing Short-Term, Faculty-Led Study Abroad Programs

I don't know if [school name] will ever do the trip again but I think just, I recommend traveling to everybody I can. Getting the SA experience, especially the one here from [school name], I recommend to as many students as I can because I think it is such a Eureka kind of moment in your life. It changes you. I think it's difficult to go and not change in some way or another.
[FG1-1, Male, Egypt]

After return to the home country, students who studied abroad can act as *co-designer* of future study abroad programs. That is, these students typically have to submit a reflection paper as part of their course assignments. While this post-travel reflection may reinforce a student's perceived value, students use the opportunity to make suggestions for the future. As a result, faculty leaders can utilize this information and adopt the course in the following year.

I think a roommate questionnaire with the following types of questions would be helpful in pairing up students for future trips: do you snore? Does your spouse say you snore? Can you sleep in the same room with someone who snores? Do you plan on staying out late? Are you up for dancing? Do you just want to drink beer, or do you plan to be active?
[Reflection Paper #13, Female]

IMPLICATIONS, LIMITATIONS AND FUTURE RECOMMENDATIONS

The present study does not come without several limitations. First, the approaching end of the spring semester led to difficulties to recruit a large number of focus group participants. As an unexpected result, one focus group consisted mainly of students who were enrolled in the moderator's own study abroad course. Thus, a second limitation relates to a potential response bias. Participants in focus groups may give socially desirable responses i.e., saying what they believe the moderator wants to hear or making up answers (Krueger & Casey, 2014). Third, the study utilizes student data from only one industry, thus comparing the results with other industries is limited. Furthermore, the focus has been on short-term, faculty-led study abroad programs which is a particular form of international education. As a result, the findings may not apply to semester-long study programs without any faculty leadership. Finally, the study is limited to university faculty and students. Díaz-Méndez and Gummesson (2012) noted that a study of value co-creation in the

Designing Short-Term, Faculty-Led Study Abroad Programs

HE context should ideally involve all actors and all factors (resources, laws, cultures etc.) since it constitutes a complex network of stakeholders (faculty, staff, students, institutional decision-makers, society etc.).

CONCLUSION

As colleges and universities globally continue to expand study abroad programs, scholars have identified a need to explore the meaning of these programs (Rowan-Kenyon & Niehaus, 2011). This study is one of a few to investigate the meaning and process of value co-creation in short-term faculty-led study abroad programs. Prior research has suggested a shift of perspective from a *value delivery approach*—doing something 'to' students, to a *co-creation approach*—doing something 'with' students. The purpose of this study was to explore 'value creation' of faculty-led study abroad programs. Based on principles of SDL and a qualitative study, this chapter developed a framework that identifies roles and resources of study abroad participants and demonstrates the process of value co-creation of such programs.

The results of this investigation are particularly important for those designing and managing short-term study tours. Given the intense efforts that are required to create and implement a study abroad course, in particular for new faculty, the results provide insights for developing a balanced approach to address both pedagogical and cultural-focused value-creating activities. The individual course leader plays a significant role as facilitator in the value creation process of students' international experience. They have to provide the input resources which refers to the course content. In addition, faculty contribute through 'joint value co-creation' (Grönroos & Ravald, 2009) by value-supporting interactions. Furthermore, faculty play a strong role not just in providing the necessary resources for the trip but also function as a guide and mentor or plainly, as one student said, as a 'mom' during the time abroad.

Although the role of the faculty instructor or course leader is critical, study abroad students integrate various operand and operant resources in the value co-creation process during their study tour. According to previous research, customers' operand resources include geographical location/place, building/space, and products. In the discussion with students, one key theme emerged as *operand resource* i.e., a student's economic situation (i.e., financial resources) and how 'frugal' they live while studying abroad. For example, due to the costs of living, students in Switzerland were saving money on hospitality eating 'Doner Kebab' or fast food instead of more expensive meals in sit-down restaurants. Faculty leaders need to be conscious of the cost of living as this may influence a student's overall experience. One solution,

Designing Short-Term, Faculty-Led Study Abroad Programs

for example, is the organization of several group dinners paid by the budget of the faculty leader. Besides reducing the expenses for students this leads to the positive effect of bonding within the group.

Overall, this study provides important contributions for the institution's administration, its offices for international programs and the faculty to design, manage and evaluate short-term faculty-led study abroad programs. For example, the findings can be incorporated in workshops to prepare faculty for their upcoming travel.

REFERENCES

Aarikka-Stenroos, L., & Jaakkola, E. (2012). Value co-creation in knowledge intensive business services: A dyadic perspective on the joint problem-solving process. *Industrial Marketing Management*, *41*(1), 15–26. doi:10.1016/j.indmarman.2011.11.008

Andrews, C. P. (2007). Service learning: Applications and research in business. *Journal of Education for Business*, *83*(1), 19–26. doi:10.3200/JOEB.83.1.19-26

Arnould, E. J. (2008). Service-dominant logic and resource theory. *Journal of the Academy of Marketing Science*, *36*(1), 21–24. doi:10.100711747-007-0072-y

Baron, S., & Harris, K. (2006). A new dominant logic in marketing: Pedagogical logic implications. *The Marketing Review*, *6*(4), 289–300.

Baron, S., & Harris, K. (2008). Consumers as resource integrators. *Journal of Marketing Management*, *24*(2), 113–130. doi:10.1362/026725708X273948

Bettencourt, L. A., Ostrom, A. L., Brown, S. W., & Roundtree, R. I. (2002). Client co-production in knowledge-intensive business services. *California Management Review*, *44*(4), 100–128. doi:10.2307/41166145

Bobbitt, L. M., Inks, S. A., Kemp, K. J., & Mayo, D. T. (2000). Integrating marketing courses to enhance team-based experiential learning. *Journal of Marketing Education*, *22*(1), 15–24. doi:10.1177/0273475300221003

Bowden, J. L.-H., & D'Alessandro, S. (2011). Co-creating value in higher education: The role of interactive classroom response technologies. *Asian Social Science*, *7*(11), 35–49. doi:10.5539/ass.v7n11p35

Chalcraft, D., & Lynch, J. (2011). Value propositions in higher education: An S-D logic view. *Proceedings of the Academy of Marketing Conference*.

Costello, J. (2015). Students' stories of studying abroad: Reflections upon return. *Journal of International Students, 5*(1), 50–59.

Cubillos, J. H., & Ilvento, T. (2013). The impact of study abroad on students' self-efficacy perceptions. *Foreign Language Annals, 45*(4), 494–511. doi:10.1111/j.1944-9720.2013.12002.x

Díaz-Méndez, M., & Gummesson, E. (2012). Value co-creation and university teaching quality: Consequences for the European Higher Education Area (EHEA). *Journal of Service Management, 23*(4), 571–592. doi:10.1108/09564231211260422

Dollinger, M., Lodge, J., & Coates, H. (2018). Co-creation in higher education: Towards a conceptual model. *Journal of Marketing for Higher Education, 28*(2), 210–231. doi:10.1080/08841241.2018.1466756

Dziewanowska, K. (2017). Value types in higher education: Students' perspective. *Journal of Higher Education Policy and Management, 39*(3), 235–246. doi:10.10 80/1360080X.2017.1299981

Etgar, M. (2008). A descriptive model of the consumer co-production process. *Journal of the Academy of Marketing Science, 36*(1), 97–108. doi:10.100711747-007-0061-1

Fagerstrøm, A., & Ghinea, G. (2013). Co-creation of value in higher education: Using social network marketing in the recruitment of students. *Journal of Higher Education Policy and Management, 35*(1), 45–53. doi:10.1080/1360080X.2013.748524

Finsterwalder, J., O'Steen, B., & Tuzovic, S. (2010). Service-learning through multiple client-sponsored projects in an MBA marketing course. *New Zealand Journal of Adult Learning, 38*(2), 71–91.

Ford, R. C., & Bowen, D. E. (2008). A service-dominant logic for management education: It's time. *Academy of Management Learning & Education, 7*(2), 224–243. doi:10.5465/amle.2008.32712620

Geissler, G. L., Rucks, C. T., & Edison, S. W. (2006). Understanding the role of service convenience in art museum marketing: An exploratory study. *Journal of Hospitality & Leisure Marketing, 14*(4), 69–87. doi:10.1300/J150v14n04_05

Govekar, M. A., & Rishi, M. (2007). Service learning: Bringing real-world education into the B-school Classroom. *Journal of Education for Business, 83*(1), 3–10. doi:10.3200/JOEB.83.1.3-10

Gray, K. S., Murdock, G. K., & Stebbins, C. D. (2002, May). Assessing study abroad's effect on an international mission. *Change Magazine*, 45-51.

Greer, C. R., Lusch, R. F., & Vargo, S. L. (2016). A service perspective: Key managerial insights from service-dominant (S-D) logic. *Organizational Dynamics*, *45*(1), 28–38. doi:10.1016/j.orgdyn.2015.12.004

Gremler, D. D., Hoffman, K. D., Keaveney, S. M., & Wright, L. W. (2000). Experiential learning exercises in services marketing courses. *Journal of Marketing Education*, *22*(1), 35–44. doi:10.1177/0273475300221005

Gribble, C., & Tran, L. (2016). *International Trends in Learning Abroad*. Melbourne: Universities Australia.

Grönroos, C. (2008). Service logic revisited: Who creates value? And who co-creates? *European Business Review*, *20*(4), 298–314. doi:10.1108/09555340810886585

Grönroos, C., & Ravald, A. (2009). *Marketing and the logic of service: Value facilitation, value creation and co-creation, and their marketing implications*. Working Paper 542. Hanken School of Economics. Retrieved from https://ideas.repec.org/p/hhb/hanken/0542.html

Hopkins, J. R. (1999). Studying abroad as a form of experiential education. *Liberal Education*, *85*(3), 36–41.

Hughes, T., & Vafeas, M. (2018). Service-dominant logic as a framework for exploring research utilization. *Marketing Theory*, *18*(4), 451–472. doi:10.1177/1470593118764019

IIE. (2018). *Open Doors 2018*. Retrieved from https://www.iie.org/Research-and-Insights/Open-Doors/Open-Doors-2018-Media-Information

International Research and Analysis Unit. (2016). *The global context of tertiary student mobility*. Retrieved from https://internationaleducation.gov.au/research/Research-Snapshots/Documents/Global%20context%20of%20tertiary%20student%20mobility.pdf

Karns, G. L. (2005). An update of marketing student perceptions of learning activities: Structure, preferences, and effectiveness. *Journal of Marketing Education*, *27*(2), 163–171. doi:10.1177/0273475305276641

Katula, R. A., & Threnhauser, E. (1999). Experiential education in the undergraduate curriculum. *Communication Education*, *48*(3), 238–255. doi:10.1080/03634529909379172

Kelley, S. W., Donnelly, J. H., & Skinner, S. J. (1990). Customer participation in service production and delivery. *Journal of Retailing*, *66*(3), 315–333.

Kirschner, P. A., Sweller, J., & Clark, R. E. (2006). Why minimal guidance during instruction does not work: An analysis of the failure of constructivist, discovery, problem-based, experiential, and inquiry-based teaching. *Educational Psychologist*, *41*(2), 75–86. doi:10.120715326985ep4102_1

Koskinen, L., & Tossavainen, K. (2004). Study abroad as a process of learning intercultural competence in nursing. *International Journal of Nursing Practice*, *10*(3), 111–120. doi:10.1111/j.1440-172X.2004.00470.x PMID:15149458

Krueger, R. A., & Casey, M. A. (2014). *Focus groups: A practical guide for applied research* (5th ed.). Thousand Oaks, CA: Sage.

Lemmons, K. (2015). Short-term study abroad: Culture and the path of least resistance. *Journal of Geography in Higher Education*, *39*(4), 543–553. doi:10.10 80/03098265.2015.1084607

Lengnick-Hall, C. A., Claycomb, V., & Inks, L. W. (2000). From recipient to contributor: Examining customer roles and experienced outcomes. *European Journal of Marketing*, *34*(3/4), 359–383. doi:10.1108/03090560010311902

Lusch, R. F., & Vargo, S. L. (2006). Service-dominant logic: Reactions, reflections and refinements. *Marketing Theory*, *6*(September), 281–288. doi:10.1177/1470593106066781

Lusch, R. F., & Wu, C. (2012). A service science perspective on higher education linking service productivity theory and higher education reform. *Center for American Progress*. Retrieved from http://www.americanprogress.org/wp-content/uploads/issues/2012/08/pdf/service_science.pdf

Matthews, K. E., Garratt, C., & Macdonald, D. (2018). *The higher education landscape: Trends and implication*. Discussion Paper. University of Queensland.

McColl-Kennedy, J. R., Vargo, S. L., Dagger, T. S., Sweeney, J. C., & van Kasteren, Y. (2012). Health care customer value cocreation practice styles. *Journal of Service Research*, *15*(4), 370–389. doi:10.1177/1094670512442806

Mezirow, J. (1991). *Transformative dimensions of adult learning*. San Francisco, CA: Jossey-Bass.

OECD. (2018). The future of education and skills. *Education*, *2030*. Retrieved from http://www.oecd.org/education/2030/E2030%20Position%20Paper%20(05.04.2018).pdf

Ordanini, A., & Pasini, P. (2008). Service co-production and value co-creation: The case for a service-oriented architecture (SOA). *European Management Journal, 26*(5), 289–297. doi:10.1016/j.emj.2008.04.005

Payne, A. F., Storbacka, K., & Frow, P. (2008). Managing the co-creation of value. *Journal of the Academy of Marketing Science, 36*(1), 83–96. doi:10.100711747-007-0070-0

Pengelly, K. A. (2018). Loving neighbor as self: Translating the study abroad experience into intercultural friendships on the home campus. *Journal of International Students, 8*(3), 1108–1128. doi:10.32674/jis.v8i2.136

Prahalad, C. K. (2004). The co-creation of value: Invited commentaries on 'evolving to a new dominant logic for marketing'. *Journal of Marketing, 68*(1), 18–27. doi:10.1509/jmkg.68.1.18.24035

Prahalad, C. K., & Ramaswamy, V. (2004). Co-creation experiences: The next practice in value creation. *Journal of Interactive Marketing, 18*(3), 5–14. doi:10.1002/dir.20015

Rabiee, F. (2004). Focus-group interview and data analysis. *The Proceedings of the Nutrition Society, 63*(4), 655–660. doi:10.1079/PNS2004399 PMID:15831139

Ranjan, K., & Read, S. (2016). Value co-creation: Concept and measurement. *Journal of the Academy of Marketing Science, 44*(3), 290–315. doi:10.100711747-014-0397-2

Redden, E. (2013). *International study up.* Retrieved from https://www.insidehighered.com/news/2013/11/11/survey-finds-increases-international-enrollments-study-abroad

Ritz, A. A. (2011). The educational value of short-term study abroad programs as course components. *Journal of Teaching in Travel & Tourism, 11*(2), 164–178. doi:10.1080/15313220.2010.525968

Rowan-Kenyon, H. T., & Niehaus, E. (2011). One year later: The influence of short-term study abroad experiences on students. *Journal of Student Affairs Research and Practice, 48*(2), 213–228. doi:10.2202/1949-6605.6213

Seaman, J., Brown, M., & Quay, J. (2017). The evolution of experiential learning theory: Tracing lines of research in the JEE. *Journal of Experiential Education, 40*(4), NP1–NP21. doi:10.1177/1053825916689268

Sidorchuk, R. (2015). The concept of 'value' in the theory of marketing. *Asian Social Science, 11*(9), 320–325. doi:10.5539/ass.v11n9p320

Simpson, M. C., & Pham, K.-Q. (2007). The creative campus: Experiential learning by short study-abroad courses. *32nd Improving University Teaching Conference*.

Stebleton, M. J., Soria, K. M., & Cherney, B. T. (2013). The high impact of education abroad: College students' engagement in international experiences and the development of intercultural competencies. *Frontiers: The Interdisciplinary Journal of Study Abroad, 22*, 1–24.

Thomas, L., MacMillan, J., McColl, E., Hale, C., & Bond, S. (1995). Comparison of focus group and individual interview methodology in examining patient satisfaction with nursing care. *Social Sciences in Health, 1*, 206–219.

Tuleja, E. A. (2008). Aspects of intercultural awareness through a BA study abroad program: Going 'backstage'. *Business Communication Quarterly, 71*(3), 314–337. doi:10.1177/1080569908321471

Tuzovic, S., & Kuppelwieser, V. (2014). The marketing blog competition: Integrating educational blogging and analytics in the classroom. *Journal of Innovative Education Strategies, 3*(1), 43–59.

Vandeveer, R., & Menefee, M. L. (2006). Study abroad, international internship and experiential learning: A world-class adventure in learning. *Proceedings of the 37th Southwest Decision Science Institute Conference*. Retrieved from http://www.swdsi.org/swdsi06/Proceedings06/Papers/IE 07.pdf

Vargo, S. L., & Lusch, R. F. (2004). Evolving to a new dominant logic for marketing. *Journal of Marketing, 68*(1), 1–17. doi:10.1509/jmkg.68.1.1.24036

Vargo, S. L., & Lusch, R. F. (2006). Evolving to a new dominant logic for marketing. In R. F. Lusch & S. L. Vargo (Eds.), *The Service Dominant Logic of Marketing: Dialog, Debate and Directions* (pp. 3–28). New York, NY: M.E. Sharpe.

Vargo, S. L., & Lusch, R. F. (2008). Service dominant logic: Continuing the evolution. *Journal of the Academy of Marketing Science, 36*(1), 1–10. doi:10.100711747-007-0069-6

Vargo, S. L., & Lusch, R. F. (2016). Institutions and axioms: An extension and update of service-dominant logic. *Journal of the Academy of Marketing Science, 44*(1), 5–23. doi:10.100711747-015-0456-3

Vargo, S. L., & Lusch, R. F. (2017). Service-dominant logic 2025. *International Journal of Research in Marketing, 34*(1), 46–67. doi:10.1016/j.ijresmar.2016.11.001

Vargo, S. L., Maglio, P. P., & Archpru Akaka, M. (2008). On value and value co-creation: A service systems and service logic perspective. *European Management Journal, 26*(3), 145–152. doi:10.1016/j.emj.2008.04.003

Warnaby, G., Baron, S., & Konjier, P. (2009). Toward an understanding of customer perspectives on organizational operant resources. In *Proceedings of the Australian & New Zealand Marketing Academy Conference* (pp. 1-7). Melbourne: Academic Press.

Wikström, S. (1996). The customer as co-producer. *European Journal of Marketing, 30*(4), 6–19. doi:10.1108/03090569610118803

Wilden, R., Akaka, M. A., Karpen, I. O., & Hohberger, J. (2017). The evolution and prospects of service-dominant logic: An investigation of past, present, and future research. *Journal of Service Research, 20*(4), 345–361. doi:10.1177/1094670517715121

Williams, T. R. (2005). Exploring the impact of study abroad on students' intercultural communication skills: Adaptability and sensitivity. *Journal of Studies in International Education, 9*(4), 356–371. doi:10.1177/1028315305277681

Zimmermann, J., & Neyer, F. J. (2013). Do we become a different person when hitting the road? Personality development of sojourners. *Journal of Personality and Social Psychology, 105*(3), 515–530. doi:10.1037/a0033019 PMID:23773042

Chapter 4

The Academic Second Language (L2) Socialization and Acculturation of International Exchange Students

Jane Jackson
The Chinese University of Hong Kong, Hong Kong

ABSTRACT

As internationalization efforts intensify across the globe, the number of higher education (HE) students who are gaining some form of international educational experience is on the rise. A large percentage of study abroad participants are from East Asian nations (Mainland China, Hong Kong SAR, Japan, Korea, Macau SAR, Taiwan), and most enroll in English language enhancement modules or English-medium content courses during their stay abroad, depending on their level of proficiency. To better meet their needs and ease their adjustment in an unfamiliar academic and social environment, it is imperative for researchers to conduct systematic studies that delve into study abroad experience. This chapter reports on a mixed-method study that investigated the second language socialization and acculturation of international exchange students from a Hong Kong university who took part in a semester-long stay in their host country. The findings have implications for both home and host institutions.

DOI: 10.4018/978-1-7998-1607-2.ch004

Copyright © 2020, IGI Global. Copying or distributing in print or electronic forms without written permission of IGI Global is prohibited.

The Academic Second Language (L2) Socialization and Acculturation

INTRODUCTION

In the past few decades, the number of students who have been studying outside their home country for part of their tertiary education has increased dramatically. Among them, a significant number are from East Asian nations (Hong Kong SAR, Japan, Korea, Macau SAR, Mainland China, and Taiwan) and most study in a second language (L2) while abroad, with English the most common medium-of-instruction. To facilitate their L2 socialization and acculturation in the host environment, it is imperative for study abroad researchers to conduct systematic studies that help us to acquire a deeper understanding of student needs, expectations, and challenges. The analysis of this data can provide useful direction for pedagogical interventions both in home and host institutions.

This chapter reports on a study that investigated the developmental trajectories of undergraduates from a bilingual (Chinese-English) university in Hong Kong who joined a semester-long international exchange program. Many elements have been scrutinized, however, in this work discussion largely centers on the participants' perceptions of, attitudes towards, and reactions to diverse educational practices.

BACKGROUND AND LITERATURE REVIEW

As this chapter centers on the academic L2 socialization of international exchange students, the literature review covers the following topics: acculturation and L2 socialization, culture confusion, and 'cultures of learning', with particular attention paid to L2 study abroad participants.

Acculturation and L2 Socialization

Berry, Poortinga, Breugelmans, Chasiotis and Sam (2011, p. 464) defined acculturation as 'changes in a cultural group or individuals as a result of contact with another cultural group'. This contact may bring about changes in both parties e.g., study abroad students and host nationals, particularly in individuals who are receptive to novel ideas and 'ways of being'.

Within the context of border crossings, Berry et al. (2011) depict adaptation as the process whereby newcomers employ strategies to deal with the natural 'ups and downs' of acculturation. Some scholars distinguish between *psychological* adaptation i.e., the nurturing of personal well-being and self-esteem, and *sociocultural* adaptation i.e., the ability to cope with everyday life in the wider society (Ward,

81

Bochner, & Furnham, 2001). The acculturation process involves varying degrees of discomfort as individuals adjust to the unfamiliar. Acculturative stress may be defined as 'a negative psychological reaction to the experiences of acculturation, often characterized by anxiety, depression, and a variety of psychosomatic problems' (Berry et al., 2011, p. 465).

Academic mobility often involves more than one language. Thus, acculturation may include L2 socialization, that is, the process by which newcomers become familiar with the linguistic conventions, sociopragmatic norms e.g., verbal expressions of politeness, cultural scripts e.g., common greetings and responses in social interactions, and other behaviors that are prevalent in the new culture (Duff, 2014; Kinginger, 2017). As border crossers gain exposure to the host environment, they may hone their intercultural communicative competence i.e., their ability to communicate effectively and appropriately in an L2 with individuals who have a different linguistic and cultural background. Individuals who open themselves up to new ideas and practices may develop a sense of belonging in the host environment and experience a broadening of their sense of self. Over time, some may develop a more inclusive and intercultural identity (Jackson 2018; Kim, 2018).

Culture Confusion

Transitioning from one's home environment to a new context may bring about culture confusion, a sense of loss, disorientation, and identity misalignments (Bennett, 1998). The strain of adjusting to unfamiliar practices can affect the newcomer's emotional, psychological, behavioral, cognitive, and physiological well-being, at least, temporarily. This phenomenon has traditionally been referred to as transition shock, a broad term which encompasses culture shock, role shock, language shock, and identity shock (self-shock). Interestingly, a number of contemporary acculturation specialists (e.g., Neuliep 2018) argued that 'culture confusion' is a more appropriate term for the natural process of cultural orientation among temporary border crossers.

In the host environment, L2 students who participate in an international exchange program may experience various forms of culture confusion in both academic and social domains (Jackson, 2013, 2014, 2018). When students travel abroad, they bring with them the language, values, beliefs, attitudes, and habits that they developed in their home environment through the process of enculturation or primary socialization. In a new cultural, linguistic, physical, and social environment, they are apt to experience acculturative stress as they confront ideas and behaviors that differ from what they are used to. Adler (1975, p. 13) defined culture shock as 'a set of emotional reactions to the loss of perceptual reinforcements from one's own culture, to new cultural stimuli which have little or no meaning, and to the misunderstanding of new and diverse experiences'. This experience can be unsettling and how newcomers

The Academic Second Language (L2) Socialization and Acculturation

respond can impact the quality and outcomes of their stay abroad. Some may find transitions overwhelming and, in extreme situations, flee the host environment for the safety of home. In others, the 'fluctuations of stress and adaptation' may spur deep reflection, personal growth, and identity expansion (Kim, 2018; Ward, 2015).

In the host environment, border crossers may also experience role confusion, that is, a state of bewilderment about the norms of behavior in the new environment e.g., the social 'rules' of politeness (Byrnes, 1966). For example, study abroad students are apt to be exposed to roles and responsibilities that differ from what they are used to in their home environment, which can be uncomfortable for some and liberating for others (Jackson, 2014).

Language confusion ('language shock') refers to the daunting challenge of understanding and communicating in an L2 in a new linguistic environment (Smalley, 1963). Not having adequate L2 skills to fully express one's thoughts and emotions can be frustrating, exhausting, and humbling, especially for adults. In their home country, students may use a L2 in class and rarely in social settings. In the host country, they may discover that they are ill-prepared for informal, social situations and fast-paced conversations with first language (L1) speakers (Jackson, 2013, 2014; Montgomery, 2010). Even if newcomers speak the same L1 as host nationals, differences in accent, cultural scripts, vocabulary, norms of politeness, dialects, humor, vocabulary, slang, and communication styles can serve as barriers to effective communication and relationship-building. Nonverbal behaviors e.g., body language and paralanguage, can also be confounding for newcomers. For some, language and cultural confusion can lead to disorientation, and, in extreme cases, the desire to return home earlier than planned.

Exposure to an unfamiliar linguistic and cultural environment can raise awareness of one's sense of self and serve as a catalyst for reflection on one's place in the world. For Zaharna (1989, p. 501), identity shock (or self-shock) refers to 'the intrusion of inconsistent, conflicting self-images', which can involve 'loss of communication competence', 'distorted self-reflections in the responses of others', and 'the challenge of changing identity-bound behaviors'. Identity confusion is a more contemporary term to describe this phenomenon.

Efforts to convey one's personality and preferred self-identities through an L2 can be challenging, and lead to misunderstandings (Jackson, 2018; Zaharna, 1989). As study abroad students try to communicate their authentic selves in the new environment, they may discover that they are not perceived as they would like. For example, they may regard themselves as fluent in the host language but are frequently reminded that they are L2 speakers. This can be very discouraging for some and yet motivating for others who then seek out ways to enhance their linguistic competence.

83

Cultures of Learning

When students participate in study abroad programs, they bring with them their own experiences and attitudes towards teaching and learning that have been cultivated in their home country over many years e.g., expectations regarding the roles and responsibilities of students and teachers, ideas about the most effective ways to learn, perceptions of the qualities and actions of a 'good' teacher. Jin and Cortazzi (2006) defined a 'culture of learning' as:

[T]aken for granted frameworks of expectations, attitudes, values and beliefs about how to teach or learn successfully and about how to use talk in interaction... A culture of learning frames what teachers and students expect to happen in classrooms. (p. 9)

At the host institution, international exchange students may encounter unfamiliar educational practices. Some newcomers may welcome the opportunity to explore diverse practices, whereas others may find new behaviors and expectations difficult to understand and accept. For example, students may initially be dismayed and very critical of educators in the host environment who provide much less support and guidance than what they are accustomed to e.g., no PowerPoint slides or lecture notes, less explicit directions for assignments. Newcomers may also feel uneasy if they are expected to speak up more frequently in discussions; or conversely, they discover that the norm is for students to remain quiet and let the teacher do most of the talking (Cortazzi & Jin, 2011; Jackson, 2013; Parris-Kidd & Barnett, 2011). How study abroad students react in these situations can vary and, ultimately, affect their willingness to engage in the host environment. A complex mix of internal and external elements can influence the quality and degree of study abroad learning.

THE PRESENT STUDY

Background

As in many other parts of Asia, the number of students from Hong Kong universities who are joining international exchange programs has been on the rise in recent years. To help determine how to enhance their international educational experience, the present study tracked the developmental trajectories of undergraduates from a Hong Kong university who joined a semester-long international exchange program. While this project examined many issues, this chapter addresses the following questions:

The Academic Second Language (L2) Socialization and Acculturation

- *What are the participants' perceptions of, attitudes towards, and reactions to unfamiliar educational practices prior to and during the international exchange program?*
- *What impact do their international exchange experiences have on their perceptions and attitudes towards diverse educational practices?*
- *What are the implications for the preparation and support of outbound international exchange students from this region?*

Research design and methodology

The present study employed a mixed-method sequential explanatory design (Creswell, 2014; Ivankova & Greer, 2015), beginning with the collection of quantitative data to develop a broad picture of the participants' views and experiences before and after their stay abroad. Qualitative data was also amassed and analyzed to help explain and elaborate on the quantitative results.

Participants

The full cohort consisted of 246 outbound semester-abroad students from a comprehensive, bilingual (Chinese-English) Hong Kong university. There were 149 females (60.6%) and 97 (39.4%) males, with a mean age of 20.41 years and a mean Grade Point Average (GPA) of 3.32 (out of 4), signifying above average academic performance. All of the participants were ethnic Chinese; 186 (75.6%) spoke Cantonese as a L1 and 60 (24.4%) Putonghua (Mandarin). In the full cohort, all spoke English as an additional language. Ninety-nine (40.2%) had never travelled outside their home country, while 147 (59.0%) had some travel experience, which typically consisted of a few days or weeks in Asia e.g., short trips with family members or friends, or participation in organized tours. Fifty-three (21.5%) had studied abroad; in most cases, this entailed a micro- or short-term stay abroad e.g., an English or Putonghua summer immersion program.

The participants came from the following faculties: 134 (54.4%) Business Administration, 51 (20.7%) Social Science, 24 (9.8%) Arts, 19 (7.7%) Science, 13 (5.3%) Engineering, and 5 (2.0%) Education. When the exchange program got underway, 52 (21.1%) were in their 2nd Year of studies, 144 (58.5%) in their 3rd Year, 46 (18.7%) in their 4th Year, 2 (0.8) in their 5th Year, and 2 (0.8%) in postgraduate studies. For their semester-long exchange program, the participants went to the following destinations: 82 (33.3%) to the US, 28 (11.4%) to Canada, 24 (9.8%) to China, 16 (6.5%) to Australia, 14 (5.7%) to the Netherlands, 11 (4.5%) to France, 8 (3.3%) to South Korea, 8 (3.3%) to Sweden, 8 (3.3%) to the UK, 8 (3.3%) to Finland, 7 (2.8%) to Singapore, 7 (2.8%) to Switzerland, 6 (2.4%) to New Zealand, 5 (2.0%)

85

The Academic Second Language (L2) Socialization and Acculturation

to Denmark, 5 (2.0%) to Mexico, 2 (0.8%) to Czech, 1 (0.4) to Germany, 1 (0.4) to Ireland, 1 (0.4) to Norway, 1 (0.4) to Thailand, 1 (0.4) to Japan, and 1 (0.4) to South Africa. While abroad, nearly all did their coursework in English. For their exchange program, 182 (74.0%) lived on campus, 31 (12.6%) off-campus, and 3 (1.2%) in a homestay.

To gain deeper insight into their international experience, a sampling of students (35), 21 (60.0%) females and 14 (40.0%) males, were interviewed in-depth before and after the semester abroad. The gender ratio mirrored that of the full cohort (see Table 1 for the code number and profile of each interviewee).

Major code: BCHE Biochemistry; CENG Computer Engineering; CHLL Chinese Language & Literature; COMM Journalism & Communication; ECON Economics; ELED English Studies and English Language Education, GPAD Government & Public Administration; IBBA Integrated BBA Program; IERG Information Engineering; LSCI Life Sciences; MATH Mathematics; MBTE Molecular Biotechnology; PACC Professional Accountancy Program; PHYS Physics; PSYC Psychology; QFIN Quantitative Finance; RELS Religious Studies; RMSC Risk Management Science; SEEM Systems Engineering & Engineering Management; SOCI Sociology; TRAN Translation.

The mean age of the interviewees was 20.75 and the average GPA was 3.4 (out of 4). Similar to the full cohort, all of the interviewees were ethnic Chinese students who spoke English as an additional language; 19 (54.3%) spoke Putonghua as an L1 and 16 (45.7%) Cantonese. Nineteen were born in Mainland China, while the rest were born and raised in Hong Kong. Twenty-two (61.1%) had never travelled outside their home country; 14 (38.9%) had travel experience, which typically consisted of a few days or weeks in Asia. Ten (27.8%) had previous study abroad experience; in most cases, this entailed a micro- or short-term stay e.g., an English or Putonghua summer immersion program.

When the exchange program got underway, 5 (14.3%) of the interviewees were in their 2nd Year of studies, 20 (57.1%) in their 3rd Year, 9 (25.7%) in their 4th Year, and 1 (2.9%) in the 5th Year. They came from the following faculties: 11 (31.4%) Business Administration, 10 (28.6%) Science, 7 (20%) Social Science, 3 (8.6%) Arts, 3 (8.6%) Engineering, and 1 (2.9%) Education. Among the interviewees, 17 (48.6%) studied abroad in the US, 6 (17.1%) in Canada, 2 (5.7%) in Australia, 2 (5.7%) in South Korea, 2 (5.7%) in the UK, 2 (5.7%) in Finland, 1 (2.9%) in China, 1 (2.9%) in New Zealand, 1 (2.9%) in Singapore, 1 (2.9%) in Mexico and 1 (2.9%) in South Africa. In the host country all of the interviewees did coursework in English. A few also took a language enhancement course in the host language. For example, S6 and S14 studied Finnish, S7 and S12 Korean, and S9 Spanish. For their stay abroad, 25 (71.4%) lived on campus, 5 (14.3%) off-campus, and 2 (5.7%) in a homestay.

The Academic Second Language (L2) Socialization and Acculturation

Table 1. Profile of interviewees

Code No.	Sex	L1	Birth-Place	TOEFL/ IELTS Scores	Faculty	Major	Year of Study	Host Country
S1	M	P	PRC	97/7.0	Business Administration	IBBA	3	Canada
S2	F	P	PRC	105/7.5	Business Administration	PACC	3	USA
S3	F	P	PRC	93/6.5	Business Administration	IBBA	3	Canada
S4	F	P	PRC	109/7.5	Social Science	PSYC	3	USA
S5	M	P	PRC	104/7.5	Science	RMSC	3	USA
S6	M	C	HK	105/7.5	Education	ELED	4	Finland
S7	M	C	HK	112/8.0	Social Science	GPAD	2	Korea
S8	M	C	HK	104/7.5	Business Administration	QFIN	3	Canada
S9	F	P	PRC	98/7.0	Science	MBTE	4	Mexico
S10	M	C	HK	94-101/7.0	Science	BCHE	4	Australia
S11	M	C	HK	98/7.0	Engineering	CENG	5	Singapore
S12	F	C	HK	93/6.5	Arts	RELS	4	Korea
S13	F	P	PRC	102/7.5	Science	MATH	4	USA
S14	M	C	HK	78/6.0	Social Science	SOCI	4	Finland
S15	M	P	PRC	100/7.0	Engineering	IERG	3	USA
S16	F	C	HK	104/7.5	Social Science	PSYC	4	South Africa
S17	F	C	PRC	79-93/6.5	Social Science	ECON	4	New Zealand
S18	F	P	PRC	105/7.5	Business Administration	PACC	3	USA
S19	F	P	PRC	98/7.0	Business Administration	IBBA	3	USA
S20	F	P	PRC	113/8.0	Science	RMSC	3	USA
S21	M	P	PRC	112/8.0	Business Administration	PACC	3	USA
S22	F	C	PRC	102-109/7.5	Arts	TRAN	2	U.K.
S23	F	P	PRC	92/6.5	Engineering	SEEM	3	U.K.
S24	F	P	PRC	106/7.5	Science	RMSC	3	USA
S25	F	P	PRC	115/8.5	Science	LSCI	3	Canada
S26	M	C	HK	103/7.5	Business Administration	PACC	3	Australia
S27	F	P	PRC	102/7.5	Science	RMSC	3	Canada
S28	F	C	HK	92/6.5	Business Administration	IBBA	2	USA
S29	M	C	HK	79-93/6.5	Social Science	GPAD	2	USA
S30	F	P	PRC	101/7.0	Business Administration	PACC	3	Canada
S31	M	C	PRC	103/7.5	Arts	CHLL	3	USA
S32	F	P	PRC	111/8.0	Social Science	COMM	3	USA
S33	F	C	HK	104/7.5	Business Administration	IBBA	2	USA
S34	M	P	PRC	103/7.5	Science	PHYS	3	USA
S35	F	P	PRC	100/7.0	Science	MATH	4	USA

Note: L1 = C, Cantonese; P, Putonghua; Birthplace: HK, Hong Kong; PRC, Mainland China English language proficiency test results: NB. If the students provided a TOEFL score, the IELTS band equivalent is provided, and vice versa.

INSTRUMENTATION AND DATA COLLECTION

Pre-Study Abroad Data

Prior to studying abroad, the full cohort completed the *Pre-International Exchange Questionnaire* in the pre-departure session organized by the home university, and students who were absent were later invited to complete it online. This in-house instrument addressed such topics as: reasons for studying abroad; aims, expectations and level of preparedness for their stay abroad; concerns about living and studying abroad; expected challenges and gains; previous international/education abroad experience, and intercultural contact; perceptions of their intercultural competence; interest in international/global affairs; L2 proficiency and use; language, culture, and identity; and family background. Most of the items in the questionnaire were closed; several open-ended questions were included to gather more information about the respondents' perceptions and experiences. With their written consent, their application forms were also reviewed to gather more background information and insight into their study plan (a short essay outlining their aims and expectations for their international exchange experience).

Before departing for the host country, 35 students from a range of disciplines took part in semi-structured interviews that were conducted in Cantonese, Putonghua or English, depending on the preference of the interviewee. The average length of the pre-study abroad interviews was 85 minutes. Topics included: aims and expectations for study abroad; identity;

intercultural contact; L2 proficiency and use; social networks; level of preparedness for life/study abroad; perceptions of intercultural competence; previous international experience; and other issues of relevance to the international exchange experience that the interviewees wished to discuss.

Study Abroad Data

To better understand what was happening during the stay abroad, the interviewees also responded to monthly email prompts during the exchange period. In this way, they were prompted to provide details about their observations and reactions to teaching and learning practices and other phenomena related to the main themes of the study.

Post-Study Abroad Data

Immediately after their semester abroad, the participants were invited to complete the online *Post-International Exchange Questionnaire* (an in-house instrument) to gather information about their international exchange experience. This instrument primarily consisted of closed questions with a few open-ended ones. To facilitate the assessment of their learning, the instrument included many items that were similar to those in the *Pre-International Exchange Questionnaire*. Topics included: aims, expectations and level of preparedness for the stay abroad; assessment of goals achieved/perceived gains; challenges faced while living and studying abroad; L2 proficiency and use; perceptions of intercultural competence; social networks; language, culture, and identity; and suggestions for the preparation of future international exchange students.

After they had returned to Hong Kong, the students who were interviewed previously were invited to share their views about their international exchange experience in individual interviews. As in the first session, these interviews took place in the language of their choice. The average length of the post-study abroad interviews was 101 minutes. Topics covered a range of topics, including: current intercultural contact and future plans; intercultural communication skills; intercultural contact and adjustment; L2 development and usage; language, culture, and identity (change); level of preparedness for study abroad/re-entry; overall impression of their international experience; perceived gains and challenges encountered abroad; reentry challenges and adjustment; social networks; their academic, social and intellectual development; and suggestions for the preparation and support of future exchange students/ returnees. Similar to the pre-study abroad interview, the participants were invited to talk about additional issues related to their international exchange experience or re-entry that interested them.

Data Analysis

NVivo, a qualitative software program, facilitated the organization, coding, and triangulation of the quantitative and qualitative data e.g., study plans, interview transcripts, open-ended survey questions, emails, pre- and post- questionnaire results. The statistical data obtained from the pre- and post-questionnaires were processed using SPSS. The study plans and interview transcripts were subjected to thematic content analysis, along with responses to open-ended questions in the in-house questionnaires and sojourn emails. When processing the qualitative data, a thematic, 'open coding' approach (Bazeley & Jackson, 2013; Grbich, 2013) was employed, and the analysis was not confined to preconceived notions and categories (Miles, Huberman, & Saldana, 2013). As the relationship between items became clear, new categories emerged and others were modified. In addition to full-cohort pre- and post-study abroad profiles, triangulation of various types of data made it possible to track the stories of each interviewee.

FINDINGS

While the study gathered data related to multiple issues and themes, this section focuses on the participants' L2 socialization, acculturation, and evolving perceptions of and attitudes towards diverse educational practices. Selected quantitative results are presented, along with excerpts from the qualitative data that illustrate the participants' views and experiences in their own words. The application essays/ study plans were written in English and excerpts are in their original form except for a few amendments due to spelling and grammatical errors. For interviews that were conducted in Cantonese or Putonghua, the English translations are provided. Efforts were made to retain the nuances in the translations, which were checked by two bilingual (Chinese-English) research assistants. Given the large amount of quantitative and qualitative data amassed, only a small percentage can be presented here.

Pre-Study Abroad Aims, Expectations and Concerns

Study Abroad Goals

In the application form, the students were required to supply a brief study plan, which offered insight into their aspirations for their stay abroad. Most wished to study abroad to experience life in another culture, enhance their L2 proficiency, broaden their horizons, and become more independent and self-reliant. Many wished to gain exposure to cultural differences as the following excerpts reveal:

Despite the possible cultural shock at the first stage of being abroad, the exchange program will provide many benefits, enabling me to taste cultural differences, nourish my language and interpersonal skills, and, most importantly, allow me to get access to cutting-edge research and meet great minds. It will not only contribute to my academic life, but also equip me with a global perspective. (S13)

The Academic Second Language (L2) Socialization and Acculturation

Different universities have their unique ways to deliver knowledge and nurture future talents based on their vision of how a university education should be.... I firmly believe that a different curriculum in another university can supply me with different ways to gain knowledge and enable me to compare my major studies here with those in the host university. (S33)

Similar to S33, others expressed the desire to experience diverse teaching and learning styles in an international setting:

I would like to learn more about how students in other countries study accounting and see how it is different from here. I'd also like to attend courses in other subjects to more broadly experience the different teaching methods and learning atmosphere in a foreign university. (S26)

I want to explore different teaching and learning styles and ways to solve problems in a different culture. (S28)

While many of the participants had high expectations for the 'foreign education' that they expected to experience, some (e.g., S10) were skeptical and wished to see for themselves what they could gain from international educational experience:

It is always said that foreign education is good. Sometimes, I wonder what is so good about it. From my experience, foreign students, especially Hong Kongers who study abroad, act more confidently, particularly in speaking. What is the hidden story behind this? Or is it just an illusion owing to my prejudice? I want to find answers to these questions. (S10)

Some explained that the exchange period would enable them to learn more about the host country and education system, and help them to see if they were 'suitable' for a longer stay abroad. For these individuals, the semester abroad would serve as a trial run for future postgraduate studies or employment abroad.

Going on exchange is a good chance to test myself; to see whether I like to live abroad, how I like the place, how fast I can adapt to a new environment, how suitable I am to develop a global career etc. Through practice, I can know myself much better, and thus plan for my future development. (S9)

I enjoy my field of study and hope to continue my studies in North America after graduation since it has the most advanced knowledge and abundant academic resources in science and technology. I want to be familiar with the universities there before I become a postgraduate student in order to better adapt to their style of studies. I would like to find out how their math classes differ from ours, how their students study, and see what the facilities and policies in the university are like. (S35)

A number of the participants hoped to form a closer connection to their chosen field of study, discover more about themselves and provide clarity about their future career path:

I can get a better understanding of engineering by taking engineering courses abroad since people in different countries may have different perspectives towards the discipline. This may give me a different view about what engineers do and I will learn more about my major from a new perspective.... I also want to explore western culture and deepen understanding of myself as well as the world. (S23)

In their study plan, a few stated that even though they would not transfer credits back to their home university they were determined to take full advantage of the freedom this afforded them. S34, for example, resolved to make the most of opportunities in the academic arena:

As I will be free from the pressure of my GPA during the exchange period, I would like to take some really advanced math courses to challenge myself, in addition to my major courses. I will, for the first time after entering the university, learn things purely out of interest and passion. This freedom, I believe, will be extremely beneficial for my future career. (S34)

In the pre-study abroad questionnaire, which the participants completed soon after they had been accepted to join an international exchange program, they were asked to indicate their aims for their semester abroad. The respondents were provided with a list of common reasons to go on exchange and asked to rank them in terms of their degree of importance for them personally. They were also invited to add additional aims that were not in the list. *To travel and see many new places, to become more mature and independent,* and *to experience life in another culture* were ranked as the top three aims, while the three least important were *to enhance knowledge and skills in their discipline, to develop their leadership skills,* and *to improve one's practical academic skills.* Interestingly, academic motives were generally deemed less important.

In pre-study abroad interviews, 35 of the participants discussed their aims for their stay abroad. While a few had set specific goals and targets for learning—language enhancement, exposure to courses not offered in their home university, growth in independence—many were rather vague, and it was evident that that they had given

The Academic Second Language (L2) Socialization and Acculturation

it little thought. Some commented that their time in the host country would be too brief to accomplish much, and several explained that they had not engaged in goal-setting because they would not need to transfer credits to the home institution and were unconcerned about academic results. These individuals appeared to view the international exchange program as a break from their 'real studies' in Hong Kong:

I don't think I'll attain any specific goal as I'll only go there for one semester. (S7)

I haven't set any academic goals because the GPA I get there won't be transferred back. (S19)

I'm not going on exchange because I want to accomplish a lot. I don't have any big goals. I'll only be there a few months. Basically, I just want to enjoy my time there. I've heard that the learning style is less stressful and very different from Hong Kong so I just want to experience it. (S22)

In contrast, some of their peers had set concrete academic aims for the semester-long exchange period. In addition to enhancing their L2 proficiency, they wished to gain first-hand experience with different teaching and learning styles:

Academically, I want to improve my English-speaking ability. I also hope to experience the American teaching style, observe the relationship between students and teachers, and see how students interact with each other. (S5)

In line with what they had stated in their study plan, some of the interviewees expressed the desire to discover more about their suitability for their chosen career and postgraduate studies in the host country. Some were quite strategic in their plans.

I want to take some interesting courses and learn about what kind of research they are doing in psychology and how it differs from what we do here. I hope to discover an interesting direction for my future research. I'm thinking about doing a Master's degree in the US and this exchange can help me decide if this is a good plan for me. (S4)

As for academic goals, I want to take statistic courses and get some credits transferred back. I also want to find out whether I'm really interested in statistics. If I become interested in doing postgraduate studies there, I'll try to connect with some professors. If they could write a reference letter for me that would be great! (S20)

A number of the interviewees planned to take courses in their host institution that were not available at their home institution in Hong Kong. Many hoped to benefit from a different learning environment, which they anticipated would be less examination-oriented and more interactive:

I want to experience the learning environment in New Zealand. Many people say that the learning environment in Hong Kong is too focused on exams, so students don't participate much in classrooms. I want to experience the difference over there. (S17)

By doing projects with other college students there and communicating with them, I hope I can get a better understanding of the education model that's used in Canada. I want to experience the North American teaching style. This is my main motivation for studying abroad. From what I understand, teachers there do not simply pass knowledge to students. They also share their vision, beliefs, and life experiences. Teachers in different countries must have very different value systems and views of the world. When they teach, they will tell some of their personal experiences or talk about cases that have happened around them. I'm very interested to know their thinking, teaching style, and ways of looking at problems. (S25)

I'm going to study in an English-speaking country where the business courses are case-based and require active participation. This is quite unlike courses here where students only need to listen to the teachers and few students respond to questions so I hope I can improve my oral English in this way. (S30)

Anticipated Challenges in the Host Environment

In the pre-study abroad questionnaire, the full cohort was provided with a list of possible challenges that they may face in the host environment, which drew on previous study abroad research. The respondents were asked to rank their key concerns and add any that were not in the list. As Table 2 illustrates, a language barrier, culture shock (cultural confusion), and intercultural interactions were cited as the greatest challenges they expected to encounter, followed by managing finances, personal safety and security, and homesickness. Around a third expected that participation in class would be a significant challenge for them. Only 18 (7.3%) were worried about handling a heavy workload.

In the pre-study abroad interview, which was conducted closer to the departure date, the interviewees disclosed concerns about living and studying abroad. Many expressed doubts about their ability to cope with language and cultural confusion, and worried that they would be homesick. Those who had less confidence in their proficiency in the medium of instruction were especially anxious about their ability

The Academic Second Language (L2) Socialization and Acculturation

Table 2. Expected challenges abroad (N = 246)

Challenges anticipated in host environment	f	%
Language barrier	102	41.5
Coping with culture shock	97	39.4
Interacting with people from other cultures	89	36.2
Managing my finances	85	34.6
Personal safety and security	81	32.9
Homesickness	81	32.9
Participating in class	79	32.1
Accommodation problems	60	24.4
Racial discrimination	31	12.6
Heavy workload	18	7.3

to adjust to the academic environment. For example, S35 said, *'I feel a little bit nervous. It'll be a bit difficult for me to fully understand lectures in English'*.

Many of the interviewees doubted their ability to follow and contribute to fast-paced discussions in English, their L2, at least, in the beginning of their stay:

As most of the students there will speak English as a first language, they'll be very active in answering questions or expressing their ideas in class. They'll be able to say whatever they want; however, for me, I'll need more time to organize my speech, and I'm afraid that I won't be able to express myself clearly. It'll be a challenge to be in this kind of situation, but I'll do my best. (S5)

I feel a bit uneasy about what it will be like in my classes there. I might lag behind in the beginning as all of the discussions will be conducted in English, and that will be really challenging for me; however, I think I should be able to catch up after a few weeks. (S32)

Nearly all of the interviewees aspired to make friends with host nationals as well as international students from many parts of the world. Lacking confidence in their language and intercultural communication skills, some worried about their ability to develop and sustain meaningful multicultural relationships.

I'm quite nervous. I don't have a clear idea about what the locals are like. I haven't communicated with any before. I've heard they're pretty aggressive, and I'm a little worried about that. I'm kind of scared about what it will be like to be in classes with them, especially when we have discussions and have to work on projects together. I feel pressured because I'm not very confident in my English. (S33).

I think I'll feel some pressure there. Inevitably, there will be some obstacles when communicating with native speakers. The local students may not want to have me in their group when doing projects or presentations. I totally understand, because I don't want to do projects with exchange students here. The main aim of most exchange students is travelling and relaxation, so they often contribute very little. Also, my English will not be as good as theirs. (S1)

S1's remarks also convey his perception of study abroad as primarily a time for *'travelling and relaxation'*, a notion that appeared frequently in the analysis of the post-study abroad data.

Post-Study Abroad Reflections

Post-Study Abroad Perceptions and Experiences

After returning from the semester abroad, the full cohort was invited to complete the *Post-Study Abroad International Exchange Questionnaire*. Additionally, the participants who were interviewed previously were interviewed again. The returnees were prompted to identify the obstacles they encountered during their international exchange experience and to reflect on the ways they benefited from their stay abroad.

Challenges in the Academic Environment

In the post-study abroad questionnaire, the respondents (N = 91) were asked to identify and rank the greatest challenges that they had faced while abroad. Similar to the pre-study abroad instrument, they were provided with a list of items and invited to add other obstacles they had encountered that were not on the list. Table 3 presents the results in order of frequency.

In line with their pre-study abroad expectations, the results indicated that language and culture confusion, followed by class participation, were the most challenging aspects of their stay abroad for the full cohort.

A review of the post-study abroad interview transcripts revealed that most of the students found it difficult to adjust to the academic environment, at least in the first month. In sync with the questionnaire results, most experienced transition confusion (e.g., language and culture confusion, identity misalignments) and, in particular, had difficulty coping with fast-paced discussions both in the academic arena and in social contexts.

The Academic Second Language (L2) Socialization and Acculturation

Table 3. Challenges abroad (N = 91)

Challenges anticipated in host environment	f	%
Language barrier	46	50.5
Coping with culture shock i.e., adjusting to cultural difference	32	35.2
Participating in class e.g., class discussions	30	33.0
Managing my finances	28	30.8
Interacting with people from other cultures	28	30.8
Heavy workload	21	23.1
Personal safety and security	16	17.6
Homesickness	16	17.6
Accommodation problems	16	17.6
Making friends with people from other cultures	8	8.8
Racial discrimination	6	6.6

Linguistic Challenges

While in the host country, most of the participants attended L2-medium courses, with English the most common language of instruction. A few also enrolled in language enhancement or culture-related courses related to the host culture, such as Korean, French or Spanish classes, etc.

At their home university many courses are offered in Chinese (Cantonese or Putonghua) as well as English. Students may also study other foreign languages. For local students, the primary language used outside of class is Cantonese. While abroad, many of the participants found themselves in classes where L1 speakers of English were in the majority; feeling under pressure, some deemed their English language proficiency inadequate. These individuals found it difficult to integrate into the host environment both in and outside of class. Further, individuals who perceived themselves to be fluent in English prior to their stay abroad were dismayed when they were constantly asked to repeat themselves. Disappointingly, they realized that they were viewed as L2 learners and outsiders in the host environment.

A small number of the participants were overwhelmed by the amount of reading required in their English-medium courses and felt lost. For example, in his post-study abroad interview, a Chinese Language and Literature major who studied in the US said: In the course 'Approach to literature', I couldn't get a good grade because the readings were too much for me. I couldn't keep up'. (S31)

The Academic Second Language (L2) Socialization and Acculturation

Several of the returnees disclosed that their everyday vocabulary and grasp of specialized terminology in their L2 were inadequate, especially when compared with L1 speakers. As a result, they found it difficult to comprehend readings and follow lectures. For example, two males who were on exchange in the US remarked:

I was disadvantaged in some of my courses as the use of terms in English was much easier for native speakers, and they had a much bigger vocabulary. (S15)

I found it challenging to adjust to the academic environment there. I had to check dictionaries a lot. It took me forever to get through the readings. It was really difficult for me. (S29)

S29's revelations suggest that his academic reading skills e.g., skimming and scanning, were not well developed. Rather than look for the main idea in readings, he was spending a great deal of time looking up individual words, and, not surprisingly, was unable to keep up in his courses.

Interestingly, only a few of the interviewees indicated that they had experienced problems with their writing. They explained that they had to write brief reports/essays in their courses or had quizzes or examinations, which did not require much writing. Although a few struggled because their L2 writing skills were weak, most remarked that the teachers made allowances for L2 writers when assignments were graded.

Although only a few interviewees found L2 reading and writing difficult in the host environment, the majority deemed listening and speaking to be quite demanding. In particular, it was challenging for them to follow lectures and participate in class discussions. For lectures that were delivered in English, the interviewees found the following elements problematic: unfamiliar accents and communication or speech styles, the use of unfamiliar terms and vocabulary, a rapid rate of speech, and discourse that drew on cultural knowledge that they did not possess e.g., examples and jokes. The following students, for example, found it difficult to understand lecturers or classmates who spoke with accents that were unfamiliar to them.

In New Zealand, I had to participate in case discussions. I could feel the people there were quite nice, but I didn't always understand what they were saying. Actually, their accent was a bit difficult for me to comprehend. (S17)

In lectures and discussions, I had to listen really well to try to catch their accents. It was really difficult for me. (S28)

98

The Academic Second Language (L2) Socialization and Acculturation

Cultural Gap

Most interviewees found lectures and class discussions irritating at times as the lecturer's examples and jokes drew on cultural knowledge that they did not possess. Comments such as the following were typical:

I often felt annoyed when having lessons in the US as I had great difficulty understanding what the teachers said even though I tried my very best to be attentive. I could hear their words but couldn't get their meaning. I didn't know what the teachers were talking about, especially when the talk was somehow related to the culture. There were too many cultural elements incorporated into the lectures. (S2)

One teacher's lessons were too difficult for me even in the very end. He spoke especially fast and liked giving examples which I knew nothing about. They could be about some famous people, magazines or books, but I knew nothing about them. Even when others laughed, I didn't know why. This course was not really suitable for me. There was too much background information that was a mystery to me. (S8)

In their post-study abroad interviews, some of the students disclosed that lecturers in their host institution made little or no effort to integrate local and international students. Accordingly, the newcomers felt on the periphery.

I had some difficulty with my studies during my exchange. I couldn't understand the content of the courses, not because it was very difficult, but because there was a lot of cultural stuff incorporated into the teaching, such as the history of finance in America. We, the few Asians who were in the course, felt very confused in the lessons when the teacher told jokes or stories. We just couldn't get the point. I don't think the jokes were funny, but the Americans laughed themselves to death. I could feel the teacher was very knowledgeable, but I just couldn't understand a bit of what he said. If an American student listens to the story of the 'Monkey King' he surely doesn't understand what it is, you know? This is why I think learning in Hong Kong is easier as the cases that teachers use are mostly based in Asia. Even if they use a European case, they will introduce some background information beforehand. (S21)

Humor is often difficult to translate across cultures. Initially, many of the exchange students found satire, jokes, idiomatic expressions, social discourse, and argumentation styles confounding and very frustrating. This served as a barrier to their integration in both academic and social contexts and hampered the development of meaningful multicultural relationships.

Many of the interviewees believed that their academic results were negatively impacted by their lack of local cultural knowledge. This made it difficult for them to follow lectures and perform well in examinations. The frustration of S13 is evident in the following interview excerpt:

In the US, my GPA was very low. In Hong Kong, I've maintained a GPA of 3.5 (out of 4) but I only got less than 3 there. I just couldn't follow some of the teachers. For the courses that I could understand, I got a B. I only got a C for the ones that I couldn't follow. It was okay when the teachers stuck to the course content, but I couldn't get their points if they talked about cultural stuff. In the exams, there were a lot of culture-related things and that was difficult for me. (S13)

Discussion-Based Pedagogy

Most of the interviewees indicated that discussion-based pedagogy e.g., case discussions, was the greatest academic challenge they faced in their host institution. Many attributed their limited participation in discussions to multiple factors, including: the fast pace of interactions with frequent interruptions by other students, little or no understanding of cultural-based content/examples/humor; lack of certainty about when to 'jump into' a discussion, insufficient time to think and respond before the discussion had moved on to other topics; an inability to follow the discussion in their L2 due to limited proficiency; fear of making comments that would not be understood or would be perceived as 'stupid'; concern about wasting time in class, a heightened level of communication anxiety, lack of familiarity with the open-ended nature of discussions, shyness, and little or no incentive if they did not need to transfer credits to their home university. Most of the interviewees gave multiple reasons for their own reticence or reluctance to participate.

Some of the participants explained that they did not take an active role in discussions because they did not care about grades since they would did not transfer credits back to their home university.

In Canada I just didn't have much incentive to take the initiative and raise my hands in discussions as the participation mark was not important for me. I wasn't going to transfer credits, so I was just not motivated to join in. (S8)

I didn't participate much. I really slacked off in my studies because I didn't have to transfer credits, although I did learn things through immersion. (S18)

The Academic Second Language (L2) Socialization and Acculturation

In the host environment, most of the interviewees observed unfamiliar roles and behaviors of students and teachers, and their reactions to these differences varied. Many of the newcomers experienced what Byrnes (1966) refers to as role shock (role confusion). For example, many of the students who were studying in English-speaking countries remarked that local students tend to ask questions whenever they are unsure about something and they may even interrupt a lecturer, a practice that they considered impolite. Many of the interviewees stated that they waited until they felt certain that their question or comment was 'worthy' of taking up class time. The fear of losing face in front of their peers and teachers limited their participation in class.

Locals have an active learning style and in class they tend to ask questions right away if they have doubts. (S3)

The American students just take over and speak right after the instructors finish their lectures. Moreover, they ask questions when they come across any problems. In discussions, they aren't afraid to interrupt other speakers, even instructors. (S24)

One challenge that I faced in the academic environment is that I needed to participate in class discussions. Asian students also have a lot of questions, but they usually take some time to formulate them and won't say anything until they are pretty sure that they are good questions. Then they will ask. But the American students ask questions whenever they feel that they don't understand something. Then, they solve their problems immediately. (S34)

Many of the exchange students found it difficult to adjust to discussions that were much more free-flowing and open-ended than what they were accustomed to in Hong Kong or Mainland China. For example, some newcomers found that their US-American lecturers served as facilitators rather than transmitters of knowledge and this was an unfamiliar teaching style for them. Further, many of the students seemed to expect their lecturers to identify a single, preferred solution to a problem or issue at the end of a discussion. They were perplexed and uneasy when they were left with a range of possible alternatives. Confused about the rationale for this mode of teaching and learning, they perceived their lecturers to be ill-prepared or lazy and deemed their classes to be a waste of time.

The lectures allowed room for many discussions and even some debates. These took up a lot of class time and I wasn't sure what the main point was in a lot of these talks. (S6)

101

The students speak up a lot more there and their comments are very different from each other, but in Hong Kong we gradually arrive at a common conclusion. (S19)

Most of the interviewees experienced difficulty adjusting to fast-paced discussions with speakers often interrupting each other, however, a few of the exchange students appreciated the amount of interaction they observed.

I've become a lot bolder with asking questions. Now, I just speak out if I have any thoughts because I think this contributes to the class. I'm also more willing to speak out since I'm now more confident with my English. Before, I only listened, and would just ask questions after the class ended. Affected by Western culture, I think speaking out during class is a good thing, so I now push myself to do it. Maybe this habit will diminish after a period of time but since I've already developed this learning style, it has become very normal for me to ask questions in class. (S18)

Classes were much more interactive than in Hong Kong, and the pace of discussions much faster. It was quite good. Discussions were meaningful. In Hong Kong, when a teacher asks a question, there's usually dead air, with little response. The local students asked questions and spoke out in a more active manner than Hong Kong students. (S27)

After a period of adjustment, some of the newcomers embraced a more active learning style. By the end of the semester, they asked more questions in discussions and were more vocal in debates.

Classroom interaction is very intense in the US. In tutorials in my home university, I would prefer more people to voice out their opinions but the lack of time and the unwillingness of classmates to answer questions or discuss things discourages interaction. At home, students usually post lengthy comments on the online forum when reminded that the discussion will close soon but this is different from instant interaction in class. Lengthy analysis and comments on the forum help to get higher grades, but that is totally different from a debate that happens in class. In the US, interaction in class was much more exciting and triggered more thoughts and ideas. Since classroom participation is emphasized, students must talk and voice out their opinions. They compete with each other to answer questions, and the professors ask a lot of questions and chat with them. This process is much more interactive than in Hong Kong and I think this was the most beneficial part of studying there. (S31)

The Academic Second Language (L2) Socialization and Acculturation

Several interviewees declared that they expected to be more active in discussions in Hong Kong after they returned home, provided that they did not annoy their teachers and classmates. Some added that they did not wish to be regarded as show-offs in their home environment.

Host Receptivity and Sense of Belonging

Although many of the students focused on problems they had encountered in the host environment (e.g., 'uncaring teachers' who offered little guidance/handouts and spoke too fast), some described the teachers and local students as very helpful, which eased their adjustment. For example, the following student who studied in New Zealand appreciated the efforts that her hosts made to speak more slowly. This helped her to follow conversations and feel more comfortable in the new environment.

In the beginning, I really couldn't understand what they were talking about, but they were nice and slowed down their pace of speech. That really helped and gradually I became more comfortable expressing my ideas in discussions. Also, the relationship between teachers and students was better there. People were really friendly. It seems that they really value communication and are willing to talk with you. (S17)

Several of S17's peers also praised the closer, more informal relationship between teachers and students in their host institution. While a few of the interviewees were uncomfortable with the use of their lecturers' first name by local students, others embraced the reduced power distance that this conveyed.

Classes in the US felt more comfortable. The relationship between teachers and students was more equal, and the atmosphere more relaxing and active, with students even calling the teachers by their first name! (S4)

Not surprisingly, the exchange students who perceived their hosts to be welcoming and accommodating were more satisfied with their international educational experience, and much more willing to use their L2 to initiate intercultural interactions. Many of these individuals indicated the desire to do postgraduate studies abroad, often in the same institution. A perceived high-level of host receptivity appeared to have a positive impact on their intercultural attitudes, willingness to use their L2, and degree of investment in their academic learning and social development.

103

PEDAGOGICAL IMPLICATIONS AND RECOMMENDATIONS

The findings of the study have implications for both home and host institutions. With regard to the preparation of students for international exchange programs, it is important to encourage the setting of realistic, attainable goals e.g., personal, academic, and social, for study abroad. Before departing for the host country, it would also be helpful for students to have more awareness and understanding of diverse educational practices e.g., the rationale for discussion-based pedagogy and collaborative group work, the use of e-learning. Encouraging students to refrain from making snap judgments about unfamiliar teaching and learning practices would be a helpful starting point. Developing the habit of observing and engaging in deep reflection could ease their acculturation.

It is important for program administrators to explain the broad aims of international exchange programs. This study found that students who do not plan to transfer academic credits back to their home institution may not be motivated to actively participate in their courses. After they returned to Hong Kong, some regretted wasting their time abroad. Notably, only a few students who were not transferring credits recognized that the exchange program provided them with a great opportunity to learn without the pressure of maintaining a high-grade point average. In pre-departure sessions, explicitly addressing this issue should help raise awareness of the need to set concrete goals that are not just driven by grades/exam results. This could also be a topic of discussion in host country orientations for inbound international exchange students.

Host institutions can significantly impact the quality of the learning experience and the degree of (non)integration of international exchange students. In addition to developing an understanding of the challenges that newcomers may face, it is important for teaching staff to be mindful to individual differences and avoid the pitfalls of stereotyping (Jackson & Chen, 2018). Armed with enhanced knowledge and sensitivity, lecturers can incorporate classroom activities, assignments, and assessment options that cater to diverse learning styles. Further, it is important to discuss the rationale for these elements as well as expected roles and responsibilities. As the transfer of credits can affect the motivation of exchange students, the responsibility for all students to contribute in courses must be clear to everyone. To foster meaningful integration and respectful intercultural dialogue, lecturers can intervene in classroom interactions e.g., form diverse groups that welcome the contributions of both local and international students. In the host environment, exchange students can enrich the learning experience of local students and vice versa. Without intervention, however, students may remain in their own ethnic enclaves and the full aims of internationalization will not be realized.

The Academic Second Language (L2) Socialization and Acculturation

More research is needed to optimize the potential of internationalization. Increasing participation rates in international exchange programs is insufficient. More attention should be paid to developing creative and effective ways to better integrate local and international students in academic/social settings. Local and international students and teachers can learn from each other.

LIMITATIONS AND FUTURE RESEARCH DIRECTIONS

Although qualitative and quantitative data were collected and triangulated, the present study relied on the semester abroad students to recount their international exchange experiences and reactions to diverse educational practices. Caution must be exercised when interpreting self-reports as first-person data presents *versions* of reality (Ochs & Capps, 1996; Pavlenko, 2007). 'Regardless of their elaborateness, tellings of personal experience are always fragmented intimations of experience' (Ochs & Capps, 1996, p. 21). When recalling past experiences, individuals are constrained by their memory, degree of self-awareness, and contextual factors e.g., the location and timing of the interview, the status of the interviewer.

To advance our understanding of study abroad learning, there is a pressing need for collaborative, inter-institutional projects e.g., ethnographic investigations, longitudinal mixed-method studies that track and document the learning of international exchange students from their home environment, through study abroad experience, and until at least six months after their return home. Studies that involve researchers from both the home and host institutions could enrich our field and benefit study abroad students. The information gleaned from research of this nature could provide direction for pre-study abroad orientations and suggest ways to optimize the learning of L2 participants.

CONCLUSION

The present study offered a window into the linguistic, sociocultural, psychological and environmental variables that played a role in the adjustment and (non)participation of the students in the host environment. A complex array of internal and external factors influenced their degree of L2 socialization and acculturation in the academic arena. Variations in their expectations, study abroad goals, motivation, attitudes towards learning, degree of openness, willingness to communicate in the host language, and personality characteristics e.g., degree of extroversion brought about divergent developmental trajectories. Although the depth of their investment in academic learning played an important role in determining what they gained from

The Academic Second Language (L2) Socialization and Acculturation

their stay abroad, external elements e.g., degree of host receptivity, amount of support provided for international students, cultural distance, also influenced how their stay abroad unfolded. Significantly, even among students with a similar linguistic and cultural background, there were many differences in how they reacted to the host environment and unfamiliar educational practices, raising further awareness of the complex, idiosyncratic nature of study abroad.

Prior to taking part in the international exchange program, most of the participants had mixed feelings about what they may encounter in the academic arena in their host country. Most divulged concerns about their ability to adjust to unfamiliar academic practices, especially fast-paced discussions. Post-study abroad, only a few interviewees stated that they did not find the host environment challenging and perceived the academic learning situation to be quite similar to Hong Kong or Mainland China. Most, however, did identify multiple differences, and their reactions to them varied markedly, as did their degree of acculturative stress and study abroad learning.

In the host environment, some of the newcomers successfully employed strategies that helped them to cope with the psychological strains of acculturation (Berry et al., 2011). Demonstrating a higher level of Willingness to Communicate (WTC) in their L2 (Yashima, Zenuk-Nishide, & Shimizu, 2004), these individuals tended to be open to new ways of being, including unfamiliar educational practices and cultural scripts. Some revealed that they felt liberated in the host environment as they were able to take courses of interest that were not linked to their major. A few who did not need to transfer credits to the home university challenged themselves in advanced courses, without worrying about grades. Finding their hosts receptive, these individuals experimented with new modes of learning and gradually developed a higher degree of self-efficacy in their L2, intercultural sensitivity, and heightened self-awareness (Ehrman, 1996).

By the end of the semester, the individuals who had felt welcomed in the host environment generally become more engaged in their L2-medium courses. Their positivity and intercultural mindset enabled them to more fully benefit from different educational practices and develop meaningful multicultural friendships (primarily with other international students). This, in turn, affected their degree of acculturation and integration in the host environment. After they returned to Hong Kong, they interacted with international students, instead of shying away from intercultural encounters as they had done before their stay abroad. Several also claimed to be active in English-medium discussions and even invited international students to join in group projects with them.

In contrast, a number of the participants disclosed that they had not been motivated to participate in class activities abroad and had exerted little effort in their classes because they would not be transferring credits back to the home environment and

The Academic Second Language (L2) Socialization and Acculturation

were unconcerned about grades. Their desire to learn appeared to be largely confined to instrumental motives, and without the pressure of grades/exams, they exerted little effort. Demonstrating scant interest in their academic performance, they did not take full advantage of learning opportunities in the host environment.

Many of the interviewees disclosed other reasons for their reticence or lack of participation in the host environment, especially in academic discussions. Some experienced communication apprehension and heightened anxiety in classroom situations, and most found it difficult to understand cultural content. Lack of confidence in their L2 proficiency limited the oral participation of these newcomers, especially when there were many L1 speakers present. In addition, a number of the exchange students were overcome with acculturative stress (Berry et al., 2011). Perceiving their hosts to be unwelcoming, they resisted new practices and spent most of their free time with co-nationals or on their own. When group work or projects were required in a course, they sought out co-nationals, avoiding collaborations with locals. Consequently, they gained less exposure to the host language and culture.

By raising awareness of differences in the developmental trajectories of Chinese study abroad students, this research challenges the stereotype of the 'deficient', passive Chinese exchange student that dominates much of the literature. As noted by Cortazzi and Jin (2011) and Jackson and Chen (2018), ethnic Chinese study abroad students are often portrayed as homogeneous and discussions about Chinese education are over-simplified and over-generalized, largely ignoring numerous variations in teaching and learning situations in Greater China. The limitations of didactic forms of teaching and learning are often emphasized, with many claims made about the lack of creativity, agency, and autonomy in Chinese learners. Chinese students are often stereotyped as 'quiet, passive rote-learners, who are respectful of teachers and teaching materials' (Stanley, 2011, p. 95), allowing insufficient room for individual variations, of which there are many.

Undeniably, some Chinese students are reluctant to offer their views in academic discussions or express ideas that contradict those of their teachers, however, it is unhelpful to assume that *all* students who share this ethnicity will behave in this way. In fact, a number of the participants in the present study embraced affordances in the host environment; they assumed an active role in their classes and also diversified their social network. Further, it is important to recognize that the reasons for students' conduct in discussions and other academic situations are far from straightforward. A myriad of individual and external factors contributes to variations in the learning behavior and attitudes of study abroad students and can naturally result in differing learning outcomes. Sounder understanding of these elements can help to provide direction for meaningful and culturally-appropriate interventions.

ACKNOWLEDGMENT

The investigation of the learning of semester-abroad exchange students has been supported by General Research Fund grant #4440713 from the Research Grants Council of Hong Kong. Further, this study would not have been possible without the participation of the exchange students.

REFERENCES

Adler, P. (1975). The transitional experience: An alternative view of culture shock. *Journal of Humanistic Psychology, 15*(4), 13–23. doi:10.1177/002216787501500403

Bazeley, P., & Jackson, K. (2013). *Qualitative data analysis with Nvivo* (2nd ed.). Thousand Oaks, CA: Sage.

Bennett, J. M. (1998). Transition shock: Putting culture shock in perspective. In M. J. Bennett (Ed.), *Basic concepts of intercultural communication* (pp. 215–224). Yarmouth, ME: Intercultural Press.

Berry, J. W., Poortinga, Y. H., Breugelmans, S. M., Chasiotis, A., & Sam, D. L. (2011). *Cross-cultural psychology: Research and applications* (3rd ed.). Cambridge, UK: Cambridge University Press. doi:10.1017/CBO9780511974274

Byrnes, F. C. (1966). Role shock: An occupational hazard of American technical assistants abroad. *The Annals, 368*, 95–108.

Cortazzi, M., & Jin, L. (2011). Conclusions: What are we learning from research about Chinese learners? In L. Jin & M. Cortazzi (Eds.), *Researching Chinese learners: Skills, perceptions and intercultural adaptations* (pp. 314–318). Basingstoke, UK: Palgrave Macmillan. doi:10.1057/9780230299481_15

Creswell, J. W. (2014). *Research design: Qualitative, quantitative and mixed methods approaches* (4th ed.). Thousand Oaks, CA: Sage.

Duff, P. A. (2014). Second language socialization. In A. Duranti, E. Ochs, & B. Schieffelin (Eds.), *The Handbook of Language Socialization* (pp. 564–586). Oxford, UK: Wiley-Blackwell.

Ehrman, M. E. (1996). *Understanding second language acquisition*. Oxford, UK: Oxford University Press.

Grbich, C. (2013). *Qualitative data analysis* (2nd ed.). London, UK: Sage.

The Academic Second Language (L2) Socialization and Acculturation

Ivankova, N. V., & Greer, J. L. (2015). Mixed methods research and analysis. In B. Paltridge & A. Phakiti (Eds.), *Research methods in applied linguistics* (pp. 63–81). London, UK: Bloomsbury.

Jackson, J. (2012). Education abroad. In J. Jackson (Ed.), *The Routledge handbook of language and intercultural communication* (pp. 449–463). London, UK: Routledge. doi:10.4324/9780203805640

Jackson, J. (2013). Adjusting to differing cultures of learning: The experiences of semester-long exchange students from Hong Kong. In L. Jin & M. Cortazzi (Eds.), *Researching intercultural learning: Investigations in language and education* (pp. 235–252). Basingstoke, UK: Palgrave Macmillan. doi:10.1057/9781137291646_13

Jackson, J. (2014). *Introducing language and intercultural communication*. Abingdon, UK: Routledge. doi:10.4324/9781315848938

Jackson, J. (2018). *Interculturality in international education*. New York, NY: Routledge. doi:10.4324/9780429490026

Jackson, J., & Chen, X. (2018). Discussion-based pedagogy through the eyes of Chinese international exchange students. *Pedagogies, 13*(4), 289–307. doi:10.108 0/1554480X.2017.1411263

Jin, L., & Cortazzi, M. (2006). Changing practices in Chinese cultures of learning. *Language, Culture and Curriculum, 19*(1), 5–20. doi:10.1080/07908310608668751

Kim, Y. Y. (2018). Integrative communication theory of cross-cultural adaptation. In Y. Y. Kim (Ed.), *The International Encyclopedia of Intercultural Communication* (Vol. 2, pp. 929–941). Hoboken, NJ: John Wiley & Sons.

Kinginger, C. (2017). Language socialization in study abroad. In P. A. Duff & S. May (Eds.), *Language Socialization, Encyclopedia of Language and Education* (3rd ed.; pp. 227–238). New York, NY: Springer.

Miles, M. B., Huberman, A. M., & Saldana, J. (2013). *Qualitative data analysis* (3rd ed.). Thousand Oaks, CA: Sage.

Montgomery, C. (2010). *Understanding the international student experience*. Basingstoke, UK: Palgrave Macmillan. doi:10.1007/978-0-230-36500-1

Neuliep, J. W. (2018). Culture shock and reentry shock. In Y. Y. Kim (Ed.), *The International Encyclopedia of Intercultural Communication* (Vol. 1, pp. 618–626). Hoboken, NJ: John Wiley & Sons.

Ochs, E., & Capps, L. (1996). Narrating the self. *Annual Review of Anthropology*, *25*(1), 19–43. doi:10.1146/annurev.anthro.25.1.19

Paige, R. M., & Vande Berg, M. (2012). Why students are and are not learning abroad: A review of recent research. In M. Vande Berg, R. M. Paige, & K. H. Lou (Eds.), *Student learning abroad: What our students are learning, what they're not, and what we can do about it* (pp. 29–58). Sterling, VA: Stylus.

Parris-Kidd, H., & Barnett, J. (2011). Cultures of learning and student participation: Chinese learners in a multicultural English class in Australia. In L. Jin & M. Cortazzi (Eds.), *Researching Chinese learners: Skills, perceptions and intercultural adaptations* (pp. 169–187). Basingstoke, UK: Palgrave Macmillan. doi:10.1057/9780230299481_8

Pavlenko, A. (2007). Autobiographic narratives as data in applied linguistics. *Applied Linguistics*, *28*(2), 163–188. doi:10.1093/applin/amm008

Smalley, W. (1963). Culture shock, language shock, and the shock of self-discovery. *Practical Anthropology*, *10*, 49–56.

Stanley, P. (2011). Meeting in the middle? Intercultural adaptation in tertiary oral English in China. In L. Jin & M. Cortazzi (Eds.), *Researching Chinese learners: Skills, perceptions and intercultural adaptations* (pp. 93–118). Basingstoke, UK: Palgrave Macmillan. doi:10.1057/9780230299481_5

Vande Berg, M., Paige, R. M., & Lou, K. H. (2012). Student learning abroad: Paradigms and assumptions. In M. Vande Berg, R. M. Paige, & K. H. Lou (Eds.), *Student learning abroad: What our students are learning, what they're not, and what we can do about it* (pp. 3–28). Sterling, VA: Stylus.

Ward, C. A. (2015). Culture shock. In J. M. Bennett (Ed.), *The SAGE Encyclopedia of Intercultural Competence* (Vol. 1, pp. 207–210). Los Angeles, CA: Sage.

Ward, C. A., Bochner, S., & Furnham, A. (2001). *The psychology of culture shock*. London, UK: Routledge.

Yashima, T., Zenuk-Nishide, L., & Shimizu, K. (2004). The influence of attitudes and effect on willingness to communicate and second language communication. *Language Learning*, *54*(1), 119–152. doi:10.1111/j.1467-9922.2004.00250.x

Zaharna, R. S. (1989). *Self-shock: The double-binding challenge of identity*. International.

Chapter 5
Facilitating International Healthcare Experiences:
A Guide for Faculty, Administrators, and Healthcare Providers

Jon P. Wietholter
iD https://orcid.org/0000-0002-4364-3909
West Virginia University, USA

Renier Coetzee
University of the Western Cape, South Africa

Beth Nardella
West Virginia University, USA

Douglas Slain
iD https://orcid.org/0000-0002-4318-7165
West Virginia University, USA

ABSTRACT

International healthcare experiences (IHEs) provide opportunities for students to experience healthcare in unfamiliar and sometimes challenging settings. Students have reported multiple benefits through completion of IHEs including increased personal and professional development, increased cultural sensitivity, and increased self-awareness and self-confidence. While many benefits have been noted, there are also many challenges in developing, implementing, and sustaining IHEs including financial considerations, safety concerns, and apprehensions regarding the impact the IHE is having on foreign patients and healthcare workers. This chapter's aim is to summarize the currently available literature on IHEs and to provide subjective reflections from students and international colleagues associated with IHEs connected to the authors' institutions.

DOI: 10.4018/978-1-7998-1607-2.ch005

Copyright © 2020, IGI Global. Copying or distributing in print or electronic forms without written permission of IGI Global is prohibited.

INTRODUCTION

Interest in global health among health professions students has increased considerably over the past two decades. It was relatively rare for United States (US) students to study overseas until the 1960s (Bruno & Imperato, 2015). However, the explosion of new technology and travel modalities over the last few decades have made it much easier to communicate and interact with people and places that were previously unreachable. Fortunately, there are growing opportunities for health professions students to study or train abroad and this chapter will focus on international healthcare experiences (IHEs) for US students training in health professions programs due to the authors' involvement with multiple US-based programs.

BACKGROUND

The healthcare education literature is replete with articles extoling the benefits of student participation on IHEs (Hampton et al., 2014; Smith-Miller, Leak, Harlan, Dieckmann, & Sherwood, 2010; Thompson, Huntington, Hunt, Pinsky, & Brodie, 2003). Students' reasons for participating in IHEs are varied, but are often chosen for altruistic motives, adventure, desire to travel, personal growth, skill improvement, and to develop cultural sensitivity (Flaherty, Leong, & Geoghegan, 2018; Peluso et al., 2018). Most of these motives are quoted from students living in high-income countries. Although these same motives may apply, students from low to middle-income countries who participate in IHEs often do so for professional development or to gain experience in a country of hopeful future employment (Peluso et al., 2018).

IHEs typically range from a few days to a year and can differ substantially from one another (Crump, Sugarman, & WEIGHT, 2010). IHEs are normally administered by US colleges or universities, or by a contracted partner (Rhodes, DeRomana, & Ebner, 2014). In response to increased student demand for global experiences, schools in the health professions appear to be increasing their global content and IHE offerings (Audus et al., 2010; Drain et al., 2007; Kelleher, 2013). In 2008, it was reported that 87% of US medical schools offered IHEs and as of 2012, more than 30% of medical school graduates had completed an IHE (Ackerman, 2010; Hampton et al., 2014). This reflects an increase of nearly 25% since similar surveys were performed in the late 1970s (Kao, 2014). Students may even select which school to attend based on international opportunities (Drain et al., 2007; McKinley, Williams, Norcini, & Anderson, 2008). Current trends in study abroad or global experience programs for US students have displayed an overall decline in Western European countries while the demand for programs in Asian or Southern hemisphere countries has increased (Rhodes et al., 2014). Interest in primary care and serving underserved populations has been shown to increase after IHE participation (Ackerman, 2010; Chin-Quee, White, Leeds, MacLeod & Master, 2011).

The increased interest in global health and international experiences has also fueled a growing 'voluntourism' industry which allows students, healthcare professionals, and non-healthcare personnel to provide services including healthcare in resource-poor settings. Some of these third parties have even aligned with health profession schools to provide a conduit for students to gain academic-credit for global health experiences (McCall & Iltis, 2014). Pre-health students, in particular, are often drawn to these opportunities. Unfortunately, voluntourism has often been criticized when it permits healthcare provision by inadequately trained individuals. This is a serious ethical concern that schools and students need to consider (Dell, Varpio, Petrosoniak, Gajaria, & McCarthy, 2014; McCall & Iltis, 2014).

The inclusion of philanthropic organizations or third-parties in the development, implementation, and funding of IHEs may be required for success (McKimm & McLean, 2011). These third-party providers, who coordinate activities on the ground for many international programs (Hampton et al., 2014), may be governmental or non-governmental organizations (NGO). Amizade is an NGO based out of Pittsburgh, Pennsylvania. Amizade has relationships with communities in several countries across the world. They partner with over 50 institutions and help coordinate and supervise multiple undergraduate service-learning programs and interprofessional clinical rotations for students in Schools of Medicine, Nursing, Pharmacy, Dentistry, Public Health, and other Allied Health programs (e.g., Physical Therapy). The benefits of working with qualified intermediary organizations are vast.

In international work, partnerships are of the utmost importance. Good partnerships take years to develop and significant resources to foster. As the nature of healthcare is sensitive, when foreign students are involved, extra care must be taken to respect the rights and feelings of patients. Therefore, it is essential to have 'local expertise' in the region, allowing for consistency and trust. All stages of these partnerships should be regularly evaluated by program faculty (Crabtree, 2013). Third-party providers can also help establish a framework for pedagogy on global citizenship and the ethics of clinical service abroad, and can offer cultural and historical information on host communities to better prepare students for immersion.

Global engagement has become a common feature in college strategic plans and entire courses focusing on global health are now being described in the literature (Addo-Atuah, Dutta, & Kovera, 2014; Drain et al., 2007; Owen et al., 2013; Schellhase, Miller, Ogallo, & Pastakia, 2013). Health professions schools interested in establishing IHEs should first examine global engagement programs currently offered at their institution. Pre-existing global relationships in other divisions of the college or university may provide opportunities for multidisciplinary/interprofessional IHEs. Identification of global partners is often easy; the difficult task is assessing the capacity for safe and mutually rewarding partnerships. Many IHE programs are initiated by a few dedicated individuals and the development of a high-quality program can take years (Evert, Bazemore, Hixon, & Withy, 2007). Ultimately, many programs strive for the development of sustainable programs that can provide continuous benefits to students, global partners, and patients. Regardless of structure and duration of IHE offerings, schools must evaluate any potential impact on a wide range of stakeholders including faculty, students, sponsors, global partner organizations, and the patients being served. Importantly, a high ethical standard must be maintained so that efforts are not hampered by unintended consequences (Crump et al., 2010).

Students and programs must consider the ethical and safety issues that are associated with health professions students being put into situations in developing countries where they—either assumed on their own or at the request of others—provide care that they are not adequately trained to give (Dell et al., 2014). This may occur more often when students are not closely supervised. Students placed in these situations may additionally develop anxiety and a sense of guilt. Many students are often ill-prepared and may become apprehensive about participating in IHEs. Thorough preparation and supervision is a must before allowing learners to participate in IHEs (Chuang et al., 2015; Thompson et al., 2003).

Student personal safety and risk education is an essential part of preparing students for IHEs. They must be made aware of safety issues that can adversely affect them: crime, traffic accidents, sexual assault, infectious diseases, and scams (Dell et al., 2014; Thompson et al., 2003). Students traveling to developing countries should be advised to have formal travel medicine consultation (Flaherty et al., 2018). Student safety and effectiveness can be enhanced by providing them with thoughtful pre-trip preparation (Carey, Carter-Templeton, & Paltzer, 2015; Dell et al., 2014).

From an educational standpoint, accreditation standards from the Liaison Committee on Medical Education ([LCME], 2018), the Accreditation Council for Pharmacy Education ([ACPE], 2016), and the American Association of Colleges of Nursing ([AACN], 2018) all focus on the particular need for cultural sensitivity and/or competence, an understanding of health disparities, and the need for interprofessional collaborative skills. In the US, interprofessional education has also become an essential requirement in most health professions curricula (Bonner, 2014). While there are no standards requiring a global health component, IHEs are an opportunity for students to practice in an interprofessional environment while hopefully becoming more culturally sensitive (Crump et al., 2010).

Facilitating International Healthcare Experiences

Global health is a dynamic entity with involvement of an increasing number of stakeholders. With the expansion of different healthcare professions into the global arena, there appears to be a lack of standardization in competency development across disciplines. In an effort to address this issue, the Consortium of Universities for Global Health (CUGH) charged its Competency Sub-Committee of the Education Committee to foster the development of competencies for global health education and professional development (Jogerst et al., 2015). These efforts have resulted in the CUGH Global Health Education Competencies Tool Kit, which continues to develop as a resource for global health training in health professions education.

With this as the relevant background, the primary objective of this chapter will be to review IHEs available to US students in the literature and subjective and/or objective benefits of these experiences while also providing subjective evaluations from foreign counterparts and students who have completed IHEs associated with the authors' institutions.

IHE CLASSIFICATIONS

Acute Care IHEs

Acute care IHEs are defined as experiences completed primarily within a hospital setting. There are many IHEs offered across the US through many different universities; this chapter will solely focus on existing publications summarizing these IHEs. Such publications have become more commonplace in the literature over the last 20 years with a focus on experiences of pharmacy, medical, and nursing students.

In 2011, it was estimated that 23.1% of all US medical students participated in some form of international experience annually since the year 2000 (Jeffrey, Dumont, Kim, & Kuo, 2011). Through participation in IHEs, surveyed medical students have been shown to potentially enhance public health knowledge, increase utility of the history and physical examination in diagnosis and management, and increase appreciation for family and culture roles in patient care (Thompson et al., 2003). Additionally, two review articles on IHEs primarily evaluating quantitative and/or qualitative data have suggested multiple benefits to student nurses through completion of an IHE. These benefits included enhanced personal and professional growth, enhanced insight on care of another culture, improved communications skills, and increased confidence levels (Button, Green, Tengnah, Johansson, & Baker, 2005; Kulbok, Mitchell, Glick, & Greiner, 2012).

While the following is not an exhaustive list of acute care IHE publications, the subsequent summaries each: (a) describe the hospital-based collaboration that was the setting for the IHE; (b) describe student responsibilities within the IHE; and (c) describe subjective and/or objective benefits students gained through completion of the IHE.

- The University of Maryland School of Pharmacy (UMSOP) developed an APPE in Melbourne, Australia at The Royal Melbourne Hospital (RMH) in 2008. During this program, UMSOP students completed a renal transplant rotation. Activities included participation in topic discussions and literature evaluations, provision of patient-centered pharmaceutical care, discharge medication counseling, and admission medication reconciliation. Subjectively, participants of the IHE expressed increased cultural awareness, clinical knowledge, communication skills, confidence levels, problem-solving skills through circumvention of language barriers, and personal and professional development (Bress et al., 2011).
- The West Virginia University School of Pharmacy (WVUSOP) formed an initial partnership with Nelson Mandela Metropolitan University (NMMU) in Port Elizabeth, South Africa in 2009. During this program, students participated in the provision of pharmaceutical care in adult medicine wards through chart reviews and attendance at daily patient-care rounds while also providing presentations to South African practicing pharmacists and pharmacy students on unique patient cases and differences between the US and South African healthcare systems. A non-validated survey instrument has shown a significant increase in students' ability to apply knowledge of human immunodeficiency virus (HIV) and tuberculosis treatments to patient care, overall medication knowledge base, ability to perform as a clinical pharmacist, motivation to continue to help underserved populations, ability to complete self-assessment for continued improvement, and comfort level in dealing with individuals from a different culture (Wietholter, Coetzee, McCartney, Gegg, & Schwinghammer, 2014).
- Surgeons from Oregon Health and Science University (OHSU) partnered with the Surgical Gastroenterology Department of the Sanjay Gandhi Post-graduate Institute of Medical Sciences in Lucknow, Uttar Pradesh, India providing medical students an elective rotation focused on international surgical care. The authors summarized this is the first international surgical clerkship that paired US students directly to surgeons from the host country.

Facilitating International Healthcare Experiences

Medical students spent between 1-3 months in India where they were involved in bedside teaching and clinical rounds, surgical ward duties, outpatient clinic observation(s) and operating room instruction, which is similar to a surgical elective experience in the US. Students, via a qualitative survey, described the experience's positive impact on their ability to build collaborative relationships, their desire to serve impoverished patients, and the potential to make international surgery part of their career (Moren et al., 2015).

- Emory University School of Medicine (EUSOM) collaborated with Project Medishare and Hopital St. Therese in Hinche, Haiti since 2008, providing 2nd and 3rd Year medical students an opportunity to aid in surgical management of patients (Chin-Quee et al., 2011; Leeds et al., 2011). Student responsibilities have included obtaining donated medications and/or supplies necessary prior to departure for the IHE, gathering the history and physical examination, presenting patient information to the attending surgeon, assisting and/ or observing multiple surgical procedures, and providing postoperative patient care. Suggested benefits to student participants included enhanced communication, interdisciplinary cooperation, technical skills, and increased patient responsibility relative to their current stage of medical training in the US (Chin-Quee et al., 2011). From a qualitative standpoint, no short-term patient complications were noted during the first three years of the experience covering 64 surgical procedures on 54 patients and all patients were discharged home (Leeds et al., 2011). Additionally, an evaluation was undertaken to examine whether performance on the IHE impacted the academic performance of participating students compared to students who did not. No statistically significant differences were noted in the National Board of Medical Examiners (NBME) subject examination or oral examination scores, or in overall grade (Leeds, Hugar, Pettitt, Srinivasan, & Master, 2013). Due to its early successes, the IHE was expanded in 2012 to include 2nd, 3rd and 4th Year medical students. While 2nd and 3rd Year students completed a similar experience as previously described above, 4th Year students completed a four-week IHE as an elective course. Additional 4th Year student responsibilities included the provision of postoperative follow-up care, which differed from their core clerkship rotations completed in the US, and participation in nightly bedside teaching rounds during the second operative week of the IHE. Students reported increased patient care responsibilities and that the experience of providing care to underserved patients was extremely rewarding (Hugar, McCullough, Quinn, Kapadia, & Pettitt, 2014).

117

In summary, there are multiple descriptions of IHEs in the literature; however, few have documented whether they are definitively acute care IHEs taking place primarily within a hospital setting. Overall, the reported benefits to students are widespread and consistent regardless of discipline. Acute care IHE participants report how post-program they have developed a greater capacity for interpersonal and intercultural understanding and how the program has provided unique opportunities for their professional development. Moreover, IHEs may contribute to developing a more mature, compassionate, and empathetic healthcare practitioner (Hugar et al., 2014).

Ambulatory Care and Medical Mission IHEs

In addition to acute-care IHEs, students often participate in shorter, ambulatory care IHEs which take place in clinics or community health settings. These are oftentimes in populations that are hard to reach or in limited resource settings and can provide services including health screenings, health promotion, and health-based education (Cone & Haley, 2016). Students often see these experiences as a way to give back to the global community and spend time learning about a new culture firsthand (Hammersley, 2014). As many students approach global service-learning with good intentions, it is imperative they learn the dangers of repeating past mistakes in development (Crabtree, 2013). Courses with readings/texts on global citizenship, ethics, and community-driven service, combined with historical, social, and cultural information will provide students with the knowledge and understanding essential to a high-quality program and a positive experience.

Medical mission IHEs can provide learning experiences that are not only educationally robust, but also personally and professionally enriching. Many times, these IHEs force learners outside their comfort zone through exposure to a different culture, patient population, changing physical environment that may be poverty stricken and/or volatile, and unique practice models. Additionally, they provide the opportunity to develop work flow, problem-solving and leadership skills, and an opportunity to collaborate with practitioners from different countries and disciplines (Brown & Ferrill, 2012). Furthermore, medical mission IHEs provide multiple opportunities for identification and refinement of these skills (Brown, Brown, & Yocum, 2012). Medical missions also provide a unique opportunity to experience disease states that may not be encountered in the learner's home country or ones that may be common but left untreated for years due to the lack of accessibility, funds to acquire care, or even the knowledge that a need exists. Most medical mission trips are based in low- and middle-income countries that have inherent barriers which can reduce the accessibility of medical care to a majority of their population (Smith et al., 2018).

Facilitating International Healthcare Experiences

Similar to acute care IHEs, the following summaries each: (a) describe the ambulatory care or medical mission-based collaborative setting; (b) describe student responsibilities within the IHE; and (c) describe the subjective and/or objective benefits to students.

- East Tennessee State University College of Pharmacy partnered with Global Health Outreach, an international medical relief organization, to provide an APPE that covers 10-15 days in multiple global locations requiring medical assistance. During this IHE, students are responsible for organizing, managing, and operating a clinic-based pharmacy which includes medication dispensing, preparation of unit dose medications, and providing counselling to patients when necessary. In certain settings, students could also be responsible for welcoming patients, taking vital signs, and recording the patient's chief complaint. Students commented that the experience expanded their knowledge of pharmacy beyond what they could have learned had they stayed in the US, taught them how to be adaptable and flexible, increased their compassion and patience, and made them consider the whole patient situation rather than just the current complaint. Additionally, they felt that the IHE improved their ability to work within an interprofessional team (Flores & Courtney, 2014).

- The North Dakota State University Colleges of Pharmacy, Nursing and Allied Science partnered with a Christian medical mission organization to develop an APPE in clinics in several small rural communities in Guatemala. During the experience, fourth-year pharmacy students were responsible for reviewing medication orders, dispensing medications and counseling patients while on the ground for 10 days in Guatemala. This medical mission IHE included physicians, nurses, dentists, and social workers. Reflections were used to identify areas of growth during the rotation and these showed improvement in interdisciplinary approaches to patient care, pharmacy workflow, and communication. Students also stated that the mission clarified for them the impact that they could make in their profession. Additionally, the Inventory for Assessing the Process of Cultural Competence – Student Version was used, and every student who completed the assessment increased their score after completion of the IHE. Furthermore, students showed four main themes representing particular learning domains documented via the Photovoice research method which asks students to capture learning visually by using photography. These four domains were attitude, professional growth, cultural competence shift, and in-the-field experiences leading to emotional experiences (Werremeyer & Skoy, 2012; Werremeyer, Skoy, & Kelly, 2016).

- The University of Louisiana at Monroe College of Pharmacy developed an elective course entitled 'Medical Outreach Experience'. The students spent ten weeks completing training and preparation prior to a one-week international outreach experience held in Mirebalais, Haiti. The experience included working in five multidisciplinary clinics and students rotated through each area of the clinic including triage, clinician assessment, pharmacy, and crowd management. Upon returning, students spent two weeks reflecting on the IHE along with writing a paper and presenting their experience. The overarching theme of the reflections was how the experience positively impacted their career aspirations going forward. Students reported the experience provided the opportunity to see pharmacy practice from a different perspective regarding direct patient care and multidisciplinary interactions. It was also found to be a humbling experience and induced feelings of appreciation for the resources available to them at home (Perry, Storer, Caldwell, & Smith, 2013).
- The Jamaica Medical Mission trip occurred annually and involved medical professionals from multiple universities and healthcare systems. Students from schools of medicine, dentistry, optometry, nursing and pharmacy participated in this medical mission IHE that lasted 10 days in Jamaica on an annual basis. Each discipline provided their own individualized expertise, but students were required to work together in an interprofessional fashion. For example, upon arriving at the clinic, a patient was triaged by nursing to either the dental or medical station. After an initial assessment, the patient was presented to pharmacy personnel who reviewed the patient's chart and provided medication-based recommendations. All students had oversight from licensed practitioners within their particular discipline. Student pharmacist recommendations were tracked throughout the experience and 73% of these recommendations were accepted by prescribers, with many of these focusing on sexually transmitted infections and/or hypertension management (Smith et al., 2018).

In summary, ambulatory care and medical mission IHEs have the opportunity to leave long-lasting impacts even though they are often short-term in nature. Provision of health education and long-term preventative medications such as immunizations can be the focal point of ambulatory care IHEs and can impact the populace in a positive manner for longer-term time frames than just during the actual time of the IHE (Cone & Haley, 2016). The necessity to work together as a team in these types of learning situations creates an opportunity to build respect for other disciplines and an understanding of ways to leverage the strengths that each medical professional possesses (Davis et al., 2015).

Facilitating International Healthcare Experiences

INTERNATIONAL COLLEAGUES' VIEWPOINTS

Due to the authors' involvement in multiple types of IHEs, it was deemed pertinent to gather perceptions from international colleagues. Questions were asked to gain perspective on the rationale(s) for their involvement in an IHE, how/if the US students have made an impact, what changes have been implemented as a result of the IHE, and future plans for the IHE.

Regarding rationale for participating in an IHE, one colleague mentioned the lack of domestic and international partnership opportunities for students and institutions. He went on to describe why public universities in particular are more aggressive in collaborating with other institutions on IHEs.

Public universities in Brazil are often charged in their mandate to establish partnerships with foreign organizations and institutions. They are more interested in creating partnerships to facilitate academic exchanges and also foresee the potential in more research opportunities. Public universities are often more interested in the bilateral networking than just facilitated programs.

Additionally, a lack of clinical pharmacy presence within the healthcare system was mentioned as a major reason behind IHE involvement by another colleague. Three main values have guided the IHE from inception: provision of excellent patient care, development of pharmacy leaders through mentorship and training, and collaboration(s) that provide a supportive environment to enhance pharmacy education.

Clinical pharmacy services continue to advance in developed countries. However, in South Africa there is a shortage of pharmacists and limited work has been done in the field of clinical pharmacy. The South African Pharmacy Council has recommended that all pharmacy schools review their undergraduate programs to address the need of clinical services provided by pharmacists. Thus, the continued vision of the IHE is to provide a program for international pharmacy students to work and learn in a resource constrained environment while aiding in the improvement and expansion of clinical pharmacy services throughout South Africa.

Colleagues also discussed the impact that US students have had via participation in IHEs. They expressed a view that it appears that students have had both indirect and direct influence within the systems they have practiced in. Momentary impact while students are present in the international environment is an obvious noticeable impact. Additionally, financial benefits to the local communities have been noted.

The municipality of Belterra on several occasions has been unable to financially support fluvial family health trips to the 3000+ people that live in the FLONA (Tapajos National Forest). Funds were directed to the municipal's health team to support the trip thus providing an experiential learning opportunity for the students with local health professionals serving as preceptors and oversight.

While the short-term benefits are clearly important in the evaluation of IHEs, the long-term impact should be their focus and these are more difficult to define and/or discern. Certain long-term benefits including a change in the education of both students and educators within the affiliated international institutions were mentioned by one colleague.

The collaborations with US academic institutions have led to partnerships to assist in the training of students as teaching resources are limited in South Africa. Current teaching staff is mentored by US faculty members who have assisted with developing teaching materials and aid in the design of the clinical curriculum. The aim is to provide an opportunity to teach in a different setting, and to assist in growing the clinical program in a sustainable fashion. Students completing an IHE will hopefully model to local faculty how clinical training should take place. For example, therapeutic case labs will be presented by foreign students with the aim to provide training on the specific topic to students, but also to benchmark for local staff on how it should be done. These students are supervised by senior local staff as well as US faculty and staff.

Additionally, one of the local hospitals that hosted US students during an IHE has begun to expand the role of South African pharmacists within the institution. This was largely based off the experience of having US students' IHE participation and has led to more focused clinical training for South African pharmacists within the hospital, including provision of both antimicrobial stewardship and direct patient care.

The program will continue to focus on training participants to be global healthcare practitioners who are able to provide leadership in resource-constrained settings worldwide. One of the goals is to expose international students to healthcare settings in developing countries as well as give them the opportunity to be involved in the clinical management of patients with various diseases including HIV and tuberculosis. Students will participate in a variety of clinical services, but also be integral in developing new and sustainable clinical services. Students will also get the opportunity to strengthen their teaching skills while teaching and mentoring South African pharmacists and pharmacy students who are embarking on a more clinical function within the hospital sector.

Facilitating International Healthcare Experiences

When evaluating potential next steps of these IHEs, colleagues mentioned the need to cement current relationships with US institutions and expand programs within their own institutions moving forward. Sustainability of these IHEs is extremely important and there is an ongoing request to increase the number of US students participating in IHEs, either through currently involved institutions or other universities to provide sustainable clinical services to the hospital and ensure that positive changes take place. An example of one change that was implemented is summarized below:

Final year South African pharmacy students complete a 10-week block of clinical rotations in the public healthcare sector of South Africa. These clinical rotations provide students the opportunity to directly interact with patients and other healthcare professionals. This is relatively new for undergraduate pharmacy student training in South Africa. During these clinical rotations, US APPE clerkship students get the opportunity to work closely with South African students providing them opportunities to interact and learn more about the local culture and healthcare system. Often APPE students do peer mentoring as clinical training is more advanced in the US Pharm.D program as compared to the program in South Africa.

Additionally, an ongoing prerequisite for future development was the need for a continued focus on finding preceptors that can provide appropriate guidance to IHE participants.

From our organization's point of view, finding strong oversight from our preceptors has been a constant battle. Ideally, we'd like to have preceptors that are able to fill in the cultural context, bridge the clinical interactions, and teach our students. We have never found ideal clinical preceptors.

Overall, gathering feedback from the international colleagues who are practicing in the environments our students are participating in during IHEs is a necessity. There are multiple pearls of wisdom, both positive and negative, that can be gathered from our international colleagues in regard to the development and sustainment of IHEs. Hopefully with their continued evolution, the impact of participating in an IHE will be felt by both participants and the patients they cared for over the years and decades to come.

STUDENTS' VIEWPOINTS

The literature is replete with indications that IHEs are often positive and life-changing experiences for the students on both a professional and personal level (Crump et al., 2010; Gourley, Vaidya, Hufstader, Ray, & Chisholm-Burns, 2013; Kelleher, 2013; Peterson, 2017). Students who participate in IHEs are more likely to assist in the care of underserved patients at the global or local level, gain knowledge in tropical diseases, cross-cultural issues, public health, and healthcare delivery, gain new clinical, critical thinking, and communication skills, and increase interest in volunteerism and humanitarianism (Chuang et al., 2015; Crump et al., 2010; Davis et al., 2015; Peluso et al., 2018; Peterson, 2017; Thompson et al., 2003). Health professions students who have participated in IHEs have often opted for primary care careers instead of more lucrative specialties and it has also been suggested that IHEs can restore a student's idealism (Hampton et al., 2014; McKinley et al., 2008; Ramsey, Haq, Gjerde, & Rothenberg, 2004).

There are many potential reasons students may want to participate in IHEs including the unique nature of the experience, an ability to experience unique cultures and healthcare systems, expansion of interprofessional collaboration, enhanced faculty accessibility due to reduced student to faculty ratios, the ability to foster a desire to help underserved communities in future career endeavors, improved clinical skills, an opportunity to enhance cultural competency, and a desire to increase self-awareness and/or self-confidence levels (Abedini, Gruppen, Kolars, & Kumagai, 2012; Arif, Dilich, Ramel, & Strong, 2014; Hugar et al., 2014; Jeffrey et al., 2011; Leeds et al., 2013; Peluso et al., 2018). Individuals that have completed IHEs and have had positive experiences will often promote global engagement to others, with publications showing 96-100% of participants recommending their experience to future students (Gourley et al., 2013; Haq et al., 2000).

To further evaluate students' opinions after completion of IHEs, five questions were posed to participants of programs the authors are affiliated with to gather input on their rationale for participation, noted strengths and weaknesses of the IHE, its impact on future professional plans, and clinical and cultural preparation prior to departure. Contained below are the discovered themes from the completed surveys and selected quotes from participants who have completed an IHE.

Several main themes arose out of the students' responses. Not surprisingly, almost all students wanted to participate in an IHE to experience a new culture. Many of those students also wanted to learn how the healthcare system in another country works. While most students polled were concerned about their professional development, others were inspired to serve or make a difference.

Facilitating International Healthcare Experiences

1. What Was Your Rationale for Participating in the IHE You Completed?

While in school, I felt secluded to my own bubble. I was constantly absorbed in what project to work on and what test to study for next, and have always been fascinated by other cultures. The opportunity to experience this firsthand is something I just couldn't pass up. Leaving my comfort zone and arriving in a country I knew very little about was absolutely mind-blowing and I am forever changed from it. From this adventure, I was expecting to make an impact on the people and places that we visited; yet they made an even larger impact on me.
–Trinidad and Tobago, 2013

Throughout my adolescence, foreign culture always fascinated me. Different languages, different foods and different ways of life inspired me to learn more about what influenced the daily lives of people from around the world. As I became passionate about my career in pharmacy, it was only natural that I began to have the same curiosity about pharmacy practice in other countries. This provided the opportunity to gain an inside view of the area of pharmacy that interested me most in a healthcare setting and patient population completely different from ours in the US.
–South Africa, 2012

My rationale for completing an IHE stemmed from a passion to help serve underprivileged populations and to better understand other cultures. I had a desire to learn about different beliefs, values, and attitudes. I knew that culturally-sensitive care in another country would expand my global health competence and teach me how to practice pharmacy in a different context, without the resources available in the US. I wanted to learn how to help manage patients with limited access to medications and technology. I also wanted to learn more about South Africa's healthcare structure, medical approaches, and how to apply these approaches to healthcare back home.
–South Africa, 2013

In relation to students' goals to experience a new culture, the strongest programs were those with opportunities to be immersed in that new culture. A strong program combines discussions of global citizenship with critical reflection. Students also listed good mentors and partnerships as strengths of their programs. When a program is organized and has a variety of opportunities in different settings, students tend to feel more comfortable. They enjoy getting a better view of cultural differences while seeing the full scope of medical care available to the local citizens. People and partnerships are essential to the success of an IHE just as they are in clinical service in the US.

125

2. What Were the Overall Strengths of the IHE?

The biggest strength of my IHE in South Africa was the opportunities for pharmacist intervention in the patients' care plans. We were able to approach the physicians with our recommendations for each patient, which was often truly valued by the physicians. As a pharmacy student on rotations, there is nothing more fulfilling than making a recommendation, having it accepted, and seeing the patient benefit clinically from that recommendation. Lastly, our preceptors, both in South Africa and the US were excellent in giving us guidance throughout our time in South Africa. I think an essential part of acclimating during an IHE is having someone to listen as you reflect on your daily experiences and feelings.
–South Africa, 2014

This program does an amazing job of teaching you to deal with new and unexpected situations. No matter how much you think you have prepared or how much you think you know about a place there will always be new unexpected challenges that arise. This is true while working in the US but is multiplied many times over when participating in an IHE. This program helped to build my confidence and adaptability better than any others I had in school. It fostered the skills necessary to work in an increasing globally integrated world. It gave me real world experience working with other professionals and patients that did not speak the same language or share the same cultural backgrounds as I did and taught me how to overcome these barriers. This provided me with a wealth of professional knowledge, taught me to be a more adaptable pharmacist, and a better global citizen.
–South Africa, 2011

Teamwork amongst healthcare professionals is the chief strength of the IHE. It was refreshing to see how each healthcare profession had a positive impact on a patient's treatment plan.
–Guatemala, 2011

Many of the weaknesses listed were expected. Students discussed issues with transportation and program organization. As most of the IHEs took place in developing nations, these types of challenges should be anticipated. Most students, however, did learn to be open-minded and more flexible as a result of these experiences. There was also a wide variety of preceptor participation in the student programs. Some programs use US faculty or healthcare providers while others hire local, bilingual preceptors. Finally, in programs in non-English speaking countries, many students felt the language barrier. All students who travelled to Brazil reported that if they were to do one thing differently before departure, it would be to study the language more.

Facilitating International Healthcare Experiences

3. What Were the Overall Weaknesses of the IHE?

For me, the most noteworthy weakness of this IHE was realizing how many people, students, politicians, etc. truly lack an accurate understanding of international healthcare policies, and even international work in general. Returning home was exceedingly difficult because of my changed perspectives about race, inequality, poverty, politics, and education.
–Brazil, 2014

The only weakness I can come up with is the length of the experience. I wish that we could've stayed for longer than four weeks to continue to build on the relationships that I was forming with both patients and practitioners. In addition, it is important to remember to be flexible and open-minded. If a person is not flexible and open-minded, he/she will likely find multiple weaknesses in an international experience.
–South Africa, 2013

With IHE programs, it can be hard to adjust to the experience when you arrive. However, I found this to be a much easier process than adjusting after the international experience. I felt that I learned so much from my experience, but it was hard to explain to my peers, families, and friends.
–Jamaica, 2011

IHEs greatly impacted professional plans, all in positive ways. Almost all students responded that the programs fostered their interest in international work. Many commented on how the programs helped them to choose a direction such as Public Health or Infectious Diseases. Others became more committed to volunteer work in order to give back to their communities. These decisions were aligned with commitments to working with the underserved or those in rural areas. Attention to patient advocacy and greater empathy were also noted by the students.

4. How Did Your IHE Impact Your Future Professional Plans?

I knew I would have an unforgettable experience on my IHE, but I never thought the events would forever change the course of my life. I was not sure what career path I wanted to take before I took my IHE trip. I knew I wanted to do something in health and wellness, but I had not narrowed that down. This experience led to the realization that doctors, nurses, and healthcare in general is powerless without proper legislation and tools to provide the public with services. This led to my decision to get my Master's in Public Health in Health Policy, Management and Leadership.
–Brazil, 2014

127

The IHE I completed as a pharmacy student has had a significant impact on my professional path thus far as well as my future career goals. My very first exposure to the pediatric population took place during the IHE when we spent approximately one week of our clinical time working in a women's and children's hospital in Port Elizabeth. I felt immediately drawn to the pediatric patients that we met and cared for and was suddenly fascinated with a patient population that I previously had been somewhat nervous to care for. My interest in pediatrics developed further as I completed other APPE rotation experiences and became a focus for my future career goals. My path to practicing in pediatrics was certainly influenced by the IHE I completed as a student and I am fortunate to now practice in an institution where my clinical and cultural experiences are put to use on a daily basis. Additionally, I have recently joined the Global Health Initiative (GHI) at Dana Farber Cancer Institute/Boston Children's Hospital and will be representing oncology pharmacy in future GHI activities. My experience as a pharmacy student was key in developing my interest in global health and continues to be an influence in my professional career. –South Africa, 2010

My plan was to pursue a post-doctoral fellowship program afterwards. Having experienced this rotation in Santarém, Brazil really opened my eyes to the global aspect of healthcare, and even expanded and solidified my interests for my future career goals. Within the pharmaceutical industry, global medical affairs and global scientific communications quickly became an area I gravitated towards. The experience of learning a new language, being immersed in another culture, and learning how their healthcare system is organized and functions allowed me to realize how passionate I really am about becoming a part of a team that works on a large, even global, scale. Not only working within our own country, but also in relations with other regions and countries quickly became an area I am very interested in. –Brazil, 2014

Program coordinators have much to learn from the experiences of their students. While few felt the effects of culture shock and/or reverse culture shock, almost all of the students polled felt they were not culturally prepared. This is not surprising. Even those who spent time engaging with material about the host country and felt culturally prepared before arrival noted that it is actually not possible to be fully prepared. Clinical preparation is important in any rotation. All students polled responded that they felt clinically prepared or as clinically prepared as possible for the IHE.

Facilitating International Healthcare Experiences

5. Did You Feel Prepared for the IHE Both Clinically and Culturally? Having Completed the IHE, What Would You Have Done Differently in Preparation for Your Experience?

Despite coming to South Africa with knowledge of the challenges I was likely to encounter and the disease states I would likely see, it was still a difficult transition. This clinical experience was very different from any I had before. Although I had the information I needed, culture shock was definitely a factor for me. Prior to the rotation, I had watched several documentaries on South Africa to get a better picture of what to expect; however, I don't think anything could have prepared me emotionally for the deep connection I developed for South Africa and the people. I'm not sure preparing any differently would have made the experience any different. Although you can read every article and watch every documentary you come across, being actively involved is truly the only way to fully understand their culture and healthcare system.
–South Africa, 2014

Overall, I did feel prepared. I think that no matter how prepared one may feel, traveling to a foreign country is going to be a culture shock. Looking back, I wouldn't have done anything differently. The culture shock was a positive experience for me. When I really got to take part in the food, the music, the language barrier, the dogs roaming the streets, the lack of water pressure for a shower (or just to flush the toilet for that matter), their social life, their school systems, and just their everyday life, it really was a lot to take in. Had I truly been prepared for everything I was going to see, hear, and do, the experience wouldn't have been as rich, moving, or simply shocking. I had never been so sad to leave somewhere yet happy to be home in my life.
–Trinidad and Tobago, 2013

I can confidently say that my educational, rotational, and internship experiences prepared me very well clinically for this rotation experience. Culturally, I made efforts to familiarize myself with the landscape, climate, culture, and even language of this region before packing my bags. I read throughout the majority of my 'Portuguese for Dummies' handbook, and got through as many lessons on my 'Mango Languages' application. Even so, I really don't feel like I was fully prepared culturally. It's one thing to study the language and culture, but you never really understand or appreciate any of these things until you live it. We certainly lived the culture during our time in Santarém, and I loved every minute of it. I really don't think there's anything I would have changed about my preparation efforts. I landed in Santarém with an open mind and eagerness to explore that I got to utilize to my full potential.
–Brazil, 2014

129

In summary, student participation in IHEs was overall positive and enriching. Not only did the students find IHEs rich in cultural and educational experiences, they were able to gain exposure to other healthcare systems leading to a better appreciation of the healthcare system in the US and also reported the IHE helped them to become well-rounded healthcare providers. These findings are in line with other publications, with many students considering IHEs as the best part of their education (Drain et al., 2007).

ISSUES, CONTROVERSIES, PROBLEMS

While the vast majority of this chapter paints IHEs in an extremely positive light, there are barriers, challenges, concerns, and limitations to these experiences that are important to consider.

Safety

Prior to participants leaving their home country, several things must be taken into consideration regarding safety to avoid illness and injury while traveling abroad during an IHE. Participants should research any precautions that need to be taken before departure, and the availability of equipment/supplies at the host site. For example, quantities of appropriate surgical glove sizes and sharps containers are aspects often overlooked when practicing in the US, but inadequate amounts of each may become an extremely important component of safely completing an IHE (Leeds et al., 2013). Additionally, participants should become familiar with the diseases endemic to the area they will be visiting and which vaccinations may be required prior to departure. The websites of the World Health Organization (WHO) (http://www.who.int/en/) and the Centers for Disease Control (CDC) (http://www.cdc.gov/) are excellent sources of information. Students should also review the US Department of State website (http://travel.state.gov) for any other recommendations regarding travel abroad. Registering with the local US embassy or consulate is recommended in case of emergency or safety concern (Leow et al., 2012). Further, medical insurance policies should be reviewed to evaluate coverage during the IHE. If the policies are inadequate, it is recommended that students procure short-term medical insurance that provides evacuation in case of an emergency.

When traveling to other parts of the world it is prudent to identify societal changes that may impact the learner. According to the WHO, more people are killed each year due to violence or unintentional injuries than those who may acquire an infection. A common cause of injury or death is traffic accidents, particularly in developing countries or in locations where driving rules differ (Panosian, 2010). Learners should

Facilitating International Healthcare Experiences

take appropriate precautions if choosing to utilize personal transportation methods (e.g., renting a car) during their stay. For example, many insurance policies do not cover riding in open-air vehicles such as motorcycles. Along with traffic accidents, interpersonal violence is another potential risk for students who are traveling to a foreign environment (Ackerman, 2010). Exercising due diligence is the simplest way to prevent an incident from occurring. Focusing efforts on reducing items that may entice potential assailants, travelling in groups, and not venturing out late at night to unfamiliar locations would be the first steps toward increased safety during an IHE. Logistically, faculty should discuss safety concerns with the host communities as part of relationship development (Cone & Haley, 2016). Pre-departure orientation with students should include information on packing appropriately (Cone & Haley, 2016), safety concerns such as psychological and physical health (Dell et al., 2014), student responsibilities (Johnson et al., 2017), and logistics. By implementing these different tactics to mitigate risk, students will reap the benefits of an IHE.

Financial Considerations

Completing an IHE can be an expensive endeavor and while few programs finance IHEs, many require students to pay for all expenses (Arif, Gill, & Reutzel, 2013). From airfare to short-term housing accommodations to transportation expenses, IHEs can cost thousands of dollars and may be seen as a barrier to participation (Owen et al., 2013). While fundraising, student loans, and scholarships from institutions are options to aid in the costs of an IHE, they often will not cover the entire experience.

Stress

Putting students in a foreign environment with different cultural norms can be stressful. Aspects such as being absent from social support systems or dealing with new and/or unfamiliar products/medications can create an added element of stress to IHE participants (Bress et al., 2011). Students may not be prepared for the clinical workload that will be expected of them, potentially hampering their ability to effectively function within the IHE (Jeffrey et al., 2011). Recent data indicates that mental health issues are being increasingly recognized in students and that some of these disorders may be problematic under additional stress sometimes associated with an IHE (Rhodes et al., 2014). Appropriate preparation prior to departure for an IHE is a necessity to minimize the stress that students will encounter. Pre-departure orientation that includes topics such as culture shock and depression is essential.

Preceptor Availability

As previously mentioned, another major concern is the lack of quality preceptors available to provide strong oversight. Finding quality preceptors for US-based experiences is a difficulty for many institutions and this is no different for those in an international environment. Many preceptors are unwilling to spend the time necessary to develop, maintain, or travel for an IHE and it may interrupt their typical day-to-day operations (Arif et al., 2013). Additionally, the financial considerations mentioned above for student participants may extend to preceptors as well. Developing IHEs with faculty and hosts who are dedicated to the experience can lead to more sustainable programs that benefit the participants and the host communities (Ackerman, 2010).

Noted Limitations of IHEs

It is extremely important to mention that there is minimal data about the objective benefits gained from healthcare students completing an IHE regarding patient-care outcomes (Ackerman, 2010; Kelleher, 2013; Mutchnick et al., 2003; Wallace & Webb, 2014). Certain publications suggest that short-term IHEs can be ineffective or even damaging to the healthcare systems and/or patient population(s) being served (Abedini et al., 2012; Ackerman, 2010; Garbern, 2010; Green, Green, Scandlyn, & Kestler, 2009; Leeds et al., 2013; Wallace & Webb, 2014). Additionally, IHEs can lead to dependence of the local population on 'free' healthcare to the detriment of local healthcare providers and small businesses attempting to earn a livelihood (Cone & Haley, 2016; Green et al., 2009).

Multiple authors have mentioned the need for sustainable programs rather than one-time IHEs (Ackerman, 2010; Audus et al., 2010; Cisneros et al., 2013; Suchdev et al., 2007). This would enable stronger and ever-evolving relationships between both parties. This includes evaluating resources expended by the host country on a regular basis (Ackerman, 2010; Cisneros et al., 2013; Crump et al., 2010, Dacso, Chandra, & Friedman, 2013). Taking students on an IHE can burden the local healthcare system as many of these settings are already lacking adequate numbers of healthcare providers (Leow et al., 2012; Thompson et al., 2003; Wallace & Webb, 2014). Distracting these providers from their day-to-day patient care tasks through educating foreign students completing an IHE could theoretically lead to worsened patient outcomes and further burden an already overburdened healthcare system.

The balance between providing maximal healthcare impact and the goal of educating students is a tough aspect to evaluate as the presence of relatively inexperienced students can confound the objectives of the IHEs (Chin-Quee et al., 2011; Leeds et al., 2011). Constant evaluation and reflection from the practitioners involved in the IHE should be taking place to confirm that the balance of healthcare

Facilitating International Healthcare Experiences

provision and student education isn't detrimental to patient care. One particular publication summarized that 7% of participants observed risks to patient safety and 21% observed diversions from standards of care on more than one occasion during an IHE (Leeds et al., 2013).

Suggestions for improvement should be taken seriously and implemented whenever feasible. If suggestions point toward negative impacts on patient care, the IHE should be terminated until the concerns are adequately addressed. Medical professionals must remember that our first responsibility is to do no harm, and if harm is being done, then the IHE must be reevaluated. Developing programs where the US-based contact already has professional or personal ties to a foreign counterpart will allow for a more appropriate evaluation of the feasibility of the benefits and risks (Cisneros et al., 2013). More harm than good can come from inappropriate interventions by skilled practitioners, and this risk is multiplied when students are the ones serving as the primary healthcare practitioners (Chin-Quee et al., 2011; Evert, 2014).

FUTURE RESEARCH DIRECTIONS

First and foremost, the biggest need for IHE programming is evaluation. Quality control, learning objectives, cultural competence, impact on the local community, long-term impact on the learners, overall effectiveness, etc. must be continually assessed to ensure that ethical, fair, and sustainable practices are priorities for IHE pedagogy. As IHEs grow in popularity, discipline-specific sets of standards should be drafted by each field's governing body. While costly, advisory boards or IHE consultants charged with yearly or biennial reviews of sites would help to ensure the implementation and execution of these best practices. Further, many for-profit companies and nonprofit organizations provide opportunities for students. These services, along with those sponsored by universities need to be comparatively assessed.

Continued evaluation of the potential for collaboration among multiple institutions could standardize IHEs and create a more sustainable practice model for the locations being impacted by the IHE (Audus et al., 2010; Leeds et al., 2011). Additionally, providing an opportunity for reciprocity between the international partners could lead to reasonable benefits for all parties involved, and should be a required component of any IHE (Ackerman, 2010; Crump et al., 2010; Drain et al., 2007; Green et al., 2009; Hampton et al., 2014; Thompson et al., 2003; Wallace & Webb, 2014).

Moving forward, partners abroad should be consulted regarding these collaborations (Bozinoff et al., 2014) and what they are looking for in participants. These desired skills, traits, and knowledge sets could then be required and/or taught as part of thorough pre-departure orientation. These sessions must include language and cultural information, ethics guidelines, and comprehensive training on student responsibilities and the expectations of faculty and community partners. These expanded pre-IHE lectures and immersive experiences would incorporate cultural knowledge before clinical practice is introduced (Hugar et al., 2014; Leeds et al., 2011; Schellhase et al., 2013).

Additionally, further evaluation is needed to determine the appropriate length of an IHE. There has been debate in the literature on whether the length, the intensity, or the extent of cultural differences is the most important factor regarding impact on participants (Button et al., 2005). It may take up to two weeks for students to properly adjust to cultural differences, so objectively evaluating whether anything shorter than this is beneficial would seem to be a valuable unknown component on the appropriateness of IHEs (Button et al., 2005).

Future research concerning students should be centered on the underlying traits that empower successful learners. Investigating the rationale for participation (Peluso et al., 2018), student goals and objectives, cultural sensitivity, and clinical skills prior to departure, as well as tracking students upon return, will help gauge the success of IHEs.

CONCLUSION

IHEs provide opportunities for students to broaden their horizons through healthcare practice in foreign environments. Students can reap multiple benefits through the completion of IHEs, but the limitations and challenges of these opportunities cannot be overlooked. As these programs continue to become more popular, it will become more pressing to develop guidelines on and assessment techniques for the appropriate development, maintenance, and evaluation of IHEs and their impact on faculty, students, international healthcare colleagues, and most importantly, patients.

ACKNOWLEDGMENT

The authors would like to acknowledge Micah Tae Chan Gregory, BSN, who at time of initial publication was the Brazil Site Director at Amizade for his help in the preparation of the 'International Colleagues' Viewpoints' portion of this chapter. Additionally, the authors would like to acknowledge all past IHE participants, particularly those that provided aid in the development of the 'Students' Viewpoints' portion of this chapter. Last, this research received no specific grant from any funding agency in the public, commercial, or not-for-profit sectors.

REFERENCES

Abedini, N. C., Gruppen, L. D., Kolars, J. C., & Kumagai, N. C. (2012). Understanding the effects of short-term international service-learning trips on medical students. *Academic Medicine*, *87*(6), 820–828. doi:10.1097/ACM.0b013e31825396d8 PMID:22534591

Accreditation Council for Pharmacy Education. (2016). *Accreditation standards and key elements for the professional program in pharmacy leading to the doctor of pharmacy degree.* Retrieved from https://www.acpe-accredit.org/pdf/Standards2016FINAL.pdf

Ackerman, L. K. (2010). The ethics of short-term international health electives in developing countries. *Annals of Behavioral Science and Medical Education*, *16*(2), 40–43. doi:10.1007/BF03355131

Addo-Atuah, J., Dutta, A., & Kovera, C. (2014). A global health elective course in a PharmD curriculum. *American Journal of Pharmaceutical Education*, *78*(10), 187. doi:10.5688/ajpe7810187 PMID:25657374

American Association of Colleges of Nursing. (2018). *The essentials of baccalaureate education for professional nursing practice.* Retrieved from https://www.aacnnursing.org/Portals/42/ CCNE/PDF/Standards-Final-2018.pdf

Arif, S. A., Dilich, A., Ramel, C., & Strong, S. (2014). Impact of an interprofessional international experience abroad on the attitudes of health care professional students. *Currents in Pharmacy Teaching and Learning*, *6*(5), 639–645. doi:10.1016/j.cptl.2014.05.010

Arif, S. A., Gill, T. K., & Reutzel, T. J. (2013). Barriers to offering international experiences to pharmacy students by US colleges of pharmacy. *Currents in Pharmacy Teaching and Learning*, *5*(5), 387–393. doi:10.1016/j.cptl.2013.06.009

Audus, K. L., Moreton, J. E., Normann, S. A., Sands, C. D. III, Seaba, H. H., Wincor, M. Z., ... Miller, K. W. (2010). Going global: The report of the 2009-2010 research and graduate affairs committee. *American Journal of Pharmaceutical Education*, *74*(10), S8. doi:10.5688/aj7410S8 PMID:21436917

Bonner, L. (2014). Interprofessional education: Growing focus on preparing students for team-based care. *Pharmacy Today*, *20*(12), 37. doi:10.1016/S1042-0991(15)30583-1

Bozinoff, N., Dorman, M. R., Kerr, D., Roebbelen, E., Rogers, E., Hunter, A., ... Kraeker, C. (2014, April). ...Kraeker, C. Toward reciprocity: Host supervisor perspectives on international medical electives. *Medical Education*, *48*(4), 397–404. doi:10.1111/medu.12386 PMID:24606623

Bress, A. P., Filtz, M. R., Truong, H. A., Nalder, M., Vienet, M., & Boyle, C. J. (2011). An advanced pharmacy practice experience in Melbourne, Australia: Practical guidance for global experiences. *Currents in Pharmacy Teaching & Learning*, *3*(1), 53–62. doi:10.1016/j.cptl.2010.10.005

Brown, D. A., Brown, D. L., & Yocum, C. K. (2012). Planning a pharmacy-led medical mission trip, Part 2: Servant leadership and team dynamics. *The Annals of Pharmacotherapy*, *46*(6), 895–900. doi:10.1345/aph.1Q547 PMID:22619473

Brown, D. A., & Ferrill, M. J. (2012). Planning a pharmacy-led medical mission trip, Part 1: Focus on medication acquisition. *The Annals of Pharmacotherapy*, *46*(5), 751–759. doi:10.1345/aph.1Q531 PMID:22550274

Bruno, D. M., & Imperato, P. J. (2015). A global health elective for US medical students: The 35-year experience of the State University of New York, Downstate Medical Center, School of Public Health. *Journal of Community Health*, *40*, 187–198. doi:10.100710900-014-9981-0 PMID:25564184

Button, L., Green, B., Tengnah, C., Johansson, I., & Baker, C. (2005). The impact of international placements on nurses' personal and professional lives: Literature review. *Journal of Advanced Nursing*, *50*(3), 315–324. doi:10.1111/j.1365-2648.2005.03395.x PMID:15811111

Carey, R. E., Carter-Templeton, H., & Paltzer, J. (2015). Preparing health professions volunteers to serve globally. *Journal of Christian Nursing*, *32*(4), 242–249. doi:10.1097/CNJ.0000000000000208 PMID:26548178

Chin-Quee, A., White, L., Leeds, I., MacLeod, J., & Master, V. A. (2011). Medical student surgery elective in rural Haiti: A novel approach to satisfying clerkship requirements while providing surgical care to an underserved population. *World Journal of Surgery*, *35*(4), 739–744. doi:10.100700268-011-0966-1 PMID:21301838

Chuang, C., Khatri, S. H., Gill, M. S., Trehan, N., Masineni, S., Chikkam, V., ... Levine, D. L. (2015). Medical and pharmacy student concerns about participating on international service-learning trips. *BMC Medical Education*, *15*(1), 232. doi:10.118612909-015-0519-7 PMID:26699122

Cisneros, R. M., Jawaid, S. P., Kendall, D. A., McPherson, C. E. III, Mu, K., Weston, G. S., & Roberts, K. B. (2013). International practice experiences in pharmacy education. *American Journal of Pharmaceutical Education, 77*(9), 188. doi:10.5688/ajpe779188 PMID:24249850

Cone, P. H., & Haley, J. M. (2016). Mobile clinics in Haiti, Part 1: Preparing for service-learning. *Nurse Education in Practice, 21,* 1–8. doi:10.1016/j.nepr.2016.08.008 PMID:27665303

Crabtree, R. D. (2013). The intended and unintended consequences of international service-learning. *Journal of Higher Education Outreach & Engagement, 17*(2), 43–65.

Crump, J. A., & Sugarman, J. (2010). Ethics and best practice guidelines for training experiences in global health. *The American Journal of Tropical Medicine and Hygiene, 83*(6), 1178–1182. doi:10.4269/ajtmh.2010.10-0527 PMID:21118918

Dacso, M., Chandra, A., & Friedman, H. (2013). Adopting an ethical approach to global health training: The evolution of the Botswana–University of Pennsylvania partnership. *Academic Medicine, 88*(11), 1646–1650. doi:10.1097/ACM.0b013e3182a7f5f4 PMID:24072119

Davis, L. I., Wright, D. J., Gutierrez, M. S., Nam, J. J., Nguyen, J., & Waite, A. T. (2015). Interprofessional global service learning: A pharmacy and nursing practice experience in Botswana. *Currents in Pharmacy Teaching and Learning, 7*(2), 169–178. doi:10.1016/j.cptl.2014.11.017

Dell, E. M., Varpio, L., Petrosoniak, A., Gajaria, A., & McCarthy, A. E. (2014). The ethics and safety of medical student global health electives. *International Journal of Medical Education, 5,* 63–72. doi:10.5116/ijme.5334.8051 PMID:25341214

Drain, P. K., Primack, A., Hunt, D., Fawzi, W. W., Holmes, K. K., & Gardner, P. (2007). Global health in medical education: A call for more training and opportunities. *Academic Medicine, 82*(3), 226–230. doi:10.1097/ACM.0b013e3180305cf9 PMID:17327707

Evert, J. (2014, November 20). *How does global service-learning become a dis-service in healthcare settings?* Commentary from Child Family Health International. Retrieved from http://globalsl.org/cfhi/

Evert, J., Bazemore, A., Hixon, A., & Withy, K. (2007). Going global: Considerations for introducing global health into family medicine training programs. *Family Medicine, 39*(9), 659–665. PMID:17932801

Flaherty, G. T., Leong, S. W., & Geoghegan, R. (2018). Learning to travel: Reducing the health risks of study abroad opportunities. *Journal of Travel Medicine, 25*(1), 1–2. doi:10.1093/jtm/tay085 PMID:30239844

Flores, E. K., & Courtney, L. A. (2014). Development of a partnership for international rural advanced pharmacy practice experiences. *International Journal of Health Sciences Education, 2*(1), 5.

Garbern, S. C. (2010). Medical relief trips…what's missing? Exploring ethical issues and the physician-patient relationship. *The Einstein Journal of Biology and Medicine; EJBM, 25*(1), 38–40. doi:10.23861/EJBM20102539

Gourley, D. R., Vaidya, V. A., Hufstader, M. A., Ray, M. D., & Chisholm-Burns, M. A. (2013). An international capstone experience for pharmacy students. *American Journal of Pharmaceutical Education, 77*(3), 50. doi:10.5688/ajpe77350 PMID:23610468

Green, T., Green, H., Scandlyn, J., & Kestler, A. (2009). Perceptions of short-term medical volunteer work: A qualitative study in Guatemala. *Globalization and Health, 5*(1), 4. doi:10.1186/1744-8603-5-4 PMID:19245698

Hammersley, L. A. (2014). Volunteer tourism: Building effective relationships of understanding. *Journal of Sustainable Tourism, 22*(6), 855–873. doi:10.1080/096 69582.2013.839691

Hampton, B. S., Chuang, A. W., Abbott, J. F., Buery-Joyner, S. D., Cullimore, A. J., Dalrymple, J. L., … Dugoff, L. (2014). To the point: Obstetrics and gynecology global health experiences for medical students. *American Journal of Obstetrics and Gynecology, 1*(1), 18–23. doi:10.1016/j.ajog.2013.12.018 PMID:24334202

Haq, C., Rothenberg, D., Gjerde, C., Bobula, J., Wilson, C., Bickley, L., … Joseph, A. (2000). New world views: Preparing physicians in training for global health work. *Family Medicine, 32*(8), 566–572. PMID:11002868

Hugar, L. A., McCullough, C. M., Quinn, M. E., Kapadia, S. M., & Pettitt, B. J. (2014). Scaling up short-term humanitarian surgery: A global surgery elective for senior medical students. *Journal of Surgical Education, 71*(6), 871–877. doi:10.1016/j.jsurg.2014.04.002 PMID:24913428

Jeffrey, J., Dumont, R. A., Kim, G. Y., & Kuo, T. (2011). Effects of international health electives on medical student learning and career choice. *Family Medicine, 43*(1), 21–28. PMID:21213133

Jogerst, K., Callender, B., Adams, V., Evert, J., Fields, E., Hall, T., ... Wilson, L. L. (2015). Identifying interprofessional global health competencies for 21st-century health professionals. *Annals of Global Health, 81*(2), 239–247. doi:10.1016/j.aogh.2015.03.006 PMID:26088089

Johnson, K. L., Alsharif, N. Z., Rovers, J., Connor, S., White, N. D., & Hogue, M. D. (2017). Recommendations for planning and managing international short-term pharmacy service trips. *American Journal of Pharmaceutical Education, 81*(2), 23. doi:10.5688/aj720223 PMID:28381883

Kao, J. (2014). The growth of medical student opportunities in global health. *Medical Student Research Journal, 4*, 48–50.

Kelleher, S. (2013). Perceived benefits of study abroad programs for nursing students: An integrative review. *The Journal of Nursing Education, 52*(12), 690–695. PMID:24256000

Kulbok, P. A., Mitchell, E. M., Glick, D. F., & Greiner, D. (2012). International experiences in nursing education: A review of the literature. *International Journal of Nursing Education Scholarship, 9*(1), 7. doi:10.1515/1548-923X.2365 PMID:22628353

Leeds, I. L., Creighton, F. X., Wheatley, M. A., Macleod, J. B., Srinivasan, J., Chery, M. P., & Master, V. A. (2011). Intensive medical student involvement in short-term surgical trips provides safe and effective patient care: A case review. *BMC Research Notes, 4*(1), 317. doi:10.1186/1756-0500-4-317 PMID:21884604

Leeds, I. L., Hugar, L. A., Pettitt, B. J., Srinivasan, J., & Master, V. A. (2013). International surgical clerkship rotation: Perceptions and academic performance. *American Journal of Surgery, 206*(2), 280–286. doi:10.1016/j.amjsurg.2012.10.034 PMID:23481029

Leow, J. L., Groen, R. S., Kingham, T. P., Casey, K. M., Hardy, M. A., & Kushner, A. L. (2012). A preparation guide for surgical resident and student rotations to underserved regions. *Surgery, 151*(6), 770–778. doi:10.1016/j.surg.2012.03.002 PMID:22652117

Liaison Committee on Medical Education. (2018). *Functions and structure of a medical school.* Retrieved from http://lcme.org/publications/#Standards

McCall, D., & Iltis, A. S. (2014). Health care voluntourism: Addressing ethical concerns of undergraduate student participation in global health volunteer work. *HEC Forum, 26*(4), 285–297. doi:10.100710730-014-9243-7 PMID:25079381

McKimm, J., & McLean, M. (2015). Developing a global health practitioner: Time to act? *Medical Teacher*, *33*(8), 626–631. doi:10.3109/0142159X.2011.590245 PMID:21774648

McKinley, D. W., Williams, S. R., Norcini, J. J., & Anderson, M. B. (2008). International exchange programs and US medical schools. *Academic Medicine*, *83*(10Supplement), S53–S57. doi:10.1097/ACM.0b013e318183e351 PMID:18820502

Moren, A., Cook, M., McClain, M., Doberne, J., Kiraly, L., Perkins, R. S., & Kwong, K. (2015). A pilot curriculum in international surgery for medical students. *Journal of Surgical Education*, *72*(4), e9–e14. doi:10.1016/j.jsurg.2015.04.027 PMID:26073480

Mutchnick, I. S., Moyer, C. A., & Stern, D. T. (2003). Expanding the boundaries of medical education: Evidence for cross-cultural exchanges. *Academic Medicine*, *78*(10Supplement), S1–S5. doi:10.1097/00001888-200310001-00002 PMID:14557080

Owen, C., Breheny, P., Ingram, R., Pfeifle, W., Cain, J., & Ryan, M. (2013). Factors associated with pharmacy student interest in international study. *American Journal of Pharmaceutical Education*, *77*(3), 54. doi:10.5688/ajpe77354 PMID:23610472

Panosian, C. (2010). Courting danger while doing good: Protecting global health workers from harm. *The New England Journal of Medicine*, *363*(26), 2484–2485. doi:10.1056/NEJMp1011407 PMID:21175310

Peluso, M. J., Rodman, A., Mata, D. A., Kellett, A. T., van Schalkwyk, S., & Rohrbaugh, R. M. (2018). A comparison of the expectations and experiences of medical students from high-, middle-, and low-income countries participating in global health clinical electives. *Teaching and Learning in Medicine*, *30*(1), 45–56. doi:10.1080/10401334.2017.1347510 PMID:29240454

Perry, E., Storer, A., Caldwell, D., & Smith, J. (2013). A medical outreach elective course. *American Journal of Pharmaceutical Education*, *77*(4), 78. doi:10.5688/ajpe77478 PMID:23716746

Peterson, S. C. (2017). You want to go where? A perspective on skills and competencies developed through international pharmacy education experiences. *The Canadian Journal of Hospital Pharmacy*, *70*(1), 54–55. doi:10.4212/cjhp.v70i1.1630 PMID:28348434

Ramsey, A. H., Haq, C., Gjerde, C. L., & Rothenberg, D. (2004). Career influence of an international health experience during medical school. *Family Medicine*, *36*(6), 412–416. PMID:15181553

Rhodes, G., DeRomana, I., & Pedone, B. N. (2017). Study abroad and other international student travel. In *Centers for Disease Control and Prevention CDC Yellow Book 2018: Health Information for International Travel*. New York, NY: Oxford University Press. Retrieved from http://wwwnc.cdc.gov/travel/ yellowbook/2014/chapter-8-advising-travelers-with-specific-needs/study-abroad- and-other-international-student-travel

Schellhase, E. M., Miller, M. L., Ogallo, W., & Pastakia, S. D. (2013). An elective pharmaceutical care course to prepare students for an advanced pharmacy practice experience in Kenya. *American Journal of Pharmaceutical Education*, *77*(3), 60. doi:10.5688/ajpe77360 PMID:23610478

Smith, J. N., Phan, Y., Johnson, M., Emmerson, K., West, B., Adams, J., ... Otsuka, S. (2018). Describing pharmacy student participation in an international, interprofessional medical mission trip as part of an advanced pharmacy practice experience (APPE). *Currents in Pharmacy Teaching and Learning*, *10*(7), 940–945. doi:10.1016/j.cptl.2018.04.009 PMID:30236432

Smith-Miller, C. A., Leak, A., Harlan, C. A., Dieckmann, J., & Sherwood, G. (2010). Leaving the comfort of the familiar: Fostering workplace cultural awareness through short-term global experiences. *Nursing Forum*, *45*(1), 18–28. doi:10.1111/j.1744- 6198.2009.00163.x PMID:20137021

Suchdev, P., Ahrens, K., Click, E., Macklin, L., Evangelista, D., & Graham, E. (2007). A model for sustainable short-term international medical trips. *Ambulatory Pediatrics*, *7*(4), 317–320. doi:10.1016/j.ambp.2007.04.003 PMID:17660105

Thompson, M. J., Huntington, M. K., Hunt, D., Pinsky, L. E., & Brodie, J. J. (2003). Educational effects of international health electives on US and Canadian medical students and residents: A literature review. *Academic Medicine*, *78*(3), 342–347. doi:10.1097/00001888-200303000-00023 PMID:12634222

Wallace, L. J., & Webb, A. (2014). Pre-departure training and the social accountability of international medical electives. *Education for Health*, *27*(2), 143–147. doi:10.4103/1357-6283.143745 PMID:25420975

Werremeyer, A., Skoy, E., & Kelly, G. A. (2016). Exploration of learning during an international health elective using Photovoice methodology. *Pharmacy (Basel)*, *4*(4), E39. doi:10.3390/pharmacy4040039 PMID:28970412

Werremeyer, A. B., & Skoy, E. T. (2012). A medical mission to Guatemala as an advanced pharmacy practice experience. *American Journal of Pharmaceutical Education*, *76*(8), 156. doi:10.5688/ajpe768156 PMID:23129855

Wietholter, J. P., Coetzee, R., McCartney, J., Gegg, J., & Schwinghammer, T. L. (2014). Development of an international advanced pharmacy practice experience (APPE) and lessons learned after implementation. *Currents in Pharmacy Teaching & Learning*, *6*(2), 304–312. doi:10.1016/j.cptl.2013.11.015

Chapter 6
Towards a Culturally Reflective Practitioner:
Pre-Service Student Teachers in Teaching Practicums Abroad

Karin Vogt
University of Education Heidelberg, Germany

ABSTRACT

Since 2007, it has been possible for student teachers based in Europe to complete a teaching practicum at a school abroad, supported by the European flagship mobility programme ERASMUS. The focus of this study was on 35 undergraduate preservice teachers who completed a three-month teaching practicum placement in the UK and Ireland. Data from reflective reports was content analysed and completed with focus group discussions six months after the students' stay abroad. On the basis of the reflective reports, a case study was additionally collated that focussed on their intercultural learning development. The findings indicate an interconnection of linguistic, intercultural, and professional development with professional development as the most prominent and the intercultural development as a rather neglected one. Suggestions on how to design a formal instruction element based on the principles of cultural (peer) mentoring and guided cultural reflection as part of the teaching practice experience are outlined.

DOI: 10.4018/978-1-7998-1607-2.ch006

Copyright © 2020, IGI Global. Copying or distributing in print or electronic forms without written permission of IGI Global is prohibited.

INTRODUCTION

For many years, a period of study abroad has constituted an optional or mandatory component of university degrees, particularly foreign language-related ones. It is maintained that an international education is conducive to the aim of global citizenship and helps learners prepare for a globalized world (cf. Davies & Pike, 2009; Schattle, 2009; for more critical views Lewin, 2009; Wanner, 2009). Study abroad programs are also seen as enhancing international understanding and cross-cultural awareness, given their extended period of contact between the student and locals (Carlson & Widaman, 1988; Papatsiba, 2003). A rationale for study abroad lies in assumed or expected improvement to students' target language (TL) proficiency, particularly for foreign language students (e.g., Brecht, Davidson & Ginsberg, 1995; Meara, 1994). Studies focus on progress in specific skills areas (e.g., Towell, Hawkins & Bazergui, 1996) or on outcomes indirectly related to language proficiency such as the motivation to perform well in the TL (e.g., Sasaki, 2011).

While the body of literature on study abroad has grown substantially in the last decade, little attention has been paid to periods of teaching practice abroad and their potential effect on different proficiency areas of preservice teachers. We know relatively little about the impact of teaching practicums (placement) abroad for (European) preservice foreign language teachers in terms of their language proficiency, their intercultural competence and/or their emerging professionalism. The purpose of this study was, therefore, to investigate expectations, perceptions and outcomes of 35 Germany-based preservice English as a Foreign Language (EFL) teachers who spent a teaching practice period of three months at primary and secondary schools in the United Kingdom (UK) and Ireland on the European-funded ERASMUS work experience program. After a literature review, the study design, data collection and analysis methods will be addressed before an outline of the findings. A section on didactic implications for preservice foreign language teacher training will follow with an outline of the measures taken for a guided cultural reflection of teaching practicums abroad, as well as a discussion of directions for future research in the field.

BACKGROUND

Collentine (2009, p. 218) defined study abroad as the 'context [which] takes place in countries where the L2 enjoys an important sociological and functional status, entailing a combination of planned curriculum and host family'. While this definition of a study abroad context is rather limited to university undergraduate students pursuing a more or less rigorous degree program, I would like to argue for

Towards a Culturally Reflective Practitioner

a broader definition of the term that encompasses different formats of instruction in the framework of a curriculum and also other forms of housing arrangements. A working definition for this chapter would be for study abroad to be part of a university degree program that enhances professionalization and global citizenship through increased opportunities for intercultural and experiential learning, among others.

Study Abroad Research from a Second Language (L2) Acquisition Perspective

The research findings related to second language (L2) learning processes and the potential benefits of a period of study abroad in a TL country constitutes a major research area of study abroad programs for undergraduate foreign language students. From a Second Language Acquisition (SLA) perspective, Churchill and DuFon (2006, p. 26) pointed out that according to popular assumption, the mere study abroad experience automatically leads to SLA. The amount of research on study abroad, which has increased exponentially in the last two decades, has challenged this naïve assumption. The field of research is rich and complex, with a large variety of programs in different educational systems and with different foreign languages as TLs, which account for many and varied results (e.g., Sanz & Morales-Front, 2018). However, there seem to be general tendencies of findings in study abroad, which I will try to outline.

The bulk of study abroad research in the field of SLA has tended to focus on the learner and particularly on the learners' acquisition of linguistic skills during their study abroad period e.g., as early as the 1960s (Carroll, 1967). Most studies that are concerned with linguistic gains have focused on spoken skills and more specifically on 'fluency'. For example, Segalowitz and Freed (2004) studied 40 US-based L1 speakers of English studying Spanish for one semester in a home study or study abroad context. The learners' oral performance gains were investigated e.g., gains in oral fluency by using the Oral Proficiency Interview (POI) and by measuring temporal and hesitation phenomena. In comparison, the study abroad students displayed more and longer fluent runs than the home study students and had fewer hesitations such as '*ehm*', '*well*', and '*like*'. Similar results were found by Freed, Segalowitz and Dewey (2004) and Isabelli-García (2003). However, it was found that not all study abroad learners improved in their fluency due to individual variations caused by learner differences.

Collentine (2004), in his US-based study of 46 L2 learners of Spanish, compared learners' abilities prior to and after a semester of learning the language in a formal instruction context at a US university and a study abroad context in Alicante. Collentine (2004) used the OPI and performed a corpus-based analysis on the data, as well as several discriminant analyses. The findings indicated that the home study

145

Towards a Culturally Reflective Practitioner

group showed a more marked development on discrete grammatical and lexical features whereas the study abroad group achieved increased narrative ability with study abroad learners. They were able to relate more narrative events and to produce semantically dense language.

The two studies mentioned are also instances of a more recent trend to compare study abroad and home study contexts and subsequent linguistic outcomes (e.g., Isabelli, 2002) or even a comparison of study abroad and immersion programs (e.g., Hokanson, 2000; Serrano, Llanes & Tragant, 2011). Freed et al. (2004) understood immersion programs to be superior to study abroad programs in terms of general oral performance. The greater gains in oral fluency cannot necessarily be attributed to greater out-of-class contact with native speakers of the TL. Rather, the learners' initial abilities seem to play a role, impacting on the nature and intensity of contact with native speakers (for meta-analysis of predictors cf. Dewey, Brown, Baker, Martinson, Gold & Eggett, 2014).

In terms of linguistic gains related to grammatical development, there seemed to be a weak effect on study abroad regarding overall grammatical abilities, reflected in the findings of Cheng and Mojica-Díaz (2006) on study abroad learner subjunctive abilities in their L2 Spanish or Collentine's (2004) study on the acquisition of morphosyntactic features of study abroad learners that were not found to be superior to home study learners. Conflicting results, however, were presented by Isabelli and Noshida (2005), cautioning against undue generalization. One potential explanation of this trend was offered by Barron (2003) in that study abroad learners do not have as much access to the TL as is widely assumed. In her study focused on Irish study abroad learners of German, she found that learners formed social networks with other L1 speakers of English, thus limiting their access to native speaker contacts.

Regarding the area of pragmatics, there seems to be a consensus that study abroad learners are at an advantage compared to home study learners, but that overall development is slow e.g., Hoffman-Hicks' (2000) work on study abroad learners of French who improved their command over formulaic pragmatic expressions, but also tended to use them in inappropriate contexts, thus resulting in a non-native-like behavior due to a lack of awareness.

From a broad summary of research findings from a SLA perspective, one can discern that the most important linguistic gains of study abroad learners lie in the area of oral fluency. The effect on grammatical abilities is comparatively weaker whereas study abroad learners do benefit in the area of pragmatics, but show slow progress 'overall'. The notion of a threshold in terms of a correlation between learners' prior abilities and their linguistic gains after a study abroad period seems to have become a consensus among researchers (DeKeyser, 2014). It is suggested that learners benefit more from a study abroad period if they start from an appropriate

Towards a Culturally Reflective Practitioner

linguistic proficiency level. Recently, individual differences of study abroad learners have attracted more attention and form a focus of interest in research, which is also visible in research on the 'motivation' of study abroad learners (Kinginger & Farrell, 2004) and learning strategies (Lafford, 2004) that not surprisingly, reports conflicting results as well.

Collentine (2009) identified a focus of study abroad research related to Americans abroad (e.g., Gore, 2005; Pellegrino-Aveni, 2005; Cadd, 2012; Wolcott, 2013) and only little study abroad-related research is situated in the European context (cf. Boye, 2016; Murphy-Lejeune, 2002, Ehrenreich, 2006 as exceptions). Little research has focused on the effects of study abroad on learners in European-funded ERASMUS programs, who constitute an entirely different learner population than US students in terms of prior proficiency, type of program, and learner motivation. The SALA project is a notable exception (Pérez-Vidal, 2014).

Intercultural Competence and Study Abroad

Although research on study abroad started out with a focus on SLA processes, research on study abroad and interculturality has gained momentum in the last decades. As one of the main objectives of study abroad programs is the advancement of students' cultural awareness and intercultural competence, in view of the preparation for a professional career in an increasingly globalized world, the recent attention of scholars on cultural learning processes is not surprising (Vande Berg, Paige, & Lou, 2012). The types of study abroad with a view to enhance intercultural learning and ultimately achieve global citizenship (Byram & Feng, 2006; Lewin, 2009) have diversified, with intercultural service learning (Welch Borden, 2007), short stays (Boye, 2016; de Saint-Léger & Mullan, 2018; Llanes & Muñoz, 2009) and field experiences (Smolcic & Katunich, 2017) named as only some examples.

For the purpose of this chapter, I align myself with Geertz's (1973, p. 83) definition of culture as 'the fabric of meaning in terms of which human beings interpret their experience and guide their action', fully knowing that there are many more, but to enlist them all would be beyond the scope of this chapter. The ability to understand and relate to people with diverse cultural backgrounds has been labelled differently e.g., intercultural communication competence (Chen & Starosta, 1996), intercultural communicative competence (Byram, 1997; developed further in Byram, 2008), or intercultural sensitivity (Bennett, 1993).

Byram's (1997) model of Intercultural Communicative Competence (ICC) with a component of intercultural competence consisting of attitudes, knowledge, skills and critical cultural awareness has been embraced on a European level and has found its way into the *Common European Framework of Reference for Languages*

147

(Council of Europe, 2001). Since Byram (1997, 2008) also takes the perspective of the foreign language learner, I have adopted this model of ICC as a theoretical framework for the present study with regards to interculturality.

Research studies on study abroad that consider interculturality mostly focus on students' intercultural learning outcomes, some examples of which I would like to outline. Yang, Webster and Prosser (2011) conducted a survey with 214 students during which they matched students' expectations of study abroad with their perceived outcomes. One of the findings was that the study abroad goals that the students had set correlated with the host country experiences, suggesting that students need to be encouraged to set goals that are related to their intercultural development, among others.

Hismanoglu (2011), like Egli Cuenat and Bleichenbacher (2013), attempted to link linguistic and intercultural learning outcomes of study abroad. Hismanoglu (2011) asked 35 students to fill in a multiple-choice questionnaire with possible reactions in communicative situations that 'students are likely to encounter in real life situations' (2011, p. 808) e.g., borrowing money from a friend. The answers were rated by a panel of language and cultural experts on their appropriateness. Hismanoglu (2011) found that students with higher language proficiency have better results and he also detected a significant difference in the acquisition of ICC between/among students with and without experience abroad. He concluded that experience abroad *has* an effect on fostering students' ICC.

Similarly, Brogan and Ó Laoire (2011) investigated to what extent advancement in language proficiency can facilitate or have a causal effect on intercultural learning. They analyzed how intercultural learning is visible in student reflection discourse. To this end, they administered language tests prior to the study abroad experience of 146 Irish students of German on an ERASMUS study abroad in Germany or Austria. The tests were to gauge the students' general language proficiency in German. Questionnaires were to elicit data on language learning and intercultural competence and were supplemented with one-to-one semi-structured interviews with informants and data from ongoing email contact between/among the researchers and the informants. The purpose of the email contact during the study abroad period was to implement an element of cultural mentoring to support intercultural learning on site. One main finding was that the study abroad experience promoted self-discovery with the students. From the prevalent themes of the interviews, it becomes apparent that students' awareness of their own culture had changed. The findings are indicators of intercultural learning although Brogan and Ó Laoire (2011) maintained that the students' adaptation to the host culture was challenged by the 'ERASMUS fence' (p. 272) with limited contact opportunities with TL speakers as a result and the use of students' L1 instead of the TL (cf. Baron, 2003, for similar results).

Towards a Culturally Reflective Practitioner

In the framework of the SALA project, Merino and Avello (2014) analyzed the effect of study abroad on native English (n = 26) and on Spanish/Catalan (n = 28) speakers on their intercultural awareness during after a period of study abroad and 15 months afterwards. In this longitudinal study, informants were asked to write a composition on the same culturally oriented topic (adaptation to a culture) on four different occasions in this longitudinal study. Results suggest that the study abroad context turned out to be beneficial for learners' cultural development with intercultural awareness increasing immediately after the study abroad period. Despite stereotyped and ethnocentric views that students in the study still seemed to hold, the study abroad period was responsible for a maintained interest in other cultures, compared to a formal instruction context. However, Merino and Avello (2014) also discovered a lack of long-term retention effects since the positive short-term effects of the study abroad period were not maintained on a long-term basis. The authors underline the necessity of formal instruction on interculturality not only before study abroad, but equally upon students' return in order to give them opportunities for reflection on their study abroad experience.

Another trend in research on interculturality and study abroad can be seen in a comparison of study abroad and formal instruction contexts with regard to intercultural learning outcomes. Chieffo and Griffiths (2004) conducted a survey to analyze the construct of 'global awareness' in a group of students from the US in a four-week study abroad versus formal instruction context. The study abroad group was found to be more cognizant of cultural similarities and differences, probably due to the increased number of contact opportunities with representatives of the target culture(s). Pedersen (2010) used a questionnaire to explore the individual and combined effects of study abroad and formal instruction. One group had their study abroad experience without formal instruction while one group had a combination of study abroad and formal instruction. The control groups received formal instruction only without a study abroad period. The students with a combined study abroad and formal instruction treatment acquired the greatest degree of intercultural sensitivity.

Not all studies are 'positive' in terms of intercultural learning outcomes of study abroad. Studies have found that learners do not necessarily develop their intercultural competence, but that stereotypes are confirmed or even maximized following a study abroad period (Tusting, Crahshaw & Callen, 2002). For example, Coleman (1998) analyzed the evolving intercultural perceptions among UK-based language students with different L2s, using the European Language Proficiency Survey. The students were on an ERASMUS-funded study abroad program in different countries. On their return, learners appreciated characteristics of the target culture, but up to 30% of returning students held a more 'negative' view of the TL community after their

149

study abroad experience. However, the author found differences in judgement of the target culture with different kinds of programs. For example, a work placement was linked to more positive views than a studentship (Coleman 1998, p. 59).

Teichler (1997) provided a comprehensive evaluation of the first phase of ERASMUS study abroad programs at university-level for the EU in which he used standardized research instruments in order to gauge, among other things, the perceived outcomes of students' study abroad period. While the students' personal development was rated highly, their perception of the target culture remained relatively stable. In a previously published part of the evaluation, Maiworm, Steube and Teichler (1991) found that students in their study had slightly more negative attitudes towards their 'host' country and slightly more positive views on their 'home' country after their ERASMUS study abroad. Similarly, Löschmann (2001), in his survey of British undergraduate students, found stronger stereotypes and even an emergence of new stereotypes towards the target culture after a study abroad period, concluding that the study abroad context by itself does not minimize stereotypes automatically. Löschmann (2001) highlighted the role of briefing and debriefing activities, among others.

The methodology of the research is often quantitatively oriented with self-assessment questionnaires administered to students. On the qualitative side, we find interview studies (e.g., Hammer, Bennett & Wiseman, 2003) and more recently analysis of student discourse. For example, Papatsiba (2003) collected 80 reports from students from 11 countries to see how the concept of alterity was represented in their written discourse. Merino and Avello (2014, p. 289f.) stated that 'learners' discourse—both written and oral—is a window through which we can effectively explore intercultural development'. Moreover, student narratives during and after study abroad are becoming an important instrument within this field of research (e.g., Benson, Barkhuizen, Bodycott & Brown, 2013; Mas Alcolea & Cots Caimons, 2015).

While study abroad has been researched for various decades, teaching practicums abroad have been relatively new on the research agenda. There seems to be considerably more research on teaching practicums abroad in North American contexts (e.g., Marx & Moss, 2011; Plews et al, 2010, 2014; Pritchard, 2011; Quezada, 2004) with a focus on preparing to teach culturally diverse groups in their home classroom contexts (Gay, 2000; Medina et al., 2015). Other aspects are prominent for foreign language teachers, namely developing intercultural competence in order to impart aspects of the target culture with a view to enhancing the learners' intercultural competence and lead them towards global citizenship.

Towards a Culturally Reflective Practitioner

The core characteristic of teaching practicums abroad, teaching, makes a fundamental difference to study abroad in university contexts. Teaching at a school provides and facilitates immediate and regular contact and interaction at school with mentors, colleagues, pupils and parents. This context provides outstanding opportunities for deep immersion in the TL and target culture.

While there is a growing body of research on foreign language teachers on placements abroad, preservice teachers do *not* commonly feature in studies on interculturality and study abroad with a few exceptions (for a review of research into immersion field experiences for teachers see Smolcic & Katunich, 2017, for teacher preparation see Poole & Russell, 2015) with the bulk of research located in the American and Asia-Pacific regions. Plews, Beckenridge and Cambre (2010) identified critical success factors of Mexican teachers of Spanish in Canada, finding cultural immersion as one among a variety of success factors of a Professional Development (PD) program abroad. Bournot-Trites, Zappa-Hollman and Spiliotopoulos (2018) looked into the linguistic, cultural and PD of French immersion teachers based in Canada and found that the informants in their study seemed to develop in all three areas provided their international teaching experience was properly scaffolded.

Marx and Moss (2011), in their case study of one female US student teacher completing a 15-week teaching practicum at a school in London, highlight the intercultural learning processes during the teaching practicum, applying the principles of cultural mentoring and guided cultural reflection in their study. On the basis of dialogic journals, participant observation onsite and a series of in-depth interviews at different stages of the practicum, they found that the informant in the study displayed a 'lack of understanding of the cultural construct' (Marx & Moss, 2011, p. 40) at the beginning of the placement. She required cultural facilitation by a mentor that supported her development of comparative and contextual thinking to the end of successful cultural reflection.

Two Germany-based studies considered the effects of a teaching practicum or a teaching assistant year abroad in English-speaking countries. Ehrenreich (2004) studied 22 (former) foreign language teaching assistants from Germany who were in their preservice teacher training in order to become EFL teachers. They had all spent one school year in an English-speaking country. With regards to her findings in terms of interculturality, Ehrenreich (2004) maintained that the informants made discoveries and acquired knowledge about and developed an increased affinity to the target culture, but there was no continuous development in intercultural competence, probably due to the lack of integration of theoretical concepts of intercultural competence in their teacher education. Ehrenreich (2004) added that the gains of assistantships can only be described individually, because they are determined by numerous variables. She called for better integration of teaching assistantships abroad in the home curriculum in order to improve preservice teacher education as a whole.

Work on ERASMUS teaching practicums abroad is scarce and has been conducted largely by Diehr (2013), as placements have only been funded by ERASMUS since 2007. In 2013, Diehr looked into the outcomes of teaching practicums abroad using the European Teacher Portfolio (EPOSTL). She had German preservice teachers of English assess themselves on their perceived language and intercultural outcomes of their teaching practicum in the UK. The learning processes and perceived outcomes of EFL student teachers on ERASMUS teaching practicums abroad have hardly been researched. The present study endeavors to close this gap in the literature.

THE STUDY: TEACHING PRACTICUMS ABROAD

Research Interest and Study Design

Research on the linguistic gains of study abroad is abundant, and intercultural learning outcomes have recently attracted more attention with target groups of undergraduate students (e.g., Kinginger, 2013). However, the target group of foreign language preservice teachers and teaching placements abroad have rarely been the focus of studies, therefore, we know little about the impact that teaching practicums may have on preservice teachers' professionalization as well as intercultural learning processes.

From 2010-2014, a total of 35 preservice EFL teachers completed a three-month period of teaching practice at primary and secondary schools in the UK and in Ireland. The undergraduate students at a University of Education in the Southwest of Germany were all preparing to become EFL teachers (together with another subject specialism) and were advanced learners of English at C1 level of the Common European Framework of Reference. Preservice teachers in Germany typically complete a Master's degree and sit two state examinations that will make them eligible for a post within a state school. They face their first state examination at the end of their studies, which includes several shorter periods of teaching practice and a whole semester at school. The students in question had to spend three months in an English-speaking country as a course requirement—one option was a teaching practicum at one of the university's partner schools—and as a part of the European-funded mobility program ERASMUS. The teaching practice period abroad was not mandatory, but could be credited as part of their home degree. Preservice teachers fulfilled duties such as: extracurricular activities; small-group teaching; teaching assistant activities; tutoring; and other tasks depending on their skills and the school's needs.

Students were supervised by their school mentors on location and by the university lecturer, who was the coordinator of the ERASMUS program at the same time. Before departure, they were briefed several times on organizational issues and on

Towards a Culturally Reflective Practitioner

cultural aspects e.g., school uniforms, dress code etc. The students did not have to take part in systematic formal instruction on intercultural issues prior to their departure. Students were asked about their expectations of the teaching practicums before setting off. During their stay abroad they were asked to produce student reflections (Brogan & Ó Laoire, 2011) in the form of weekly reflective journaling. By way of guiding questions (cf. appendix), they were asked to reflect on linguistic aspects, intercultural aspects and key points related to their PD as future EFL educators, taking up findings on the importance on (intercultural) guidance by e.g., Pedersen (2010) and Vande Berg (2007) who advocate the concept of intervening in students' learning by supporting students prior to, during and after their study abroad experience. Students provided the lecturer with reflective reports once a week, amounting to approximately 9-10 reports depending on the year. They were also required to send lesson plans of classes taught as well as post-lesson thoughts on their pedagogical praxis (the latter documents were not used for the purpose of this study). At the end of their teaching practice, students matched their expectations with their outcomes in their final reports. Students consented to their data being used in the study.

The underlining interest of this study was focused on the intercultural learning processes and gradual PD of future EFL teachers during their teaching practicum at schools in TL countries. Research questions can be formulated as follows:

1. *What are the expectations of EFL student teachers before their teaching practicum in the TL country? What is the subjectively perceived outcome after the teaching practicum abroad?*
2. *What instances of intercultural learning can be observed?*
3. *In what way does the teaching practice period abroad contribute to EFL student teachers' perceived PD?*

The study design is essentially qualitative with two major qualitative research instruments, namely reflective reports by students (n = 276) and focus group discussions (n = 6) with previous outgoing and present outgoing students. In line with Dörnyei (2007), qualitative research is to explore and describe the essential qualities of complex phenomena in a natural setting, in our case the learning environment that study abroad in the shape of teaching practicums provide for preservice foreign language preservice teachers.

Qualitative research, according to Merriam (2009, p. 13), is focused on 'the meaning people have constructed, that is, how people make sense of their world and the experiences they have in the world'. The present study is primarily concerned with subjective perceptions and experiences of human beings in a study abroad-setting. The fact that the teaching practice experience of the informants is situated in a complex setting like the classroom in a different cultural and linguistic context and the dialogic nature of the placements due to the constant contact between the supervisor and the students would stress the aspect of Denzin and Lincoln's (2005) approach to qualitative research as an 'interpretative, naturalistic approach to the world' (p. 3).

This study was exploratory in nature and sought to generate hypotheses about preservice teachers' intercultural and professionally-oriented learning processes. To this end, 35 preservice EFL teachers who spent a teaching practicum of three months at primary and secondary schools in the UK (Wales) and in Ireland were asked to write reflective reports on a weekly basis during their stay. The purpose was to initiate and foster reflection on a variety of study abroad-related issues. Reflections needed to capture daily routines at the students' new school environment, cultural and intercultural aspects such as cultural identity or the role of otherness, linguistic aspects such as bilingualism in Wales and in Ireland, and their own perceived PD.

Additionally, student teachers were asked to delineate their expectations of the teaching practicum before the start of the teaching practice experience and to match these expectations with their perceived outcome at the end of the teaching practice period. Student teachers received guiding questions (see Appendix) to scaffold their reflective writing and received immediate feedback in the form of comments, further information or questions for clarification by the supervisor. The purpose of the feedback was to provide an impetus for (further) reflection, to encourage ethnographic learning, but also to give encouragement and provide a protected space to verify cultural observations or to speculate on cultural meanings without being exposed to an intercultural communication situation. Additionally, the cohort of student teachers who had already completed their teaching practice abroad was matched with the departing preservice teachers for focus group discussions. The purpose of these was for the student teachers to exchange information at first hand and to reflect on their experience in a peer group setting. The focus group discussions (n = 6) took place approximately six months after the student teachers returned. All informants gave written consent to their participation in the study.

Data Collection Methods

The 276 reflective reports by the 35 students constitute the most important source of data. The structure and function of the reports come close to diary studies (Dörnyei, 2007), which are qualified by McDonough and McDonough (1997, p. 121) as a 'pervasive narrative form'. The narrative-reflective aspects as well as the personal nature of the documents are particularly relevant for the purpose of this study. Reflective texts such as reflective reports or diaries have been used in teacher education (McDonough & McDonough, 1997) and in studies on issues

Towards a Culturally Reflective Practitioner

in intercultural awareness e.g., students' expectations about homestay by Rollie Rodriguez and Chornet-Roses (2014). Using diary data seems to be an emergent trend in study abroad research (e.g., Jing-Schmidt 2015). Bolger, Davis and Rafaeli (2003) classified diary studies into three categories, namely interval-, signal- and event-contingent designs. The present study can be seen as an interval-contingent design since the informants were asked to report on their experiences at regular, predetermined intervals.

This data collection method was chosen because it was seen to be a good way of eliciting the informants' personal descriptions and interpretations of their experiences during teaching practicums. According to Dörnyei (2007, p. 157), diary methods (or reflective reports) allow the researcher to look into dynamic processes and 'study time-related evolution' within individuals. Thus, they were appropriate for delineating learning processes in complex proficiency areas such as intercultural competence or professional teacher concepts by eliciting data continuously throughout the teaching practice period. To avoid or attenuate weaknesses of the method, such as considerable variation in length or depth and in order to maintain students' motivation to provide high-quality and in-depth reports, the researcher provided some scaffolding by guiding questions and kept in regular touch with the informants (at least once a week) by giving feedback on their entries. In this manner the student teachers were given the feeling that their reports were seen as relevant and taken seriously. On a didactic level, the purpose of the feedback was to trigger further reflection processes and thus deep learning (Gipps, 1994). Starting from research insights from SLA that highlight the role of speaking and fluency in linguistic gains of study abroad, the reports represented a counterweight because they were to make students practice their writing skills as a linguistic learning objective.

After the teaching practice experience, previous outgoing students and departing students got together in a meeting during which focus group discussions (also termed 'focus group interviews' e.g., Dörnyei, 2007) took place. Usually 6-10 students were participating in 5 discussions. The method was used because it enabled the researcher to pursue a double focus. On the one hand, the 'collective experience of group brainstorming' (Dörnyei 2007, p. 144) facilitated the informants' stimulating each other's thoughts and recollections of their teaching experience. Since the format of focus group discussions allows for various degrees of structure, the researcher gave only occasional questions to the participants to answer so as to give the informants maximum freedom to discuss and pursue emerging topics. The choice of topics by the informants gave an insight into salient experiences of teaching practice abroad after an extended period of time that the students felt worthwhile mentioning.

On the other hand, the format had a practical focus as well since it gave the future outgoing students an opportunity to ask concrete questions e.g., about the appropriate dress for student teachers or what shops offer a rebate for students.

155

This way, the future outgoing students received an additional peer briefing from the previous students in the teaching practicum. The length of the focus group discussions was usually between one and two hours; not all students were present due to other commitments during term time. The focus group discussions were conducted about six months after the students' teaching practice abroad experience so that there was a chance to record their sustained experience and lasting impressions of their teaching practice period abroad. To maintain an open and uninhibited atmosphere during the discussions, data were collected as field notes. Audio recordings were deliberately not taken into account.

Data Analysis Methods

The reflective reports were content analyzed, adapting a procedure based on Mayring (2010). Mayring's (2010) qualitative content analysis is based on the creation of a system of categories that is the result of a sequenced procedure. In relation to this study:

- units of analysis were defined and identified in the material;
- relevant passages were summarized and explicated i.e., reformulated in an abstract way while retaining the original meaning; and
- explicated passages were restructured and assigned a category determined deductively i.e., starting from the research questions and those questions that arose from the narratives.

The process of explicating and structuring, as well as linking back units of analysis to the system of categories, were repeated several times in an iterative process, yielding a final system of categories as a result. Importantly, in order to enhance the reliability of the results, two researchers analyzed the data separately and established separate systems of categories. With reference to Table 1, they then shared and discussed their results, creating a common system of three main categories and subcategories.

The field notes from the focus group discussions underwent a thematic analysis. In order to take up as much of the informants' input as possible in a natural setting, a category system was not created. Instead, the emerging themes of the focus group discussions were compared with the categories from the reports to see what experiences and impressions are still present with the students six months after the teaching practice period abroad. The categories for interculturality were then linked back to Byram's (1997, 2008) framework of intercultural competence.

Towards a Culturally Reflective Practitioner

Table 1. System of categories

Language	Culture	Professionalization
language proficiency language as classroom language subject-specific terminology	cultural comparison culture in context (system, cultural procedures and behaviors, attitudes) acculturation processes otherness contact to target culture members	professional tools/routines teacher student as part of the team model learning foreign language teaching methods heterogeneous learner groups preparing teaching teacher-pupil relationship teacher personality goal setting to improve own teaching

RESULTS AND DISCUSSION

The findings will be organized into expectations and perceived gains in terms of perceived linguistic, intercultural and professional gains. Expectations of EFL preservice teachers can typically be classified into foreign language acquisition, cultural aspects and professionalization issues. This is partly due to the guiding questions for the reports, but the categories can be found in the data itself e.g., with student 1-W-10 who mentioned all three categories as a targeted learning outcome:

I see the teaching practice in Wales as a chance to improve my teaching skills, my language skills and my knowledge about other cultures.
(1-W-10)

Similarly, student 20-W-13 seemed to make a top three of target learning outcomes with the professionalization aspect clearly taking prime place:

From the teaching practice in Wales I expect that I improve my language skills, that I practice the teaching methods I have already learned and that I learn new teaching methods. I want to get to know the Welsh culture and a few Welsh words and of course I want to get to know a lot of people.
(20-W-13)

Expectations: Linguistic Aspects

In line with SLA-related literature, expectations on linguistic improvement centers on spoken language and fluency, which one student formulated as follows:

During my studies, I realized especially my use of spoken English would need a brush-up.
(21-W-13)

Respondent (21-W-13) acknowledged her lack of practice in speaking the foreign language in a university environment. Fluency forms a further focus that is to be achieved by way of practice. One student's intention was:

...most of all to improve my oral skills, to get a lot of practice in speaking and to reach the level of fluency, so that I don't have to think about what to say and that it just happens automatically.
(7-W-11)

However, we often see an interconnection of categories, which is most obvious with students linking their expected improvement of (spoken) linguistic proficiency with their professional role as a teacher. There is a tendency in the data to instrumentalize expected linguistic gains for student teachers' future classroom environment, in other words language is seen as a vehicle, as a necessity in order to function in the classroom in a professional manner. One typical example of this is one student who meticulously enumerated the areas of linguistic improvements she aimed for and to what purpose:

I want to acquire an appropriate classroom language so that I will be able to act professionally, spontaneously and self-confidently in the classroom. I would like to learn useful, comprehensible and clear chunks, sentences and expressions in order to be able to give instructions and feedback. (...) Concerning my oral communication skills, it is very important for me to improve my pronunciation, intonation and the competence to lead a conversation by using an appropriate, clear, comprehensible and accurate language. Further I want to extend my vocabulary, especially vocabulary and sentences for the classroom.
(22-W-13)

Similarly, one student linked language goals to her overall professional aim:

As a future English teacher, my ambition is to speak English as fluently and properly as possible and of course to become a good teacher (...) By teaching children, whose mother tongue is English; I am sure I will be much more confident as a foreign language teacher and in front of the class.
(12-W-12)

158

Towards a Culturally Reflective Practitioner

One other student associated the stay abroad with her professional career as a teacher:

In my opinion it is very important as an English teacher to speak English naturally and fluently. During my practicum at the [name of school] in [city in Germany], I realized that it is really necessary to go abroad as an English teacher to become a role model in speaking English.
(104-D-13)

She went on to establish a link between teachers and their teaching culture as an important feature of professionalization:

In my opinion, an authentic English teacher must have been abroad for a longer period of time and must have been able to tell something about a foreign culture based on his/her own experiences. So, I think becoming a professional English teacher implies going abroad for improving your knowledge language and culture...
(104-D-13)

From her professional ideal, she had a distinct picture of an idealized practitioner and she planned to achieve these competencies.

In their reports, the student teachers did not only determine their expected gains in different competency areas, but also voiced their concerns about various aspects of teaching practice. One language-related aspect that was prevalent in the data was the fear that they as non-native speakers of English would have to teach native speakers of the TL. One student's remark was typical of this concern before the start of the teaching practicum:

I have to teach native speakers whose English is much better than mine, which could also be a problem.
(102-D-12)

Not everybody's language-related expectations were so clear-cut, as one report suggests. The student, spending her teaching practice period in Wales, was curious about bilingualism, but also wanted to learn 'Celtic', which suggested that her prior knowledge about the target culture (and language) was rather undeveloped:

One of my main goals is to improve my language skills (...) I'm curious how bilingualism is realized in practice and how important the Welsh language is for the pupils and their education. Hopefully I learn [sic] some Celtic.
(28-W-14)

This particular student underwent a tremendous learning process since she later gave her reports witty bilingual headings in both English and Welsh.

Expectations: Cultural Aspects

In terms of culture, students in the study want to acquire knowledge and skills if we apply Byram's (1997) model of Intercultural Communicative Competence (ICC) to the data. Overall, the expectations are relatively vague, maybe also because students did not really know what encounters and opportunities for cultural learning they would have in the special context of 'their' school. However, with one category I called 'culture in context' (cf. system of categories), they were able to formulate precise expectations. Starting from their future professional environment during their stay abroad, they are interested in school-related cultural aspects, at this point on a systemic level due to lack of real insights. In the course of the stay, the reports have shown the category to have diversified considerably. The educational system in their respective environment was of great interest to the majority of students when they voiced culture-related expectations, as one typical example illustrated:

(…) I want to experience what the Welsh school system is like, [and] to compare it to the German [system] and maybe adopt some routines, tasks or methods.
(10-W-11)

Again, this can be seen as a means to an end since they hoped to use systemic aspects as a model for their own learning. The comparison of cultural aspects seemed to play a major role as the following example suggested:

I am very excited to learn how different the British school system, meaning the English and Welsh one, actually is compared to German schools.
(8-W-11)

Another major focus of the culture-related expectations by the informants in the data is the planned contact with target culture members. The student below was planning on obtaining cultural insights by socializing with local people:

Hopefully I will also make friends with some people living around here for that would be great fun and I think this would be a nice way to approach a new culture.
(9-W-11)

160

Towards a Culturally Reflective Practitioner

With some students, however, even target culture contacts were instrumentalized as one example illustrated:

I think the stay will be an enrichment regarding my later job. Building up friendships and contacts is definitely an advantage for a foreign language teacher. (14-W-12)

Here, establishing contact to local people is regarded as an investment in her professional life and not only seen as a way to develop one's own personality and to broaden one's horizons.

Expectations: Professional Aspects

Professionally oriented expectations represent by far the most prominent area with clearly formulated learning objectives and almost unanimous views on the expected gains of PD. Among the most clearly identified areas in the data range the acquisition of experience and teaching routines with a widened methodological repertoire, preferably achieved through learning on the job. Probably due to the lack of teaching experience with preservice teachers, about 40% wish for model learning because they naïvely assume that their mentors as experienced teachers know how to teach perfect lessons. The example below explicitly names model learning as one preferred way of learning combined with a trial and error approach. References to prior knowledge or theoretical frameworks that she may have encountered during her studies so far are not made, which is typical in the data.

I hope to be able to do kind of a model learning and try things out by myself. (14-W-12)

Another student actually seemed to require model learning for her search of a professional identity:

Additionally, I will expand my repertoire of teaching methods and ways to structure a day at school and school lessons (...) From the teachers, I will accompany this period of time, I will learn a lot concerning ways of teaching and coping with pupils. These positive role models I do need to define my own role as a teacher. (15-W-12)

Towards a Culturally Reflective Practitioner

The most important outcome is often formulated as teaching experience to be gained during the teaching practicum, or a repertoire of methods to be employed in the foreign language classroom, as one student posted to Ireland suggested:

My expectations from the teaching practice is to get more routine in teaching and have a real insight into the work of a teacher for a longer period of time. Furthermore, I also expect to get to know another educational system and get to know other methods which are likely for Irish teachers.
(106-D-14)

Apart from the aspect of teaching experience and related routines, the informants in the study also expect to learn about solutions for disciplinary issues, issues that they may not have broached during their formal pre-teacher education at university, but that they find challenging. Reynolds (1992) maintains that novice teachers seem to have problems to maintain discipline. Again, the approach mentioned in this context is model learning. One student observed:

I am looking forward to get [sic] to know more teaching methods, to see how teachers handle certain situations e.g., conflict solving.
(14-W-12)

Students, although they mostly do not know exactly about their duties at this point in their teaching practice, are highly motivated in general ('I want to give 100% per cent in class', 27-W-14). One student wrapped it all up:

I will try my best to do well, I hope I will get the chance to teach on a regular basis (...). This probably is my biggest wish for Wales for through teaching I am sure I can improve my language and my teaching abilities.
(9-W-11)

Students seem to be intent on a positive teacher-pupil relationship, which sometimes borders on naivety. This, in turn, seems to confirm findings of novice teachers idealizing their teacher-pupil in their early/novice years compared to more experienced teachers' relationship (e.g., Veenman, 1984). As one suggested:

I hope that they trust me and come to me if they have problems in school. I will assist them when they have problems with the subject material or with mates.
(20-W-13)

162

Towards a Culturally Reflective Practitioner

For another student, the teacher-pupil relationship was seen as the most important aspect of the teaching practicum:

I think the most important question that I have been thinking about is how the pupils will react to me. While teaching in Germany I always tried to get a good relationship with my pupils and to create a good learning atmosphere. I think it is important that students feel save in my lessons and that they like coming to my lessons.
(18-W-12)

In line with Harmer's (2001) role of a teacher, students were asked what role they would prefer. Either students did not opt for a specific role or they preferred the role that would highlight their friendly, informal relationship with their student learners:

I hope that my relationship to the class is based on a mutual acceptance which I will achieve by being more a coach or a facilitator than a lecturer...
(12-W-12)

This statement reveals the preservice teachers' typical self-concept at this stage of their careers (cf. Johnson (1994) for emerging beliefs in preservice ESL teachers; Debreli (2012) for changes in beliefs of preservice EFL teachers).

Perceived Linguistic Gains

Preservice teachers' comments in their final reports can be categorized into linguistic, cultural and professional gains. Concerning language, spoken skills are perceived to have developed. This finding is in line with the students' expectations and also the findings from SLA literature e.g., Collentine (2004) or Segalowitz and Freed (2004). Students report to speak more fluently (*'that I feel surer and I am more fluent in speaking. It has become easier to find English expressions and English words in my mind'*, 29-W-14). They develop greater confidence in speaking and taking part in a conversation due to their increased exposure to the language and the forum to practice:

I feel much more confident in having a conversation in the English language and to speak the English language than before. The environment to improve my speaking skills couldn't have been better.
(11-W-11)

Towards a Culturally Reflective Practitioner

The regular contact with TL speakers at school was seen as a key to success, something which data from different reports confirmed:

It helped a lot that my colleagues were communicative and made me feel part of the staff immediately.
(101-D-12)

Again, the linguistic gains were often seen as instrumental to teaching, as the following example suggested:

By gaining confidence in speaking English spontaneously and practicing applying the language in front of classes of native speakers I could improve my level of English, especially in the use of classroom phrases, giving instructions and explaining new concepts.
(21-W-13)

Students were aware of the fact that advancement of their linguistic capabilities would be an ongoing process:

In the long-term this means that I have not finished my English learning process yet, which will be an ongoing process throughout my whole life even when I will be working as an English teacher. This is why further trips to Wales or other English-speaking countries are absolutely necessary for my education. They will also help me to keep my passion for this language alive and to find inspiration and professionalism for my daily teaching.
(7-W-11)

This quote clearly shows how the student reflects on herself as a learner and considers lifelong learning as a necessity, but not only for her personal development ('passion for this language'). She instrumentalized her language proficiency as a tool for her professionalization, being one typical instance of interconnections of categories.

The fears of a non-native speaker having to teach native TL speakers disappeared after several days, sometimes up to three weeks, depending on the student. The data from the field notes revealed that the preservice teachers reassure the 'new' students to be assigned to teaching practice places in the focus group discussions about this previously perceived linguistic challenge.

Towards a Culturally Reflective Practitioner

Perceived Intercultural Learning Gains

The data showed that the knowledge aspect of intercultural competence (Byram, 1997) was highlighted in the students' perceived intercultural learning gains:

[M]y teaching skills, my language skills and my knowledge about other cultures have improved.
(1-W-10)

Particularly knowledge about school-related issues, the category I called culture in context, was considered as an outcome in the data, such as one student who actually described her methods of analysis closely and diversified the notion of 'school system':

I learned a lot about the foreign school system by just being there and experiencing it myself, through observing it, making notes, reflecting regularly, exploring the school building and the different classrooms, the decoration of the classroom walls, talking to the school staff and asking a lot of questions and by talking to the pupils.
(7-W-11)

The cultural knowledge acquired seems to be reciprocal, because it is typically based on cultural comparison, as one example noted:

I got to know a different educational system and was able to compare it to the one that I am used to. It was interesting to see the German educational system from a distance. There are a lot of things I appreciate over here and that I might take with me to Germany, but as well a lot of things I like better the way we do it. This stay was an opportunity for me to form my own view on things.
(14-W-12)

At times the cultural comparisons resulted in a change of perspective, according to Byram (1997) an important prerequisite to intercultural learning. The stay abroad and the familiarization with a different educational system by becoming a part of it, invoked a change of perspective with the following student:

Through my stay in Wales I learned primarily to appreciate the advantages and disadvantages of a different school system as well as those of my own school system. Before I arrived at (place name in Wales), I had seen the German school system as rather bad, but now I cannot completely agree with that.
(12-W-12)

Towards a Culturally Reflective Practitioner

The change of perspective that some students are able to make (by far not all of them) is reflected in one student's data. She reflected on the way that an external view on her cultural frame of reference, such as the one she had just taken, was conducive to her personal development:

I learned a lot about myself, what I am actually able to do and I came to know a lot about Germany and how it is seen from another perspective. I experienced what it means to be German and even to be proud of it.
(14-W-12)

Students also commented on their contact to the target culture which, for all of them, were their professional contacts at school, their host family or landlord/landlady for many and the friends and acquaintances they had made. The contacts with other members of staff at school tended to be informal and were appreciated as such:

I really like the breaks and having lunch, sitting together, and chatting about news, school events, pupils and everything you talk about with a crowd of teachers.
(104-D-13)

The students who made an effort to integrate and to take action by conducting surveys in order to find out something for their weekly reports, achieved a higher level of integration:

As to becoming friends, the people I have met in the climbing clubs are friendly and I have made friends with a few of them during my first six weeks in [place name in Wales]. Since they have weekly meets, and additional ones at the weekends, I could easily take up with the members.
(21-W-13)

At the end of the teaching practice period abroad, some even had consciously integrated aspects of the target culture into their own cultural identity. One student who had been in Ireland reported:

I would say that I assimilated my way of living to the Irish culture. I definitely got used to the Irish weather and their tea consumption. Having a cup of tea in the morning is an essential part of my everyday life and umbrellas are now only used for really heavy rain.
(102-D-12)

166

Towards a Culturally Reflective Practitioner

As mentioned before, the category of culture in context relates to systemic aspects e.g., school uniforms, behaviors and procedures such as safeguarding procedures at schools and attitudes e.g., school spirit are reflected in the focus group discussions. The data showed that it was a recurring topic in the conversations among peers, thus illustrating its centrality for the preservice teachers.

The guiding questions for the reflective reports function as a help to consciously reflect on cultural aspects. The instrument of guiding questions yields some insightful results in terms of intercultural learning gains, but also many relations of mere experience with little or no analysis of the observations made, reflected as well in the findings of Sperling's (2016) secondary analysis of the data. She found that the majority of students in the sample lacked a systematic conceptual cultural knowledge, which impeded their attribution of experiences to cultural concepts, a key to cultural awareness.

The following example, however, is indicative of successful intercultural learning processes that seem to have been triggered by a question on bilingualism in Ireland. The student minutely observed the state of bilingualism in Ireland and profited from relevant individual background research. The striking aspect is that she did this from the perspective of an outsider (herself) and from the perspective of the Irish themselves. This ability to clearly divide and switch perspectives suggests that she is apt at changing perspectives in Byram's (1997) sense and seems to be flexible in her analysis of intercultural knowledge:

While from an outsider's point of view Ireland seems to be bilingual because Gaelige is noticeably present, the Irish do not consider this to be the case. There are areas that use Gaelige as their first language, and these so-called Gaeltacht regions even have different dialects, such as parts of Mayo or the Aran Islands, but they are mostly very rural areas, which were strongly affected by historic events such as the great famine and suffered great losses in numbers of inhabitants. However, the language is overall a very important aspect of the Irish culture. The Irish are proud to have a language on their own that can differentiate them from their British neighbors and is part of their very own history. Therefore, even if they are not able to use it often, they do not want Gaelige to be ignored.
(101-D-12)

The student chose an ethnographic approach to intercultural learning (Barro, Jordan, & Roberts, 1998) and did not only talk to local teachers, but also took part in an Irish heritage trip herself to live the experience:

I originally thought that young adults would not be interested in the language at all, but talking to the Irish teachers and going to the Irish heritage trips convinced me otherwise. Once again it proves that the Irish people are very proud of their country and their traditions, regardless of their age.
(101-D-12)

This quote shows her engagement with the cultural aspect at hand, displaying her skills of discovery and interaction in Byram's (1997) sense.

A less convincing example was the answer of one student relating her own impressions and opinions on the question whether some sort of school spirit existed at her school. The student in case pointed out aspects like assemblies (which are unknown in her future professional context), school uniform (the same) and the important role of sports. She described the places where the school logo was to be found, but did not relate the aspects with one another, let alone come to a convincing conclusion that would reflect her engagement with the culture:

Not only the uniform is present all the time, if you take a closer look you will find the [name of school] logo almost everywhere. It is sewed [sic] on every part of their school uniform (...), it is printed on their journal and it is on the flag outside of school and a banner in the Assembly.
(103-D-13)

At times observations of students can be even considered as stereotypical, suggesting that undue over-generalization processes have taken place. One student discussed free time activities against the backdrop of the socio-economic situation of the families. However, the student tended to over-generalize. In her report, she gave the impression that everyone in the town in Wales she was talking about was poor and could not afford the barest necessities like decent clothes. While it may be true that unemployment in that particular industrial town tends to be higher than elsewhere, she resorted to a one-sided description of the situation:

Children in [place name] seem to be happy with those things their parents can afford. Families are very poor and you will see many people and students with holes in their trousers, dirty clothes or even old, dirty shoes. So, the children are not as demanding as they sometimes are in Germany.
(29-W-14)

168

Towards a Culturally Reflective Practitioner

Over-generalization bordering on stereotyping is also extended to behavior and communication patterns. The convention of asking *'How are you?'* when meeting someone without necessarily being interested in an answer was taken literally by the student in this example:

One of the ways of behaving I thought to be more American than British is asking for how you are doing every time you meet someone you know. Even when you do not have the time to start a conversation, people want to show their interest and motivation in speaking to you. This positive and ambitious attitude in social life seems to be significant for English people.
(21-W-13)

Apart from the fact that he was in Wales and wrongly attributes the behavior to be significant for 'English people', he attributed a positive attitude towards people in general to the conventional greeting phrase *'How are you?'*

The same misconception and related positive stereotyping is evident with a student in Dublin who took the same question as a real question and promptly over-generalized:

In terms of Irish people's mentality, I have to say again that I think they are friendlier than Germans. For example, when getting off the bus people thank the bus driver or even at supermarkets salesmen ask about your wellbeing.
(102-D-12)

The lack of knowledge about different cultural communication styles may result in over attributions and, hence stereotyping. The same students who display over-generalized statements, however, may still undergo intercultural learning processes in other areas. The intercultural learning processes seem to be described best by individual profiles, corroborating findings from Ehrenreich (2004, 2006), who highlighted the individuality of outcomes in her study of German assistant teachers in English-speaking target cultures.

As a case in point, one student who seemed to have very successful outcomes of the teaching practice abroad still displayed somewhat blatant stereotypes which, remarkably enough, had to do with her degree of acculturation. In her final report, the student evoked hetero-stereotypes about Germans, contrasting them with her (over-generalized) observation that the local people ('people here') did not conform to the 'typically German' traits of discipline, strictness and punctuality. She then concluded that she had adopted what she called 'British' behavior and had made it part of her cultural identity:

Concerning cultural adaption and the comparison between German and Welsh culture I have to mention that there are differences in some aspects in others there are not. One example for this is known as a typical German stereotype: Germans have a good discipline, are strict and always try to be on time. I think this is rather true because Germans care about things in another way as others do. So far, I have experienced this phenomenon twice, once in Ireland and now here in the UK. People here just seem not to care about several things as much as we Germans do. They just don't bother being late. By now, I can say that my behavior has change and I behave more British like I did before this stay. It might sound weird, but I've adapted the laziness and carelessness of my colleagues and friends. You might think that's not really a good thing to adapt, but in my opinion it's not too bad and I have learnt other things as well.
(1-W-10)

On the one hand, this result confirms findings on ERASMUS study abroad periods (Maiworm et al., 1998; Teichler, 1997), but it would be too easy to say that students have confirmed or developed stereotypes and thus, have not undergone any other intercultural learning.

Although there are numerous implicit instances of stereotyping or over-generalization in the data, the majority of students firmly rejected stereotyping in one report where they were asked to sketch (in a tongue-in-cheek manner) stereotypical picture of 'the typical' German/Welsh/Irish, thus highlighting a politically correct attitude on the surface while, probably unconsciously, stereotyping did creep into their cultural perceptions.

The range and depth of intercultural learning processes become obvious in the data with the concept of otherness students were invited to reflect on. Students' responses to the concept of otherness ranged from naïve:

(…) when I'm driving in my car I definitely feel different (…) the people here are definitely driving [sic] on the wrong side of the road.
(20-W-13)

…to unobservant with the student naming language as the only dividing factor:

Actually, as European I do not feel different compared to the Welsh or British people. The only thing which makes me different is the language.
(15-W-12)

Towards a Culturally Reflective Practitioner

Other students were very much aware of their otherness:

From the beginning of my stay onwards I have felt like having a post-it note on my forehead saying 'stranger'...
(25-W-13)

This made them feel insecure and inhibited, at least in the beginning. One other mature student described the phenomenon of binge drinking with younger staff and voiced his lack of comprehension of binge drinking. The same was done when he described his wonder at the fact that the pupils' parents at his school were not supposed to be informed about the learners' progress—something valued in his own cultural frame of reference as good teacher-parent co-operation—which he linked directly to the lack of respect that he says many teachers complain about. He then felt 'like an alien' (8-W-11), not understanding and maybe not attempting to understand. He related these situations to his sharp awareness of otherness.

In the data, there was also a more positive and creative approach to otherness to be found. Students exploited their sense of otherness in a positive way to try out new things or as a strategy to ask local people about cultural aspects they would not ask in Germany, as one student observed:

...because I am the other it is no problem at all, I am allowed and expected to act like this.
(14-W-12)

Students also enjoyed this status of 'the other' and felt special when locals were interested in their person and their background. One student particularly appreciated the feeling of being a somewhat cultural 'expert' or ambassador of their culture(s):

I feel like an expert because my knowledge about Germany and the German language that is normally not so unusual in my country is now important to the people in this country.
(7-W-11)

Towards a Culturally Reflective Practitioner

Closely related to this expert status, other students felt like ambassadors and monitored their behavior accordingly in order to create a good impression on local people:

Since I know that I am representing my country, I look after my behavior in order to leave a good impression. I also try to be as open as possible and have a positive attitude to show I'm willing to assimilate. In Germany, I would not have thought about it as much as I do here, as a foreigner.
(104-D-13)

The student acted consciously in order to show her willingness to integrate in her new cultural environment. She displayed a high level of reflection on the concept of otherness and thus she seems to have achieved Byram's (1997) aim of critical cultural awareness in this respect.

The willingness to integrate or establish contact with target culture members seems conducive to intercultural learning processes in the data, both on the attitudes and on the skills level of Byram's (1997) IC model. Those students who make an effort and take the initiative in contacting locals do it for two purposes in the data. They join locals in their free time activities (climbing club, choir, volunteering) to socialize and find their place in the community. The second purpose observed in the data is for students to approach locals in their immediate environment (teachers, pupils, host family, landlord/landlady) in order to garner 'expert' cultural information on a topic from weekly reports.

If students chose to do so, they often gained deeper and personalized insights into the cultural phenomenon at hand, something that is related to Byram's (1997) attitudes and advanced their skills of discovery and interaction. The role of the host family or landlord/landlady seems to be a facilitator for intercultural learning processes in their function of cultural experts and source of cultural knowledge that is readily available for students' own ethnographic endeavors.

When contact fails to be established despite the student's efforts, the individual experience may be over-generalized, confirming previous research findings (Vogt & Heinz, et al, 2004). In the data, one student spoke of a disappointing experience with someone he would have liked to make friends with, but who did not show any initiative although they had many things in common. This isolated experience was then over-generalized ('*From my point of view, many British seem to be a bit like the Americans who tend to be a bit superficial (…)*', 8-W-11) by comparing 'the British' to 'the Americans' and by attributing negative stereotypes to both groups. He did not think about other possible reasons e.g., the person being too busy in his everyday life or the person not wanting to invest time and effort in someone who would be gone soon anyway.

Towards a Culturally Reflective Practitioner

As was to be expected, the informants in the data display different degrees of integration into the target culture community and of acculturation. One student who was bicultural because of her Turkish origin made minute observations concerning cultural differences in everyday life in the third week of her stay already (i.e., food, greetings, language, school runs, traffic) and added she had already taken over some routines e.g., greeting people informally by saying *'Hey ya! You alright?'* She had already undergone intercultural learning by adopting some basic features rather quickly and thus seemed to have integrated well in this respect. Another student mentioned the openness that Byram (1997) subsumed under attitudes in his model of IC. She saw it as a necessity in order to establish contact and make friends.

There are instances in the data that are indicative of Berry's (2003) assimilation strategies in which the individual wishes to diminish the significance of the original culture to the point of denying it, to the benefit of the target culture. One student started her statement about Welshness like this:

To be in Wales means to be at home, and this is exactly how I feel since I am [sic] in Wales.
(28-W-14)

When describing aspects of Welsh identity she contrasted them to the English, but in such a way that she seemed to uniformly reject what a person with a strong Welsh identity eyes with suspicion, in the sense of being 'more Welsh than the Welsh'. One other student related an instance of reverse culture shock when back in Germany for the mid-term holidays, which she successfully reflected on:

When I was visiting my family for the mid-term break, I could detect a few changes in my behavior and reactions. While in Ireland it is often common to greet everyone, to ask them how they are doing and to have a polite tone of voice overall, Germans tend to be more direct and rougher in conversations, which is not worse, just different.
(101-D-12)

Data from field notes indicate that more students experienced this type of (mild) reverse culture shock upon re-entry after their teaching practicum abroad (Kartoshkina, 2015; Presbitero, 2016; for a similar context see Porsch & Lüling, 2017), particularly concerning communication patterns.

Sperling (2016), on the basis of a secondary data analysis (Donnellan & Lucas, 2013) collated the student teachers' intercultural learning processes and outcomes in a case study, focusing on three student teachers in the sample. She found that all three students in the case study had a rather vague idea of what the objective of intercultural learning in their teaching practice abroad would mean for them both personally

173

and as future language teachers. The expectations reports displayed the students' open and non-judgmental attitudes, one important prerequisite for the development of intercultural competence (Byram, 1997). The content analysis of their reports, however, revealed that they seemed to lack profound knowledge required to direct their focus of observation of cultural concepts and thus to make use of their skills of discovery, and to interpret their observations (skills of interpreting and relating).

As the program did not offer formal instruction that included e.g., cultural concepts on a mandatory basis, students did not receive the training that they would have required to draw on their cultural knowledge to maximize the development of their intercultural skills (of interpreting and relating and of discovery and interaction). This, in turn, resulted in potentially lower learning outcomes although all three students did undergo intercultural learning processes, albeit with heterogenous outcomes. According to Sperling (ibid), lower intercultural outcomes in the case study can be attributed to the individual cultural awareness levels which determined their ability to apply all components of intercultural competence according to Byram's model. As a consequence, Speling (2016) calls on a formal instruction component of the program that includes explicit goal setting, academic course work and activities designed to enhance self-reflection and cultural awareness, as well as guided reflection and exchange upon their re-entry. The role of a formal instruction component that would embed conceptual cultural knowledge will be taken up in the Implications section.

Perceived Professional Gains

Regarding the informants' professionally oriented outcomes, the most explicitly voiced outcomes were confidence in teaching. The preservice teachers reported to have gained experience in teaching along with a certain degree of teaching routine. One typical statement from the reports was:

I now feel more confident standing in front of the class.
(12-W-12)

This can be related to a variety of aspects in the multi-variable classroom and thus is not a reflected statement. This is closely related to the routines that students acquired and probably the model learning that took place. One student seemed to be satisfied with the outcomes in that she was able to add to her repertoire of methods:

I could practice the teaching methods I have already learnt. One new method of teaching I experienced (...)
(20-W-13)

Towards a Culturally Reflective Practitioner

The opportunity for model learning is appreciated by students and for one student resulted in efforts to work on her leadership skills:

In trying to behave like a leader I experimented with my voice and forced myself to speak louder as I would normally do. I also adapted phrases I had heard in other teachers' lessons into my own teaching.
(7-W-11)

However, it is also the fact that mentors entrusted their classrooms to the preservice teachers that was appreciated:

I am really glad that I could enjoy and observe a variety of different teaching methods and styles. I did not really expect that, but I was hoping it would be like that. The way most of the teachers let me be a part of their ideas and lessons about the current topics was absolutely great. (...) This is actually what I enjoyed most during the whole time.
(8-W-11)

The outcomes in terms of PD seem to be particularly pronounced whenever the preservice teachers felt embraced as part of the staff, as a member of the team. Students who were seen as a fully-fledged member of staff saw this circumstance as a source of great satisfaction, such as the students in the example:

I also liked the atmosphere and relationship between the staff members, as everyone was getting along with each other well. I fitted in very well and felt as a proper member of the staff, which made me really happy.
(26-W-14)

Another student who was not invited to staff meetings and not given the PIN number for entrance to classrooms did not feel the same job satisfaction, as it were, and her judgement of her professional gains was overall more negative:

Besides I did not feel like a staff member. We were not asked to join the staff meetings, they did not even give us the pin to enter the doors. So actually, I did not feel like a teacher, more as a [sic] LSA (Learning Support Assistant) (...) Unfortunately, I did not have a close relationship to the pupils.
(15-W-12)

The nature and quality of the teacher-pupil relationship seems to play an important role in the way professional gains are perceived. If preservice teachers established rapport with pupils in whatever way, they regarded this as 'success' in their PD. One rather young teacher student related her experience in teaching a gymnastics club on her own and stressed the teacher-pupil relationship as one facilitating aspect:

What helped me a lot was to get to know the students, to build up a relationship with them.
(107-D-14)

Similarly, students seem to link the establishment or improvement of a good rapport to the pupils with their experience during extracurricular activities. Extracurricular activities do not usually form part of the university course and are not always part of their teaching practicums in their home country. Therefore, the opportunity to join in school trips etc. was valued by the informants, as one example illustrated:

Fortunately, I was allowed to go to many school trips with different year-groups and also with my year six. Occasions like this always enriched my daily routine in school and concerning my class they helped to get to know my students better. As I thought it was very important to have a good relationship to my students in order to be able to teach them.
(9-W-11)

Again, the extracurricular experience was instrumentalized for enhancing the quality of subsequent teaching the same learner group.

One aspect that came up in the final reports concerns teaching heterogeneous learner groups or inclusive teaching. Since the German school system is still based on streaming in terms of academic ability level, but needs to accommodate more and more diverse learners, one vital interest of many informants was to find out more about dealing with heterogeneous learner groups. The fact that the Welsh and Irish systems are considerably more inclusive in terms of their learner groups, incited some students to find out more about the issue on site. Thus, students also tended to include this aspect in the reflection of their learning outcomes and in coming to a position on inclusive education:

I have seen how teachers have to balance it and that it is impossible to plan a lesson for anybody, if you want them to do all the same.
(10-W-11)

176

Towards a Culturally Reflective Practitioner

One student successfully tried to accommodate diverse learners and was proud of her learning outcome:

I liked how I motivated them to complete tasks, and that I had their full attention. This taught me how to plan lessons around various abilities of students. Therefore, I prepared differentiated lessons to allow each student to work to their full potential.
(27-W-14)

Again, model learning played a role in reassuring the preservice teachers, also in the area of inclusive education, as one student suggested:

The fact that the school had all kinds of learners with no distinction between Hauptschule, Realschule and Gymnasium [the different school types which are based on learners' academic abilities, K.V.] made it a partly demanding, but overall very helpful experience for future teaching. Additionally, (...) the inclusion of physically and mentally impaired pupils helped visualizing how inclusion can be implemented in Germany.
(101-D-12)

A more holistic approach to outcomes in professionalization was taken by students, although this was not the majority. The instances of a developed teacher personality are difficult to observe in the data. Since observations of teaching were only possible with two cohorts, indirect hints for the development of preservice teachers' teacher personality have to be exploited. The student who had set the development of his teacher personality as one goal of his stay is one case in point. He concluded in his final report that he had gained new insights in many respects, but the combination of 'new horizons' and 'changes the point of view towards education' could indicate a personal development that is linked to professionalism:

It is really unbelievable what a teaching practice abroad can teach. It teaches one a whole new culture, new people, a new area, a different educational system and most of all it opens the doors towards new horizons. It changes the point of view towards life and education.
(24-W-13)

The data from field notes invariably concerned rather practical aspects in the sense of dress code, the concept of Learning Support Assistants that is unknown in the students' local context or students' experience and impressions of extracurricular activities. Here, the reflection level was rather low with 'experienced' students giving advice to the outgoing ones in practical matters.

Towards a Culturally Reflective Practitioner

Summarizing the perceived outcomes of teaching practicums abroad in the data, we can make inferences on teaching practicums as a potential contribution to PD with EFL preservice teachers in the present study. In order not to duplicate previously related results, the emerging tendencies in the data will be highlighted.

The most striking difference to study abroad periods at university is that linguistic and cultural gains are seen as a preparation for the informants' future teaching environment. They are thus seen as instrumental to professionalization in the majority of cases (in the sense of 'I will adopt this procedure because in Germany...'). Regarding interculturality, this type of statement is often based on an implicit cultural comparison, something that, according to Hockenbury and Hockenbury (2013), implies a tendency to use one's own culture as a standard for judging other cultures. As the findings of Sperling's (2016) case study have shown, the aspect of interculturality would need more explicit attention in the shape of guided reflection and cultural mentoring particularly during the teaching practicum. This issue will be addressed in the next section on implications.

In the data, particularly the expectations reports, the students voice a wish for model learning to supplement their own apprenticeship of observation and to compensate for their limited teaching experience. However, at times this type of learning results in disappointments because the culture of teaching practice is different and, from the perspective of the preservice teachers, not desirable e.g., teacher-led arrangement of classes particularly in secondary school, because it runs contrary to their subjective theories and/or their previous knowledge from university. With students who resort to model learning in a more reflected way, this type of learning has satisfactory results. In one case the student consciously looked for a mentor whose teacher personality and self-concept would match with hers ('I singled out a role model for me', 104-D-13). As well as regarding target culture contacts, preservice teachers' own initiative at schools is vital for the outcome of the teaching practice and to their PD. For one student, mustering the courage to do so was a big step:

After the half term holidays, I realized that I had to take action to get to teach more lessons. This was a big personal step for me because I did not want to obtrude somebody [sic]. When I did this step [sic], suddenly everything went so well (...). Since then I have taught lessons every day, which is a wonderful experience. (27-W-14)

The opportunity for the teaching practice abroad is only the starting point, and it is up to the student to make the most of it in terms of gaining experience in their future professional field. Related to this point, taking an active part in teaching and in school life e.g., in extracurricular activities, seems to be a vital factor for the perceived outcome of the teaching practicum. Being embraced as part of a team

Towards a Culturally Reflective Practitioner

with both formal and informal opportunities for contact seems to be key to self-confidence, but also for job satisfaction with the preservice teachers in the sample, and seems to have a positive impact on cultural integration due to the number and quality of satisfying contact opportunities.

The length of the stay has an impact on the quality of the teacher-pupil relationship, the preservice teachers' self-confidence and self-concept as teachers as well as on the sense of belonging to the (staff) team. In many cases, the teaching practice abroad confirmed the students' wish to be a teacher or to teach the age group they had chosen:

I am studying to become a secondary school teacher and this experience here in a primary school in Wales has reassured me to do so').
(27-W-14)

In other cases, the experience makes them change their course, corroborating e.g., research by Smolcic (2013), in whose study novice ESL teachers' immersion situation led to changing goals for their future.

I think I will change my area of studies from primary teaching to special needs once I am back in Germany. (…) [D]uring my stay over here I got automatically drawn to those children who struggle.
(14-W-12)

Summary of Results and Implications

The results of the study have shown that the first and foremost goal of preservice teachers on teaching practicums abroad is professionalization, which contrasts the findings of other studies in which personal development was rated highest along with the linguistic outcome (e.g., Brogan & Ó Laoire, 2011). Hence teaching practicums abroad should be regarded as a special form of study abroad which takes account of the students' different needs and different ways of preparation of the teaching practicum.

In the present study, the linguistic gains are seen as a by-product and are viewed as an end to the students' PD in many cases. Cultural aspects are only systematically reflected on when guided by the instructor. In this sense, the weekly reports functioned as an impetus for intercultural learning with rather varied outcomes. Otherwise, students' observations remained largely on a descriptive level and related students' experiences in an unreflective way. A typical strategy is comparison to their own cultural frame of reference, but a change of perspective is not always involved. In some cases, stereotyping is prevalent. However, resorting to stereotypes or over-generalizing a cultural feature encountered does not necessarily mean that the informant does not develop different aspects of intercultural competence. Here, an individual cultural profile would be appropriate in order to depict the many complex learning processes over time in different areas of intercultural competence. In subsequent cohorts, a structured program that combined academic course work, cultural mentoring and guided (peer) reflection was adopted, but has not been systematically researched yet.

Culture in context, more precisely the school context, can be seen as an important category in which informants tend to acquire cultural knowledge and make it reciprocal by cultural comparison. Ambitions and personal efforts of the individual teacher student make a significant difference for the successful outcome of teaching practice and clearly impacts on their professionalization processes. This is also valid for intercultural learning processes when students take action and involve themselves in ethnographic cultural learning (Corbett, 2003). They tend to obtain deeper insights into specific aspects of the target culture and reach a higher level of critical cultural awareness, one goal of intercultural learning according to Byram (1997), by using and developing their skills of discovery and interaction. What is remarkable in the data is the interdependence of linguistic gains (linguistic confidence, fluency in classroom interaction, acquisition of classroom language), cultural gains in the field of culture in context in particular and PD.

Being part of the staff as a professional team seems to be a critical success factor for professional and cultural integration. The contact to staff and pupils also results in more TL contacts and thus more linguistic gains. With linguistic gains, a clear focus lies on preservice teachers' oral proficiency in order to use the (oral) language as a vehicle to teach. However, the tendency to instrumentalize experiences, knowledge and skills implies the danger of a narrow-minded and short-sighted approach to and perception of teaching practicums abroad. While the opportunity for experiential learning on the job is very much appreciated by the informants in the data, there is still the danger that other benefits of this type of study abroad are not seen and opportunities for development in other areas e.g., personal development, run the risk of being neglected by the preservice teachers. Results have clearly shown that guiding their linguistic, intercultural and professional experience in a teaching practicum abroad is conducive to maximizing the benefits of this type of study abroad.

Reflective reports are recommended for use in teaching practicums abroad, on the basis of the study findings. The reports can serve several purposes. They can be used to improve written skills of students in order to counter a heavy focus on spoken skills, as findings from SLA suggest. They are used to trigger reflection processes that would be conducive to intercultural learning and guide students' observations. When students take the initiative, reports may facilitate establishing and maximize contact with target culture members. One suggested procedure in the reports could be the following: Observations / descriptions - reflections - conclusion. In line with

Towards a Culturally Reflective Practitioner

the overall concept of the reflective practitioner (e.g., Schön, 1983), the reports are to foster reflection skills in students' professional domain (teaching in general, aspects of a self-concept, teacher personality etc.). Reports are seen as a suitable method to elicit narrative that also triggers reflective processes and have been used as instruments to develop a reflective stance on the teaching practicum abroad in other studies (e.g., Marx & Moss, 2011).

Reflective reports are seen as a suitable instrument for influencing preservice teachers' learning processes during their stay abroad. Before and after the teaching practicum, an extended period of formal instruction, particularly regarding cultural aspects, would be useful in order to improve preparation for the placement abroad and to provide face to face opportunities for joint reflection and sharing of experiences made during the teaching practicums. Although the preservice teachers in this study did have a debriefing session with peers and with the university coordinator, the fact that there was no opportunity for extended reflection in a formal instruction framework represents a shortcoming. This shortcoming was addressed by adding a formal instruction component to the program that was linked to cultural mentoring on the part of the university supervisor on the one hand and peers on the other hand, namely students with study abroad experience. This component representing a structured cultural mentoring approach takes into account Ehrenreich's (2006, p. 194) call for future teachers to be able to 'reflect on, conceptualize and articulate their views of cultural identity and of cultural otherness'. It took place during the teaching practicum phase. The number of reflective reports was reduced so as to not overburden the students in terms of workload. A component of explicit goal-setting following Yang et al. (2011) and Plews et al. (2014) was introduced. Additionally, students were enrolled in an online course while they were abroad and received the same course assignments on e.g., critical incidents as the students with experience abroad who were enrolled in the same course that was a blended learning course for them.

The students abroad received lecturer feedback on the assignments via email. In order to reflect on the content of the academic concepts and relate their newly acquired knowledge to their current experience abroad, they engaged in peer evaluation sessions with the students based in Germany. This way a reflection process was triggered that was based on these concepts but that gave them a chance to reflect on their international experience abroad and relate to them on different levels, namely on an academic level, with the university supervisor as a cultural mentor and with peers on eye level. The effect of this new program component still is to be studied. The enhancement of the program reflects findings from Pedersen's (2010) study and is related to the call for better integration of study abroad periods into the home syllabus of the university, which is also a crucial point for teaching practicums abroad (Brewer & Cunningham, 2009).

FUTURE RESEARCH DIRECTIONS

Preservice teachers as a key target group have rarely formed the focus of study abroad research. However, it became obvious from the present study that future teachers seem to be a special target group of study abroad students with needs and activities that differ from the average undergraduate student group in study abroad. Preservice teachers, particularly foreign language teachers as intercultural speakers, represent a key group of agents for social change as they are multiplicators of attitudes, knowledge and skills during their later careers. They impart culture on the basis of their more or less reflected stay so that their study abroad period has more impact in the long run than that of other groups of students. In this connection, the impact of teaching practice abroad could be investigated in longitudinal studies, considering learners at school as important stakeholders. In this connection, the effectiveness of the adapted program as described in the previous section would have to be established in an impact study.

Teaching practice abroad has to be acknowledged as a special type of study abroad, which entails an urgent need for research on this new aspect of study abroad e.g., needs analysis studies for the target group of student teachers in terms of effective preparation and debriefing procedures embedded in a formal instruction context. Related to this, greater insight is needed into the ways study abroad and formal instruction can effectively be combined for teaching practicums. To my knowledge, there are no comparative studies yet on teaching practicums abroad compared to teaching practicums at home in order to explore what added value teaching practice abroad would have in different areas. It would be interesting to further diversify and differentiate the concept of professionalization and investigate the factors of professionalization that would be furthered in a study abroad context.

The present study relied heavily on qualitative methods to investigate a complex phenomenon. While this is appropriate for the purposes of the study, research concerned with the outcomes of teaching practice abroad may use a variety of methodological instruments e.g., in a mixed-methods study design to combine the benefits of qualitative and quantitative research. In this connection, longitudinal studies would be advantageous to investigate the sustained effects of study abroad and more particularly teaching practice abroad on professionally oriented aspects such as self-concept or intercultural competence of practitioners, considering the learners as an important group of stakeholders.

CONCLUSION

The purpose of this chapter was to analyze the outcomes of teaching practicums in two TL countries as perceived by 35 preservice EFL teachers based in Germany. Reflective weekly reports and field notes from focus group discussions six months after the placement were content analyzed with a particular focus on intercultural learning processes during the study abroad and the potential contributions of teaching practicums abroad to students' PD. Due to the sample size, generalizability of the findings is limited, but still provides valuable insights that could be used for subsequent research. The central role of the professionalization aspect in the data sets teaching practicums apart as a special type of study abroad and calls for more research in this area. Intercultural learning needs to be guided in order to yield satisfactory outcomes in intercultural competence—a vital part of foreign language teachers' personal and professional profile. Preservice teachers, particularly foreign language teachers as intercultural speakers, represent a key group of agents for social change as they are multiplicators in the classroom. Every effort has to be made in order to enable them to teach the foreign language competently, but also trigger intercultural learning processes in their learners on the basis of their own critical intercultural awareness.

REFERENCES

Barron, A. (2003). *Acquisition in interlanguage pragmatics: Learning how to do things with words in a study-abroad context*. Amsterdam: John Benjamins. doi:10.1075/pbns.108

Beacco, J.-C. (2004). Une proposition pour référentiel pour les compétences culturelles dans les enseignements des langues [A suggestion for a frame of reference for cultural competencies in foreign language teaching]. In J.-C. Beacco & R. Porquier (Eds.), *Niveau B2 pour le français: Un référentiel* [Level B2 for French: A frame of reference] (pp. 251–287). Paris: Didier.

Bennett, M. J. (1993). Towards ethnorelativism: A developmental model of intercultural sensitivity. In M. R. Paige (Ed.), *Education for the intercultural experience* (pp. 21–71). Yarmouth, ME: Intercultural Press.

Benson, P., Barkhuizen, G., Bodycott, P., & Brown, J. (2013). *Second language identity in narratives of study abroad*. Basingstoke, UK: Palgrave Macmillan. doi:10.1057/9781137029423

Berry, J. W. (2003). Conceptual approaches to acculturation. In K. M. Chun, P. Balls Organista, & G. Marin (Eds.), *Acculturation: Advances in theory, measurement, and applied research* (pp. 17–37). Washington, DC: American Psychological Association. doi:10.1037/10472-004

Bolger, N., Davis, A., & Rafaeli, E. (2003). Diary methods: Capturing life as it is lived. *Annual Review of Psychology, 54*(1), 579–616. doi:10.1146/annurev. psych.54.101601.145030 PMID:12499517

Bournot-Trites, M., Zappa-Hollman, S., & Spiliotopoulos, V. (2018). Foreign language teachers' intercultural competence and legitimacy during an international teaching experience. *Study Abroad Research in Second Language Acquisition and International Education, 3*(2), 275–309. doi:10.1075ar.16022.bou

Boye, S. (2016). *Intercultural communicative competence and short stays abroad: Perceptions of development.* Münster: Waxmann.

Brecht, R. D., Davidson, D. E., & Ginsberg, R. B. (1995). Predictors of foreign language gain during study abroad. In B. Freed (Ed.), *Second language acquisition in a study abroad context* (pp. 37–66). Amsterdam: John Benjamins. doi:10.1075ibil.9.05bre

Brewer, E., & Cunningham, K. (2009). *Integrating study abroad in the curriculum: Theory and practice across the disciplines.* Sterling, VA: Stylus.

Brogan, K., & Laoire, Ó. M. (2011). Intercultural learning in the study abroad context. In A. Witte & T. Harden (Eds.), Intercultural competence: Concepts, challenges, evaluations (pp. 255-274). Bern: Peter Lang.

Byram, M. (1997). *Teaching and assessing intercultural communicative competence.* Clevedon, UK: Multilingual Matters.

Byram, M. (2008). *From foreign language education to education for intercultural citizenship.* Bristol, UK: Multilingual Matters. doi:10.21832/9781847690807

Byram, M., & Feng, A. (Eds.). (2006). Living and studying abroad. Research and practice. Clevedon, UK: Multilingual Matters.

Cadd, M. (2012). Encouraging students to engage with native speakers during study abroad. *Foreign Language Annals, 32*(1), 115–122. doi:10.1111/j.1944-9720.2012.01188.x

Carlson, J. S., & Widaman, K. F. (1988). The effects of study abroad during college on attitudes towards other cultures. *International Journal of Intercultural Relations, 12*(1), 1–17. doi:10.1016/0147-1767(88)90003-X

Towards a Culturally Reflective Practitioner

Carroll, J. B. (1967). Foreign language proficiency levels attained by language majors near graduation from college. *Foreign Language Annals, 1*(2), 131–151. doi:10.1111/j.1944-9720.1967.tb00127.x

Chen, G.-M., & Starosta, W. J. (1996). Intercultural communication competence: A synthesis. *Communication Yearbook, 19*, 353–383.

Cheng, A., & Mojica-Díaz, C. (2006). The effects of formal instruction and study abroad on improving proficiency: The case of-the Spanish subjunctive. *Applied Language Learning, 16*, 17–36.

Chieffo, L., & Griffiths, L. (2004). Large-scale assessment of student attitudes after a short-term study abroad program. *Frontiers: The Interdisciplinary Journal of Study Abroad, 10*, 165–177. Retrieved from http://frontiersjournal.com/issues/vol10/vol10-10_ChieffoGriffiths.pdf

Churchill, E., & DuFon, M. A. (2006). Evolving threads in study abroad research. In E. Churchill & M. DuFon (Eds.), *Language learners in study abroad contexts* (pp. 1–27). Clevedon, UK: Multilingual Matters. doi:10.21832/9781853598531-005

Coleman, J. A. (1998). Evolving intercultural perceptions among university language learners in Europe. In M. Byram & M. Fleming (Eds.), *Language learning in intercultural perspective: Approaches through drama and ethnography* (pp. 45–75). Cambridge, UK: Cambridge University Press.

Collentine, J. (2004). The effects of learning contexts on morphosyntactic and lexical development. *Studies in Second Language Acquisition, 26*(2), 227-248. doi: 10-1017/S0272263104262040

Collentine, J. (2009). Study abroad research: Findings, implications and future directions. In M. Long & C. Doughty (Eds.), *The handbook of language teaching* (pp. 218–233). New York, NY: Wiley-Blackwell. doi:10.1002/9781444315783.ch13

Corbett, J. (2003). *An intercultural approach to English language teaching*. Clevedon, UK: Multilingual Matters. doi:10.21832/9781853596858

Council of Europe. (2001). *The common European framework of reference for languages: Learning, teaching, assessment*. Cambridge, UK: Cambridge University Press.

Davies, I., & Pike, G. (2009). Global citizenship education: Challenges and possibilities. In R. Lewin (Ed.), *The handbook of practice and research in study abroad: Higher education and the quest for global citizenship* (pp. 61–77). New York, NY: Routledge.

De Keyser, R. M. (2014). Research on language development during study abroad. Methodological considerations and future perspectives. In C. Pérez-Vidal (Ed.), *Language acquisition in study abroad and formal instruction contexts* (pp. 313–325). Amsterdam: John Benjamins.

De Saint-Léger, D., & Mullan, K. (2018). A short-term study abroad program. In C. Sanz & A. Morales-Front (Eds.), *The Routledge handbook of study abroad research and practices*. Online.

Deardorff, D. K. (2006). Identification and assessment of intercultural competence as a student outcome of internationalization. *Journal of Studies in International Education, 10*(3), 241–266. doi:10.1177/1028315306287002

Debreli, E. (2012). Change in beliefs of preservice teachers about teaching and learning English as a foreign language throughout an undergraduate preservice teacher training program. *Procedia: Social and Behavioral Sciences, 46*, 367–373. doi:10.1016/j.sbspro.2012.05.124

Denzin, N., & Lincoln, Y. (Eds.). (2005). *Handbook of qualitative research* (3rd ed.). Thousand Oaks, CA: Sage.

Dewey, D. P., Brown, J., Baker, W., Martinsen, R. A., Gold, C., & Eggett, D. (2014). Language use in six study abroad programs: An exploratory analysis of possible predictors. *Language Learning, 64*(1), 36–71. doi:10.1111/lang.12031

Diehr, B. (2013). Go out. Get involved. Gain experience. Teacher development in school placements abroad. In J. Rymarczyk (Ed.), Foreign language learning outside school: Places to see, learn and enjoy (pp. 63-75). Frankfurt/Main: Peter Lang.

Donnellan, M. B., & Lucas, R. (2013). Secondary data analysis. In T. D. Little (Ed.), *The Oxford handbook of quantitative methods in psychology* (Vol. 2, pp. 655–677). Oxford, UK: Oxford University Press. doi:10.1093/oxfordhb/9780199934898.013.0028

Dörnyei, Z. (2007). *Research methods in applied linguistics*. Oxford, UK: Oxford University Press.

Egli Cuenat, M., & Bleichenbacher, L. (2013). Linking learning objectives of linguistic savoir-faire and intercultural competence in mobility experiences of teacher trainees. In F. Dervin & A. J. Liddicoat (Eds.), *Linguistics for intercultural education* (pp. 49–69). Amsterdam: John Benjamins. doi:10.1075/lllt.33.04egl

Ehrenreich, S. (2004). *Auslandsaufenthalt und Fremdsprachenlehrerausbildung* [Stay abroad and foreign language teacher education]. Berlin: Langenscheidt.

Towards a Culturally Reflective Practitioner

Ehrenreich, S. (2006). The assistant experience in retrospect and its educational and professional significance in teachers' biographies. In M. Byram & A. Feng (Eds.), *Living and studying abroad. Research and practice* (pp. 186–209). Clevedon, UK: Multilingual Matters. doi:10.21832/9781853599125-011

Freed, B. F., Segalowitz, N., & Dewey, D. P. (2004). Context of learning and second language fluency in French: Comparing regular classroom, abroad, and intensive immersion programs. *Studies in Second Language Acquisition, 26*(2), 275–301. doi:10.1017/S0272263104262064

Gay, G. (2000). *Culturally responsive teaching: Theory, research, and practice.* New York, NY: Teachers College Press.

Geertz, C. (1973). *The interpretation of culture.* New York, NY: Basic Books.

Gipps, C. (1994). *Beyond testing: Towards a theory of educational assessment.* London, UK: Falmer Press.

Gore, J. (2005). *Dominant beliefs and alternative voices: Discourse, belief, and gender in American study abroad.* New York, NY: Routledge.

Gudykunst, W. R. (1993). Toward a theory of effective interpersonal and intergroup communication: An anxiety/uncertainty management (AUM) perspective. In R. L. Wiseman & J. Koester (Eds.), *Intercultural communication competence* (pp. 33–71). Newbury Park, CA: Sage.

Hammer, M. R., Bennett, M. J., & Wiseman, R. (2003). Measuring intercultural sensitivity: The intercultural development inventory. *International Journal of Intercultural Relations, 27*(4), 421–443. doi:10.1016/S0147-1767(03)00032-4

Harmer, J. (2001). *The practice of English language teaching* (3rd ed.). London, UK: Longman.

Hismanoglu, M. (2011). An investigation of ELT students' intercultural communicative competence in relation to linguistic proficiency, overseas experience and formal instruction. *International Journal of Intercultural Relations, 35*(6), 805–817. doi:10.1016/j.ijintrel.2011.09.001

Hockenbury, D. H., & Hockenbury, S. E. (2013). *Discovering psychology* (6th ed.). New York, NY: Worth Publishers.

Hoffmann-Hicks, S. D. (2000). *The longitudinal development of French foreign language pragmatic competence: Evidence from study abroad* (Doctoral dissertation). Indiana University. *Dissertation Abstracts International. A, The Humanities and Social Sciences, 61*(2), 591.

Hokanson, S. (2000). Foreign language immersion homestays: Maximizing the accommodation of cognitive styles. *Applied Language Learning, 11*(2), 239-264.

Isabelli, C., & Nishida, C. (2005). Development of the Spanish subjunctive in a nine-month study-abroad setting. In D. Eddington (Ed.), *Proceedings of the 6th Conference on the Acquisition of Spanish and Portuguese as First and Second Languages* (pp. 78-91). Sommerville, MA: Cascadilla Press.

Isabelli, C. L. (2002). *The impact of a study-abroad experience on the acquisition of L2 Spanish syntax: The null subject parameter* (Doctoral dissertation). University of Illinois, Urbana-Champaign. *Dissertation Abstracts International. A, The Humanities and Social Sciences, 62*(8), 2703–A-2704.

Isabelli-Garcia, C. L. (2003). Development of oral communication skills abroad. *Frontiers: The Interdisciplinary Journal of Study Abroad, 9*, 149–173. Retrieved from http://www.fontiersjournal.com/issues/vol9/vol9-07_isabelligarcia.htm

Jing-Schmidt, Z. (2015). *Culture and identity: Chinese heritage language students in the ancestral homeland.* Paper presented at the 'The Culture of Study Abroad' Conference, Halifax, Canada.

Johnson, K. E. (1994). The emerging beliefs and instructional practices of preservice English as a second language teachers. *Teaching and Teacher Education, 10*(4), 439–452. doi:10.1016/0742-051X(94)90024-8

Kartoshkina, Y. (2015). Bitter-sweet re-entry after studying abroad. *International Journal of Intercultural Relations, 44*, 35–45. doi:10.1016/j.ijintrel.2014.11.001

Kinginger, C. (Ed.). (2013). *Social and cultural aspects of language learning in study abroad.* Amsterdam: John Benjamins. doi:10.1075/lllt.37

Kinginger, C., & Farrell, K. (2006). Assessing development of meta-pragmatic awareness in study abroad. *Frontiers: The Interdisciplinary Journal of Study Abroad, 10*, 19–42. Retrieved from http://www.frontiersjournal.com/issues/vol10

Lafford, B. (2004). The effect of context of learning on the use of communication strategies by learners of Spanish as a second language. *Studies in Second Language Acquisition, 26*(02), 201–226. doi:10.1017/S0272263104262039

Lanes, A., & Muñoz, C. (2009). A short stay abroad: Does it make a difference? *System, 37*(3), 353–365. doi:10.1016/j.system.2009.03.001

Towards a Culturally Reflective Practitioner

Lewin, R. (2009). Introduction: The quest for global citizenship through study abroad. In R. Lewin (Ed.), *The handbook of practice and research in study abroad: Higher education and the quest for global citizenship* (pp. xii–xxiii). New York, NY: Routledge.

Löschmann, M. (2001). Was tun gegen stereotype? [How to fight stereotypes?]. In G. Wazel (Ed.), Interkulturelle Kommunikation in Wirtschaft und Fremdsprachenunterricht [Intercultural communication in business and foreign language education] (pp. 147-201). Frankfurt/Main: Peter Lang.

Maiworm, F., Steube, W., & Teichler, U. (1991). *Learning in Europe. The ERASMUS experience*. London, UK: Jessica Kingsley.

Marx, H., & Moss, D. M. (2011). Please mind the culture gap. Intercultural development during a teacher education study abroad program. *Journal of Teacher Education, 62*(1), 35–47. doi:10.1177/0022487110381998

Mas Alcolea, S., & Cots Caimons, J.-M. (2015). *Me and my stay abroad: Comparing L1 and foreign language experiential narratives of European students.* Paper presented at the 'The Culture of Study Abroad' Conference, Halifax, Canada.

Mayring, P. (2010). *Qualitative Inhaltsanalyse: Grundlagen und Techniken* [Qualitative content analysis. Basics and techniques] (11th ed.). Weinheim: Beltz.

McDonough, J., & Mc Donough, S. (1997). *Research methods for English language teachers*. London, UK: Hodder Arnold.

Meara, P. (1994). The year abroad and its effects. *Language Learning Journal, 10*(1), 32–38. doi:10.1080/09571739485200351

Medina, A. L., Hathaway, J. I., & Pilioneta, P. (2015). How preservice teachers' study abroad experience lead to changes in their perceptions of English language learners. *Frontiers: The Interdisciplinary Journal of Study Abroad, 25*, 73–91.

Merino, E., & Avello, P. (2014). Contrasting intercultural awareness at home and abroad. In C. Pérez-Vidal (Ed.), *Language acquisition in study abroad and formal instruction contexts* (pp. 283–309). Amsterdam: John Benjamins.

Merriam, S. (2009). *Qualitative research: A guide to design and implementation.* San Francisco, CA: Jossey-Bass.

Moeller, A. J., & Nugent, K. (2014). Building intercultural competence in the language classroom. In S. Dhonau (Ed.), *Unlock the gateway to communication* (pp. 1-16). 2014 Report of the Central States Conference on the Teaching of Foreign Languages. Retrieved from http://www.csctfl.org/documents/2014Report/CSCTFLReport2014.pdf

Murphy-Lejeune, E. (2002). *Student mobility and narrative in Europe: The new strangers.* Frankfurt: Peter Lang. doi:10.4324/9780203167038

Papatsiba, V. (2003). *Des étudiants européens: 'Erasmus' et l'aventure de l'altérité* [European students. Erasmus and the adventure of otherness]. Bern: Peter Lang.

Pedersen, P. (2010). Assessing international effectiveness outcomes in a year-long study abroad program. *International Journal of Intercultural Relations, 34*(1), 70–80. doi:10.1016/j.ijintrel.2009.09.003

Pellegrino-Aveni, V. (2005). *Study abroad and second language use: Constructing the self.* Cambridge, UK: Cambridge University Press. doi:10.1017/CBO9780511620584

Pérez-Vidal, C. (Ed.). (2014). *Language acquisition in study abroad and formal instruction contexts.* Amsterdam: John Benjamins. doi:10.1075/aals.13

Plews, J., Beckenridge, J., & Cambre, M.-C. (2010). Mexican English teachers' experiences of international professional development in Canada: A narrative analysis. *Electronic Journal of Foreign Language Teaching, 7*(1), 5-20. Retrieved from http://e-flt.nus.edu.sg/v7n12010/plews.pdf

Plews, J. L., Breckenridge, Y., Cambre, M.-C., & Fernandes, G. (2014). Mexican English teachers' experiences of international professional development in Canada: A narrative sequel. *e-FLT, 11*(1), 52-75. Retrieved from http://e-flt.nus.edu.sg/v11n12014/plews.pdf

Poole, C., & Russell, W. III. (2015). Educating for global perspectives: A study of teacher preparation programs. *Journal of Education, 195*(3), 41–52. doi:10.1177/002205741519500305

Porsch, R., & Lüling, S. (2017). Reentry-Erfahrungen durch Lehramtsstudierende mit einer modernen Fremdsprache nach einem Auslandsaufenthalt [Reentry experience of student teachers of modern foreign languages after a period abroad]. *Zeitschrift für Fremdsprachenforschung, 28*(2), 259–283.

Presbitero, A. (2016). Culture shock and reverse culture shock: The moderating role of cultural intelligence in international students' adaptation. *International Journal of Intercultural Relations*, *53*, 28–38. doi:10.1016/j.ijintrel.2016.05.004

Pritchard, R. (2011). Re-entry trauma: Asian re-integration after study in the west. *Journal of Studies in International Education*, *15*(1), 93–111. doi:10.1177/1028315310365541

Quezada, R. L. (2004). Beyond educational tourism: Lessons learned while student teaching abroad. *International Education Journal*, *5*(4), 458–465.

Reynolds, A. (1992). What is competent beginning teaching? A review of the literature. *Review of Educational Research*, *62*(1), 1–35. doi:10.3102/00346543062001001

Rollie Rodriguez, S., & Chornet-Roses, D. (2014). How 'family' is your host family? An examination of student-host relationships during a study abroad. *International Journal of Intercultural Relations*, *39*(3), 164–174. doi:10.1016/j.ijintrel.2013.11.004

Sanz, C., & Morales-Front, A. (Eds.). (2018). *The Routledge handbook of study abroad research and practice*. New York, NY: Routledge. doi:10.4324/9781315639970

Sasaki, M. (2011). Effects of varying lengths of study-abroad experiences on Japanese EFL students' writing ability and motivation: A longitudinal study. *TESOL Quarterly*, *45*(1), 81–105. doi:10.5054/tq.2011.240861

Schattle, H. (2009). Global citizenship in theory and practice. In R. Lewin (Ed.), *The handbook of practice and research in study abroad: Higher education and the quest for global citizenship* (pp. 3–20). New York, NY: Routledge.

Schön, D. A. (1983). *The reflective practitioner: How professionals think in action.* London, UK: Temple Smith.

Segalowitz, N., & Freed, B. F. (2004). Context, contact and cognition in oral fluency acquisition: Learning Spanish 'at home' and 'study abroad' contexts. *Studies in Second Language Acquisition*, *26*(2), 173–199. doi:10.1017/S0272263104262027

Serrano, R., Llanes, À., & Tragant, E. (2011). Analyzing the effect of context of second language learning: Domestic intensive and semi-intensive courses vs. study abroad in Europe. *System*, *39*(2), 133–143. doi:10.1016/j.system.2011.05.002

Smolcic, E. (2013). Opening up to the world? Developing interculturality in an international field experience for ESL teachers. In C. Kinginger (Ed.), *Social and cultural aspects of language learning in study abroad* (pp. 75–100). Amsterdam: John Benjamins. doi:10.1075/lllt.37.04smo

Smolcic, E., & Katunich, J. (2017). Teachers crossing borders: A review of the research into immersion field experience for teachers. *Teaching and Teacher Education, 62*, 47–59. doi:10.1016/j.tate.2016.11.002

Sperling, I. (2016). *Intercultural learning during teaching practices abroad.* Unpublished manuscript.

Teichler, U. (1997). *The ERASMUS experience. Major findings of the ERASMUS evaluation research.* Luxembourg: Office for Official Publications of the European Communities.

Towell, R., Hawkins, R., & Bazergui, N. (1996). The development of fluency in advanced learners of French. *Applied Linguistics, 17*(1), 84–119. doi:10.1093/applin/17.1.84

Tusting, K., Crawshaw, R., & Callen, B. (2002). 'I know, 'cos I was there': How residence abroad students use personal experience to legitimate cultural generalizations. *Discourse and Society, 13*(5), 651-674. doi: 1177/0957926502013005278

Vande Berg, M. (2007). Intervening in the learning of US students abroad. *Journal of Studies in International Education, 11*(3-4), 392–399. doi:10.1177/1028315307303924

Vande Berg, M., Paige, R. M., & Lou, K. H. (2012). *Student learning abroad: What our students are learning, what they're not, and what we can do about it.* Herndon: Stylus Publisher.

Veenman, S. (1984). Perceived problems of beginning teachers. *Review of Educational Research, 54*(2), 143–178. doi:10.3102/00346543054002143

Vogt, K., & Heinz, B. (2004). Interkulturelle Kompetenz medial vermitteln – Ergebnisse einer deutsch-amerikanischen Untersuchung [Imparting intercultural competence using digital media – results of a German-American study]. In U. Kleinberger Günter & F. Wagner (Eds.), *Neue Medien – Neue Kompetenzen* [New media – new competencies?] (pp. 179–216). Bern: Peter Lang.

Wanner, D. (2009). Study abroad and language: From maximal to realistic models. In R. Lewin (Ed.), *The handbook of practice and research in study abroad: Higher education and the quest for global citizenship* (pp. 81–98). New York, NY: Routledge.

Welch Borden, A. (2007). The impact of service-learning on ethnocentrism in an intercultural communication course. *Journal of Experiential Education, 30*(2), 171–183. doi:10.1177/105382590703000206

Towards a Culturally Reflective Practitioner

Wolcott, T. (2013). An American in Paris: Myth, desire, and subjectivity in one student's account of study abroad in France. In C. Kinginger (Ed.), *Social and cultural aspects of language learning in study abroad* (pp. 127–153). Amsterdam: John Benjamins. doi:10.1075/lllt.37.06wol

Yang, M., Webster, B., & Prosser, M. (2011). Travelling a thousand miles: Hong Kong Chinese students' study abroad experience. *International Journal of Intercultural Relations, 35*(1), 69–78. doi:10.1016/j.ijintrel.2010.09.010

APPENDIX 1: GUIDING QUESTIONS

Expectations:

Please include answers to the following questions (you may but need not answer all of them):

- How do you feel about working with pupils of this age/skill level?
- How do you feel about your level of English proficiency?
- In what ways would you like to improve in terms of teaching skills?
- What are you most looking forward to in this teaching practice?
- What are you most worried about in this teaching practice?
- What do you expect from teaching practice in Wales/Dublin?
- What do you hope your relationship to the pupils will be like (will you try to be a coach, a manager, a lecturer/instructor ...)? How will you achieve this?
- What is the role of Wales, a place abroad in a different educational system, in it?

School Environment:

Please refer to your immediate school environment only and note the details that you have observed so far. This week's report is meant to make you reflect on the daily school routine at your school.

- What has struck you as worth adopting yourself as part of your own teaching or communicating with pupils?
- What have you noticed is different?
- What would you rather not take over?

Differences in Everyday Life:

- Have you have detected any differences in terms of everyday life compared to Germany?
- If so, what they are and how did you notice them?

Towards a Culturally Reflective Practitioner

School Spirit:

- Do you have a school uniform at your school?
- Do you think there is more of a school spirit in comparison to German schools?
- What role does discipline play?
- Would you say that the teachers are different in their approach to pupils e.g., when it comes to correcting them, as regards independent learning, peer-assessment etc.?

Cultural Identity:

I would like you to focus on cultural identity this week. I would like to ask you to reflect on the role of Welshness/Irishness as a part of people's cultural identity.

- Are there any regional differences within Wales/Ireland that you have detected?
- Have you come across people who are decidedly Welsh/Irishness (or who consider themselves as such)?
- How does that become obvious?
- Is there a big difference between the Welsh/Irish people you have got to know and other people from the UK?

Linguistic Identity/Bilingualism:

- Are there any regional differences as far as you can see?
- Do people identify with Welsh/Gaelic as their 'national' language?
- Do you think Wales/Ireland is a bilingual country? Why (not)?
- Do young people think differently than older people regarding this topic?
- How much Welsh/Gaelic do people (pupils included) speak in general and outside of their institutional contexts?
- What do people in Wales/Ireland think about Welsh/Gaelic as a language?
- What importance do they attach to it?
- Where and in what contexts do you come across Welsh/Gaelic at school and in your everyday lives?

Otherness:

- As you are in the role of 'the other' i.e., from a different country, how does this position make you feel?
- How do other people approach you knowing that you are 'different' from them?
- How do you perceive things that are different from your environment at home? And, would you say there is a difference in which you perceive things, in which you approach people etc. that you (would) do differently in your environment in Germany?

Preliminary Outcomes and Goal-Setting for Remainder of Teaching Practice:

This week I would like you to relate what your general duties at your school.

- Do you substitute sick teachers?
- Have you taken part in general school life e.g., school fêtes, open days or trips?
- What activities would you still like to take part in during the remainder of your time in Wales/Ireland?
- What subjects/projects/lessons do you teach, what clubs do you run?
- What would you say has helped you to develop and to learn most so far?
- Which of the activities did you like best?

Stereotypes:

During this week, I would like you to reflect on stereotypes (call it tongue-in-cheek, if you like). Could you now sketch the 'typical' Welshman/Irishman/Englishman/ Welsh/Irish student/housewife etc. (knowing, of course, that there is no such thing).

- Is there really a grain of truth, as people like to say, about stereotypes in your view?
- Would you now be able to recognize a German person if you saw him/her on the basis of certain characteristics (e.g., Birkenstocks a couple of years ago)?

Towards a Culturally Reflective Practitioner

Final Report:

You are asked to match your expectations with the outcomes and to reflect on how you have (or have not) achieved them. Here is a list of questions that you may refer to:

- Can you compare your worries to what happened afterwards?
- How do you now feel about working with pupils of this age/skill level?
- How do you now feel about your level of English proficiency?
- What did you most enjoy in this teaching practice?
- What linguistic/cultural skills have you developed most?
- What were you most worried about in this teaching practice?
- What were your expectations for the teaching practice in Wales and which ones were (not) met? Why?
- What were your roles and relationships with the pupils (a coach, a manager, a lecturer/instructor ...)?

Chapter 7
Development of an Enhanced Study Abroad Curriculum in Teacher Education

Yasemin Kırkgöz
Cukurova University, Turkey

ABSTRACT

This chapter describes the design of an enhanced innovative study abroad curriculum to be integrated into teacher education programs. The curriculum is based upon the results of in-depth interviews administered to teacher candidates and/or practicing teachers of English following their return from a study abroad program. It is designed to meet the needs of prospective study abroad student teachers of English and to address possible challenges that may result from their participation in such programs. The enhanced curriculum is comprised of 10 modules, each focusing on a different topic. Integrated into the enhanced curriculum are tasks and problem scenarios reflecting on the real experiences of the returned study abroad sojourners. It is expected that the curriculum will increase teacher educators' knowledge about the learning needs of prospective study abroad participants and enhance their awareness of the contribution(s) study abroad makes to create global citizens.

DOI: 10.4018/978-1-7998-1607-2.ch007

Copyright © 2020, IGI Global. Copying or distributing in print or electronic forms without written permission of IGI Global is prohibited.

INTRODUCTION

Higher Education Institutions (HEIs) have begun to recognize the need to equip students with the skills necessary to cope with the complexities of an increasingly globalized world by implementing study abroad programs, a powerful educational tool for internationalizing the higher education (HE) curriculum. Over the last few decades, the world has seen an increasing number of students traveling abroad for study. The Organization for Economic Cooperation and Development (OECD) reports that international student mobility worldwide reached 3.7 million in 2011, representing a 75% increase since 2000 (OECD, 2011). As maintained by Taguchi and Collentine (2018), 'as internationalization efforts in educational contexts intensify around the world, the number of students who study outside their home country continues to rise' (p. 564).

As a result, an increasing number of preservice student teachers, as well as practicing teachers of foreign languages, have become interested in studying abroad. Study abroad programs, defined as education that occurs outside the participant's home country, take various forms. Forms of study abroad include direct enrollment programs, exchange programs, internships, service-learning programs, special international student programs, sponsored study abroad programs, and summer study abroad programs. These programs are influenced to a significant degree by learning goals.

Correspondingly, numerous researchers are investigating the advantages of studying abroad (e.g., Asaoka, 2009; Button et al., 2005; Dwyer, 2004a, Dwyer, 2004b; Skelly, 2009; Lassegard, 2013). Studies generally, tend to focus on the generalized benefits, which include increased competitiveness in the global job market, foreign language proficiency, and intercultural knowledge and skills (Anderson, et al., 2006; Dywer, 2004). Sutton and Rubin (2001) reported that study abroad students acquire more academic-based knowledge in the areas of world geography, cultural knowledge, and global interdependence compared to those without these experiences. Douglas and Jones-Rikkers (2001) suggested that the study abroad experience results in an increased level of 'world mindedness,' namely, the sense of belonging to humankind. Study abroad experiences expose students to different cultures, helping them to gain comprehensive understandings of global contexts and global citizenship (Linder & McGaha, 2013), facilitating 'the individuals' retaining intercultural understanding over a lifetime' (Dywer, 2004, p. 151). Study abroad is widely considered an important opportunity to learn 'intercultural competences' through the first-hand experience of another culture (Davies & Pike, 2009) and an appreciation for cultural differences.

The literature also suggests that students demonstrate more language fluency upon returning from an overseas sojourn (King & Raghuram, 2013), as well as higher proficiency in intercultural communication (Williams, 2005). Students who go abroad even for short periods consistently report returning with higher levels of confidence and self-efficacy in the foreign language, increased motivation for further study (Ingram, 2005), greater independence, and more maturity over the course of an international experience.

Despite the well-documented academic and personal benefits offered by the study abroad programs on the participants' personal development, cultural acquisition, and intercultural competence, the international education literature recognizes that merely sending students abroad remains quite insufficient in achieving the required learning outcomes. Employing multi-method study, Doyle et al. (2010) identified factors that inhibited or promoted the usage of international exchange programs among New Zealand students. Data collection involved student surveys from five New Zealand tertiary institutions, and interviews with students from the New Zealand outbound exchange. Potential benefits gained from studying overseas included exposure to a different cultures and languages, the chance to see whether they would like to live and work overseas, being able to include the experience on their CV, being immersed in another language, and the opportunity to study subjects not available in New Zealand. However, the study also identified other crucial factors needed such as cost, social, cultural, and linguistic capabilities one of the major obstacles.

In a recent state of the art article entitled 'language learning and study abroad', Isabelli-Garcia, Bown, Plews, and Dewey (2018) reviewed empirical studies on undergraduate language learners' experiences abroad during a time period of a year or less. The researchers also reviewed the role that study abroad plays in undergraduate language curricula. It is concluded that curricula, syllabi, pedagogical or teaching and learning approaches, specific course materials, receive little attention in most SA research, drawing out attention to the fact that research or scholarly reports that solely or primarily focus on curriculum and pedagogy for study abroad particularly with domestic curricula, are rare. It becomes essential, therefore, for HE institutions in many countries, including Turkey, to design a study abroad curriculum, particularly for undergraduate students prior to their overseas sojourns, which would establish academically relevant and meaningful study abroad experiences. It is the main objective of this study to fill in the gap of the study abroad literature.

STUDY ABROAD PROGRAMS IN THE TURKISH CONTEXT

Within the system of HEI in Turkey, study abroad programs play an integral part in realizing the globalization and internationalization goals of Turkish HEI. The growth in Turkish undergraduate students participating in study abroad programs has been steadily increasing with more students opting for a European country (as a study abroad destination as part of an Erasmus exchange program), the US (as work and travel destinations), and Europe and the US (for teaching assistantships). These sojourners are enrolled as regular students at partner universities, based on agreements that HEI maintain with academic institutions through such auspices as the Erasmus program. The study abroad programs can take different forms; the most prominent ones are described below:

Fulbright Program

The Fulbright Program, initiated in 1946 by Senator J. William Fulbright and sponsored by the US Department of State's Bureau of Educational and Cultural Affairs, is the US Government's flagship international exchange program. It aims to increase mutual understanding between the people of the US and the people of other countries. One component of the program, the Fulbright Foreign Language Teaching Assistant (FLTA), provides young teachers of English as a Foreign Language the opportunity to refine their teaching skills and broaden their knowledge of American cultures and customs while strengthening the instruction of teaching their native language, such as Turkish as a foreign language at colleges and universities in the US. A potential Turkish applicant to the program must have completed undergraduate education and must hold the equivalent of a Bachelor's degree. Fulbright operates on a yearly application cycle, which generally (but not in all cases) opens approximately 15 months before the anticipated start of the grant, with a deadline approximately 11 or 12 months before the grant's start date. Along with their studies, FLTAs teach language courses. A Turkish native speaker teacher of English may serve as an instructor of Turkish as a foreign language class (Fulbright, 2014).

Erasmus+ Exchange

In order to achieve its internationalization of HEI, Turkey signed the Bologna Declaration in 2001, undertaking to enact reforms via the framework of the Bologna process. Student and academic exchange and mobility are an important component of the internationalization process. Turkey participated in the mobility programs in accordance with the conditions articulated in the Bologna Agreement of 26 February 2002, between the European Community and the Republic of Turkey under the terms

Development of an Enhanced Study Abroad Curriculum in Teacher Education

and conditions set out in a Memorandum of Understanding. The Memorandum took effect on April 1, 2004. As a result, full Turkish participation and integration of EU programs was achieved starting at the end of 2005. Since then, Erasmus mobility programs have been operating in Turkish universities (YOK, 2019).

Following 2004, Turkish HEIs attempted to establish an Erasmus University Charter, which gave them full participatory rights in hosting and sending students and academic personnel to EU member countries. Thus, any student studying at an HEI that is awarded the Erasmus Charter and has an agreement with a European university became eligible to apply for Erasmus. The mobility is carried out in the framework of prior inter-institutional agreements between the sending and receiving institutions. Prospective applicants must have completed at least one semester of their academic program at the time of application.

Students participating in the Erasmus program are exempt from tuition at the host university abroad where they spend their semester or a year. In addition, they are eligible for the Erasmus student mobility grant provided by the European Commission through the Turkish National Agency. All other related expenses, including travel expenses between Turkey and the host country, living expenses, and accommodation are incumbent upon the student. Participation in the Erasmus program can last a maximum of 12 months. As host universities may require an academic transcript to evaluate candidates' academic standing in the semester(s) before they actually begin the Erasmus program, candidates must demonstrate a good academic record, and are advised to avoid receiving failing grades prior to their participation in the program. Concerning selection criteria, Turkish National Agency regulations state that 50% of grade point average (GPA) and 50% of English language test scores are taken into account in identifying prospective Erasmus students.

Since 2004, 22,516 Turkish students have been able to study at universities across the EU. Although it is difficult to ascertain the number of study abroad students in various programs in Turkey, 3.7 million post-secondary students were said to be enrolled outside their country of citizenship as of 2009. According to the same source, Germany ranks first as the most desirable destination for Turkish students interested in Erasmus study abroad programs, followed by Poland, the Netherlands, France, and Italy. Çukurova University, where the present study has been conducted, is ranked among the 'Top Five' Turkish universities with the highest number of outbound Erasmus students (Erasmus, 2015).

Applicants must be registered as full-degree students at the time of their application. To be eligible to apply for the Erasmus program, undergraduate students need to maintain at least a 2.5 GPA (4.0 scale) and graduate students need to have at least a 3.0 GPA. Students participate in the Erasmus program during their same level of study (undergraduate students can participate in the program during their undergraduate studies, Master's students can participate in the program during their

Development of an Enhanced Study Abroad Curriculum in Teacher Education

Master's studies, PhD students can participate in the program during their PhD studies). Applicants are responsible for a relevant language proficiency document during their application to the host university (TOEFL/IELTS for English-language universities).

Work and Travel

This is another international exchange program arranged with the US. A full-time university student aged 18-30 can participate in the program in the US for work and travel for a period of four months during summer vacations. Students can plan their journey to their future place of work through specialized companies, which represent student interests by organizing vacancies and preparing the necessary documents. Such companies also register students in the program and help provide the necessary information (Work and Travel, 2015).

International Exchange Offices

Study abroad programs, in Turkey and many other countries, are facilitated by the International Exchange Offices (often known as the Study Abroad Office) of each university, an independent agency, or through direct application to the foreign HEI, according to the nature of the program. The application process can be lengthy, involving voluminous paperwork. Costs for programs vary, and various types of programs are available. Universities engaged in study abroad programs have international exchange offices that are responsible for addressing students' needs. To deal specifically with Erasmus and other study abroad programs, international offices are established in universities (YOK, 2004). These offices review student applications, select participants, and conduct pre-departure orientations. Students earn direct credit for coursework completed. Exchange programs can take place during one academic term or a whole year. The office is also responsible for carrying out the procedures for the Fulbright FLTA program. In contrast to the previous two programs, the application for work and travel is performed by specialized organizations that act as representatives in the interests of student candidates and are engaged in organizing the vacancies and preparing relevant documentation.

During the first step of the Erasmus program, the interested student can apply to the international office and/or Erasmus office of his/her home institution to receive advice concerning study abroad opportunities and application procedures, as well as information about Erasmus + EU grants. Student selection, placement, and registration at the partner institution are conducted with the help of the university's international office. Students may be awarded an Erasmus + EU grant to help cover the travel and subsistence costs incurred in connection with their study abroad period. Erasmus students—whether or not they receive an Erasmus+ EU grant—are exempt from paying fees for tuition, registration, and examinations, and may gain access to laboratory and library facilities at the host institution during the study abroad period.

Although study abroad curriculum integration has been initiated in the undergraduate degree programs in many countries, there is yet to be a single university in Turkey that offers a pre-study abroad curriculum, particularly in teacher education programs. The increasing number of Turkish preservice students and practicing teachers of English wishing to benefit from such programs warrants the need to explore this particular area of study with a view to developing a comprehensive Study Abroad Curriculum to be integrated in foreign language teacher education programs. This study aims to achieve this objective in order to enhance current teacher education programs.

THE PRESENT STUDY

The study abroad curriculum presented in this study is the enriched version of the previous curriculum (see Kırkgöz, 2016). The study is in two parts. Part one describes needs analysis which was conducted with a group of returned study abroad completers to find out their experiences, the effects of study abroad on the participants in terms of skills and knowledge gained through their sojourns. This part of the study is intended to give insights into designing the Study Abroad Curriculum. Part two of the study presents the framework of the innovative, multifaceted and enhanced model of a study abroad curriculum to be implemented in teacher education programs in Turkey and beyond, based on the outcomes resulting from Part One of the study. In this enhanced curriculum model, additional real-life problems encountered by study abroad participants are incorporated to be resolved by the prospective study abroad sojourners to raise their awareness towards potential challenges they are likely to experience so that they could gain appropriate coping strategies in advance.

Needs Analysis With Study Abroad Completers

An interview was administered to 30 teacher candidates who had studied abroad. The respondents were asked to reflect upon their experiences in terms of the program benefits and challenges that they experienced, and provide suggestions to be integrated into the design of an effective and innovative study abroad curriculum for prospective teachers of English planning to participate in such programs. The interview respondents were all native speakers of Turkish.

Development of an Enhanced Study Abroad Curriculum in Teacher Education

Those who responded to the interview had participated in one of the previously mentioned study abroad programs: Work and Travel to the US (n = 5), Teaching Assistantship to the UK (n = 5), and to an EU country on an Erasmus exchange program (n = 20). Five participants who had taken part in Work and Travel in the US spent four summer months working mainly in hotels and restaurants. Five participants were involved in teaching assistantships, teaching English in the UK and as English language teachers on an Erasmus exchange program. The remaining 20 undergraduate student teachers of English enrolled in various universities in Europe through the Erasmus exchange program. Interview questions included:

- *In which kind of a study abroad program did you participate?*
- *What was the aim of the program?*
- *Please describe the program in detail.*
- *What benefits did you gain from the study abroad program?*
- *Did you experience any challenges? If so, please explain what they were?*
- *What would you suggest to your peers who are planning to go on a study abroad program?*

Table 1, above, presents the results of interview findings. Content analysis of the responses to in-depth interviews conducted with the participants indicated a high level of satisfaction with the study abroad programs. Participants expressed the potential impact of such programs, reporting that each program was helpful for improving their English language (n = 28) and intercultural communication skills (n = 25), gaining an awareness and appreciation of the host country and culture, hence broadening their horizons. With respect to cultural understanding, most respondents indicated that they had learned a considerable amount about the culture and lifestyle of the host country they visited (n = 24) and that they had gained greater knowledge

Table 1. Benefits of study abroad

Benefits	Number
Improving foreign language ability	28
Improving intercultural communication skills	25
Gaining an appreciation of host country and culture	24
Gaining greater knowledge and experience in one's academic discipline	22
Enhancing problem solving skills	21
Gaining flexibility to adapt to new situation	18
Increasing tolerance for cultural differences	16
Total responses	**154**

and experience in their academic discipline (n = 22). Additionally, participants reported that studying abroad had enabled them to make friendships with students from around the country and the world, enhanced their problem solving skills (n = 21), given them greater flexibility, increased their capacity to adapt to new situations and places (n = 18), and increased their tolerance for cultural differences (n = 16). On the affective dimension, they indicated growth in their maturity, self-confidence and sense of independence. The results confirm findings of other researchers on improvements that can be obtained from study abroad programs, specifically in terms of language (e.g., DeKeyser, 1991), cultural knowledge, and awareness (Asaoka, 2009; Marriott, 1993). Despite the benefits, returning study abroad students also expressed challenges to be described in the following section.

Study Abroad Challenges

Studying abroad, though providing a rewarding experience in general, also created difficulties and challenges. These ranged from cost, education, cultural adjustment, housing, language, and mental health (as illustrated in Table 2).

Cost

Cost was cited as the number one reason students experienced difficulty abroad (n = 30). Although study abroad certainly is not cheap, it was found rather cost-prohibitive in some locations, such as Belgium, London, and Spain. The cost of studying abroad varied greatly depending on the location of the program, as indicated below by one participant who went to Belgium on an Erasmus exchange program, '*Everything was so expensive in Belgium and I had to adapt my spending accordingly*'. A similar comment was made by the following participant who spent six months in Spain on

Table 2. Challenges of study abroad

Challenges	Number
Cost	30
Education	28
Cultural adjustment	26
Housing	25
Language	24
Emotional issues	20
Total responses	**153**

Development of an Enhanced Study Abroad Curriculum in Teacher Education

a teacher assistant program, '*My accommodation rent was very high in Spain and I had financial problems*'.

Education

Several sojourners found the academic system, particularly the curriculum, challenging and slightly different from what they experienced in Turkey, and reported that it took considerable time to adapt to the experience (n = 28). The following participant, for instance, found the use of Moodle rather difficult to get accustomed to:

The university in which I was an Erasmus student, Moodle system operated to deliver information to students and the students were responsible for the visual and audio materials available in Moodle. The teacher was using the Moodle system actively giving clear explanations about what to do and what his/her expectations were. In response to that, the students had to sign in and send messages which affirm that they knew what to do for the classes. As I was not used to that system, it took me quite some time to get accustomed to [it].

Another difficulty was related to the credit transfer system, as reported by the following Erasmus exchange student who went to Poland:

I had difficulty in completing ECTS credits. Some of the lessons were taught in Polish so when I went to Poland, I had to change some of my lessons and it was difficult to cope with.

Another participant found a matching course difficult, as stated in the interview below '*I had difficulty to find courses which suit Çukurova University*'. A further difficulty stemmed from the students' unfamiliarity with the education system of the host university and the classroom pedagogy:

I had no information about how the courses would be conducted, to what extent I would be required to attend the classes. Also, it was not possible for me to take all the courses that I would like to because most of the classes were conducted via their native language though it was an ELT department. Thus, this was a source of dissatisfaction for me as I did not (and I guess I did not have to) know Spanish.

A teaching assistant in London expressed discrepancies between the education systems of Turkey and the UK in terms of thinking critically and writing more in an academic style, as expressed in the following interview:

The biggest difficulty for me was facing the different education system. The system in the UK requires more critical thinking which was quite new to me. The second difficulty was writing in English. I wasn't good at writing essays. I needed to learn more complex structures.

A similar difficulty was experienced by the following Erasmus student in Spain in relation to evaluation criteria:

Closely related to the educational system in Spain, grading system in the university I visited also caused some difficulties for me. I was not quite sure about what criteria would be taken into consideration for the evaluation of performance, what would bring in extra points and what would be taken as weakness.

Cultural Adjustment

Adjusting to cross-cultural differences, food, and lifestyle appeared to have the next most wide-ranging impact (n = 26). Participants' elation at the novelty of the destination was often 'overwhelmed by distress caused by structural adjustments, typical of the initial stages of settling-in' (Tange, 2005, p. 5). Routine tasks, carried out almost thoughtlessly in a familiar environment, assume disturbing dimensions of complexity in the host culture, as stated by the participants below:

The very first challenge for me was about adaptation to the culture. Every country has peculiar traditions and lifestyle of their own. It took some time to adapt to the lifestyle in Spain though it had some basic characteristic with Turkish culture. A very good example would be the siesta break, during which almost no store was open and nobody would be on the streets. I had difficulty in getting my needs met. This was hard to get used to.

Cultural diversity was deeply felt by those who went to the US, either through the Work and Travel program or for the purpose of FLTA, as expressed below by two participants:

The first thing I came across was the cultural diversity. America is a vast country and there are people from all over the World. Therefore, it takes a while to orient yourself into their culture or at least to form a common culture with this people. Another difficulty that I faced was the food. Although it may seem a small problem, it was one of the biggest problems that I faced. In one month's time, I lost nearly 12 kilos. I mean it could cause me a health problem before I sorted this problem out by cooking for myself.

Development of an Enhanced Study Abroad Curriculum in Teacher Education

The initial cultural adjustment of the participants is facilitated by the degree to which the participant established social networks in the host culture. In addition, participants stated that they were able to overcome this particular challenge by watching a video that enabled them to identify historical and geographical landmarks of the host country.

Housing

Housing was the next most frequent challenge (n = 25). Many students complained of the insufficient arrangements made by the international exchange office. The following interview extract expresses the opinion of many sojourners:

I had accommodation problems. Because the university there didn't have a dormitory, I had to find a flat. A better and more comprehensive accommodation arrangement could be done between the international offices of the two countries. In this way, Exchange students don't have to worry about it.

Finding an appropriate accommodation was rather difficult for many participants, and they stated that they had spent considerable time during the process.

Language

Several participants (n = 24) stated that they had communication problems, as they did not know the language of the host county, as reported below:

As misunderstood by a lot of Turkish people who have never visited an Eastern European country, not everybody has sophisticated language skills in those countries, although the number of people who can speak a second or a foreign language is a lot more than that in Turkey. Before the departure date, I picked up some necessary vocabulary such as numbers and some immediate expressions to use such as self-introduction, or asking for help. Young people are able to speak at least one foreign language, but the elderly who run markets and shops are unable to understand any language but Czech - and the elderly population is a lot higher than that of Turkey.

Another language-related problem experienced by some students was concerned with the higher level of proficiency in English of the students in the host country. This is illustrated below by a participant who went to Germany on an Erasmus exchange program:

209

German students' English level was very high in the first month. I couldn't understand what they tried to teach.

Similar language problems were expressed by other participants; this time in relation to different varieties of English. This is stated explicitly by the following participant:

Even though I studied in a private high school which provided an intensive English language instruction as a foreign language from primary to high school and on top of that, a-four-year of undergraduate study on teaching English as a foreign language, I still encountered some language barrier problems for the first few months. For example, I had difficulty in understanding some people's strong local accents. In Turkey, I was taught mostly standard British English. However, in London where I did my Master's and PhD degrees, I faced different versions of Englishes. It took me some time to adjust my ears in their tunes in terms of comprehension. Moreover, there are local vocabularies which I hadn't heard earlier for example, in the first week, I jotted down in my diary that I picked up words such as top up, terminate bus/train and jolly.

Emotional Issues

Many sojourners (n = 20) stated that, all in all, anybody who travels abroad for a long period should be prepared to encounter some emotional issues, as expressed below by the following participant:

To elucidate affective factors, I felt homesick in the first year. I was calling my parents twice in a day. However, I met such a nice group of friends at the university and I started feeling less homesick after that.

Despite all the challenges experienced, the participants strongly encouraged their peers to take the initiative to go along and enjoy the international experience no matter what challenges they may encounter. In fact, universities have international exchange offices that provide general briefings about Erasmus, which the participants found admirable; yet, considering the challenges the participants in this study faced, they suggested that a more comprehensive orientation be offered to prospective study abroad candidates.

Based upon the outcomes of the interviews, the Study Abroad Curriculum, to be presented in the following section, is designed to meet the needs of prospective study abroad student teachers of English, and to offer them experiential learning opportunities by involving them in realistic scenarios similar to those they are likely

Development of an Enhanced Study Abroad Curriculum in Teacher Education

to encounter in their study abroad destinations. Given the role and importance of study abroad in Turkish HE and the challenges experienced by the returning study abroad participants, it becomes crucial to integrate a study abroad curriculum into current teacher preparation programs in order to prepare prospective candidates in advance for their study abroad experiences.

DESIGN AND IMPLEMENTATION OF THE STUDY ABROAD CURRICULUM

Although the importance of an international experience cannot be underestimated, in many cases there is a lack of integration between the experience and the educational value that can be derived from it. Experiential learning is a pedagogy that is significant in transforming experience through a critical analysis of that activity into a worthwhile academic experience to maximize intentional learning (Montrose, 2002). In the present pre-study abroad curriculum, experiential learning provides a foundation that enhances and supports learning from experience.

Brewer and Cunningham (2009) addressed the central question of how colleges and universities can take the potential of study abroad and integrate what students are learning and experiencing abroad into the wider curriculum on the home campus. They suggest presenting a wide range of strategies aimed at effectively integrating the benefits of time spent abroad with developments in the home campus curriculum. Drawing on a wealth of study abroad experiences, they recommend intentional integration of students' educational and personal experiences abroad for transformational learning and development at home.

Following this suggestion, to promote experiential learning, the present curriculum brings together prospective study abroad students with students who have substantial study abroad experience and who had previously been asked to record their educational experiences, including various classroom settings, memorable trips etc. Former study abroad students were invited to recount their trip, including the residential situation, educational experience, some humorous events that had occurred, concrete experiences of the semester, and to reflect on meaningful key events in order to provide study abroad candidates with a broader sense about the system before leaving their countries. Additionally, the curriculum incorporates real problems based on the challenges encountered by the returned sojourners to be solved by the prospective candidates to give them useful strategies and hands-on experiential practice for transformational learning and personal development. Such case studies are presented below.

211

The curriculum is designed to help prospective Turkish study abroad teacher candidates develop skills and enable them to get the most out of their international experience. It also provides information about the study abroad process and the resources necessary to maximize their learning experience both during their time abroad and when they return home. Students are required to conduct research to tailor this class experience to fit their individual needs in relation to a chosen host culture. General intercultural communication techniques, vital in preparing students for the different views, values, and customs they may encounter, are integrated into class discussion. The students are required to fulfill the requirements addressed below.

Class Participation

Participation for the 10-week and weekly two-hour program is the first requirement. Participation in class discussion is an important and vital aspect of this course. Discussing and processing the weekly topics and understanding and contributing various points of view mark the beginning of the students' study abroad curriculum.

Initial Paper

This paper addresses the following questions in light of the introduction to the course: What are your expectations of this class? What are your personal goals for your time abroad? Given what you have read in the syllabus, how do you hope the course will assist you in achieving those goals? In what areas do you feel confident about your international experience? What apprehensions do you have?

Invitation of Former Study Abroad Students

For this assignment, a student with an international study abroad experience is invited. The candidate students conduct an interview with him/her, asking questions and taking notes to write an essay based on the interview. In addition, a panel is held with the returned study abroad students. Candidates write at least three questions on a note card for the panel to discuss.

International News Story

Each week, some students are assigned to come to class with an interesting news story from outside Turkey. This may be from the chosen host country or another. They provide the class with a summary of the event or story, the source of the news, why they thought it was worth sharing, and at least one question for the class to discuss related to the news item.

Group Movie Presentation

The class is divided into three or four groups. Each group is randomly assigned a relevant film to watch. They must then provide a 10-minute informal presentation to the class on how the film demonstrates some element of encountering another culture. As several of these films are familiar movies, the presentation is not a report on the movie's story but a critical look at how the film depicts topics discussed in class. Students are expected to show at least one extract from the film as an example during the presentation.

Reflection Paper

This chapter aims to address the following questions in light of each of the assignments they have completed for their coursework: *What were the most important ideas you encountered in this course? How will you apply them during your time abroad? What changes in your perspective on yourself, your host country, and Turkey have taken place? How and why has this occurred? What do you feel you still have left to learn before you go abroad? How will you go about learning more in that area(s)? What do you anticipate that you will only be able to learn by being in your host culture? What will you do to prepare yourself for feelings of discomfort so that you can work through them and continue your growth?*

The course incorporates a number of suggested readings, including articles, book chapters related to topics covered, and videos of study abroad destinations, as well as extracurricular activities.

DESCRIPTION OF THE ENHANCED STUDY ABROAD CURRICULUM

The curriculum comprises 10 modules which are described below:

Module 1: Increasing Awareness of the Study Abroad Program

Following a curriculum introduction, this module aims to increase prospective study abroad teacher candidates' knowledge and awareness about the study abroad programs. Candidates are informed of the mechanics and the procedures involved in applying for a particular program of the intended destination. They are provided information about the different study abroad programs discussed previously, the procedures involved in applying to each, and the role of the University's international office as a facilitating unit during the application process. In addition, they are asked to write *an initial paper* about their expectations from the intended study abroad program.

Module 2: Managing Money

This module is intended to familiarize candidates with financial issues in respective destinations, including banking, credit cards, food expenses (e.g., dining out), accommodation expenses, and exchange rates; overall, how to effectively budget for this adventure. For this module, teacher candidates are required to perform the following task:

- **Prepare a Sample Budget:** Candidates are given the cost of different items in their destination, and they are asked to prepare a weekly budget to help them with money management. A Former Study Abroad Student Interview is the final task of this module. For this task, teacher candidates with study abroad experience are invited into the class to share their experience with the prospective candidates.
- **Money-Related Problem:** The following is a real problem Özge (pseudonym) encountered on her first day visit to Krakow, Poland. Read it carefully and try to work out for a solution.

In the winter semester of the third year of my degree program, I had the opportunity to study abroad. The biggest problem started as soon as I arrived there. When I got off the bus, it was 2.00am in the morning, I had to exchange money! I hadn't exchanged my Turkish currency with Poland's currency before going there. Of course, Exchange Office was closed at midnight. The only solution was to exchange Money in an ATM. Finally, I felt relieved to find an ATM to exchange my Money. Soon I noticed that at ATM with lots of cutting money and taxes. I was able to draw 50 zloty and they cut 189 Turkish Lira. I had chosen to go to Krakow in Poland as it was one of the cheapest countries in Europe. However, what I experienced on the first day disappointed me a lot.

Module 3: Housing

The candidates are given information about different types of housing including university residence halls, university apartments, the home stay option, hotels, and so on. In addition, they are given information about the cost of living, meals, and personal expenses. For this module, teacher candidates are required to perform the following task:

Development of an Enhanced Study Abroad Curriculum in Teacher Education

- **Make Housing Arrangements:** Students are grouped according to different study abroad destinations. They are asked to look at the price, proximity to the university, and facilities offered by different types of accommodations to make their housing arrangements. The module ends with a Former Study Abroad Student Roundtable Discussion lasting 50 minutes.

Module 4: Traveling

The ability to travel and familiarity with different means of transportation is crucial in living abroad. Information about traveling and means of transportation are provided to help candidates plan their own excursions. For this module, teacher candidates are required to perform the following task:

- **On-the-Ground Travel Planning:** Candidates are grouped, and each one is given a map of the city they are planning to visit. They are asked to use different means of transportations to travel to their identified destination. One group is asked to navigate the train system and purchase tickets, and the other groups carry out the same task using different means of transportation. The module ends with a 50-minute Interview with Former Study Abroad Students.
- **Travel-Related Problem:** The following is a problem Seval (pseudonym) encountered travelling on an intercity bus in Poland. Read it carefully and try to offer a solution in your small group.

Ticket system on buses is vastly different from Turkey's ticket system. In Turkey we use a transportation card whereas in Poland individuals purchase a ticket on the bus. One day, I purchased a ticket, but I had forgotten to validate it. I got on the bus around 3 a.m. in the morning. I bought my ticket, and to my surprise the ticket conductor got on the bus and switched off the ticket machines. They disregarded the tickets everyone had and claimed they were no longer valid for that time. To add to this, they also fined me with 125 zloty. It was a nightmare and one of the worst experiences I had in Poland.

Module 5: Education

This module gives comprehensive information about the teacher education system and classroom practices in different destinations in order to facilitate candidates' early experiences. This will comprise course requirements, credit transfer, assessment requirements, critical thinking, writing exercises, etc. Use of technology in the lesson achieves alignment between the candidates' study abroad offerings and the

215

contents of the home curriculum. A network is established for study abroad students to facilitate communication between the former and future students, thus providing a bridge in knowledge. For this module, teacher candidates are required to perform the following task:

- **Understanding Academic Lectures in Different Cultural Contexts:** In this scenario student's work on listening competencies regarding lectures and seminars. For example, you are an Erasmus student studying one semester at the Bremen University. Although the lectures are given in English, the lecturer sometimes code switches into German to clarify the subject, which creates a problem for you; therefore, you are interested in improving your understanding of German. You have applied to attend the multilingual tutorial program, where you are supported by a student- tutor. This program involves self-directed learning in peer groups with tutor advice and a portfolio for independent learning. As the final task of this module, a 50-minute panel discussion on education in different destinations is organized with the returned study abroad students.

Module 6: Culture Learning—How We Perceive Ourselves and Others

Developing an ability to make correct attributions about the cultural values, beliefs, behaviors, and norms of the destination is important to minimize the potential for miscommunication. This module aims to increase candidates' knowledge of culture-specific modes of interaction, which will allow them to adjust to local norms and be tolerant of different cultures. In this module, teacher candidates are given various reading texts related to the culture of their study abroad destination to familiarize them with cultural issues and to help them become aware of the adjustment cycle of their study abroad destination. In addition, the following scenario relates to culture shock to help them prepare for this likely process:

In this scenario, you will talk to someone who has been immersed in another culture to learn if she or he experienced culture shock. Then, you will analyze that experience using the three-phase model of culture shock (disorientation, dissociation, reconnection) described in your reading of the assigned article.

The assignment includes the following stages:

Stage 1: As the first step, seek out someone who has lived for at least four months in a country with a culture different from his/her own.

Stage 2: Conduct a biographical interview with this informant. The interview progresses through three stages:

216

Development of an Enhanced Study Abroad Curriculum in Teacher Education

- **Build a Chronology:** Ask your informant to describe the basic facts of the adventure. Ask, where were you? When? Doing what?; With whom?; and Why? Take notes. From this broad beginning stage, establish a rough chronology of events for the next stage of the interview.

- **Explore for Symptoms:** Explain that you are particularly interested in the problems of adjustment to the other culture. Working with your chronology, ask questions similar to these, exploring for 'symptoms' of culture shock, its causes, and ways the informant moved toward reconnection. The following questions are stated so as not to force the informant to think in unfamiliar anthropological terms.
  - Did you begin to think that some aspects of your host's culture were better than yours?
  - Did you have any trouble or strong feelings when you rejoined your own culture?
  - Did you pick up any of your host's attitudes toward other cultures?
  - How did the host people's ways seem to you early in your stay?
  - How did you deal with those feelings?
  - How did your views of the host people's ways change? Why?
  - Were there certain times during your stay when this was most intense?
  - What depressed you, made you angry, or made you homesick?
  - What situations or events frightened or annoyed you?

- **Address Culture Shock Directly:** Toward the end of the interview, become explicit now about your interest, asking your informant to help you think about the travel, anthropologically saying, 'I'm trying to discover whether you felt culture shock; when, why, and how you expressed it; and how you got over it—if you think you did'.

Stage 3: Now, analyze your notes to look for a pattern that may resemble the three-stage process of culture shock. What is the evidence for a stage of disorientation?

- *How did the informant perceive the host culture?*
- *If the informant did not experience culture shock, why not?*
- *What aspects of the host-guest cultural differences produced the disorientation?*
- *What attitudes and behaviors of dissociation did she or he develop in response?*
- *Which, if any, of the symptoms of culture shock did the informant exhibit?*

Development of an Enhanced Study Abroad Curriculum in Teacher Education

This module ends with two useful activities. First, a movie presentation of different cultural sites such as museums, art galleries, etc. Second, a panel discussion with study abroad students who had returned. The topic is our values and others' values.

Module 7: Turkish Culture, International Perspective, and Non-Verbal Communication

It is widely recognized that non-verbal communication or body language is an important aspect of how people communicate and that there are non-verbal communication differences between cultures. Hand and arm gestures, touch, and eye contact, or lack of it, are a few of the aspects of non-verbal communication that may vary significantly depending upon cultural background. This module, therefore, discusses the different ways to communicate without speaking, and explores the effect non-verbal communication may have on our relationships.

The main task the teacher candidates carry out is to explore how other cultures may view Turkey and the Turkish culture. This task is assigned as an out-of-class activity. Pairs of teacher candidates interview foreign students in the university to explore this issue. The scenario of this module is called 'Communication in the Local Language,' as illustrated below:

You are an Erasmus student in Poland, together with international and local students. You have little competence in the local language, which is not necessary for your studies. You wish to be able to understand e-mails and to write e-mails in different languages, especially in the local language in order to improve your contact with local people and colleagues and for better integration locally.

The problem scenarios and interviews are complemented with a movie presentation on the topic and readings on Cross Cultural Communication. The module ends with a panel discussion with the returned study abroad students on their experiences of how foreigners viewed Turkish culture and features of the non-verbal communication of the country sojourners visited.

Module 8: Health and Safety

To make study abroad students feel more secure about living abroad, this module specifically addresses the issues of health, safety, and security to ensure that teacher candidates are familiar with local health and safety regulations, and have adequately been trained in emergency issues, including who to contact if an emergency situation arises. This module includes problem scenarios on safety and health issues, followed by a movie presentation on a related topic.

Module 9: Affective Aspect

Living away from home is likely to cause different emotions, including homesickness, inadequacy, or a lack of confidence in approaching new situations, as revealed through the interview conducted with the former study abroad students. As suggested by the sojourners, candidates are told to anticipate possible problems that they may confront while in the host culture. They are also encouraged to apply different strategies, such as being flexible when faced with challenges and be willing to challenge one's ideas culturally, socially, academically, and personally to make adjustments. The students are helped to set clear goals and they are enabled to broaden their horizons in terms of how to approach an issue from multiple perspectives. In this module, potential problem scenarios are given to potential candidates. This is followed with a panel discussion with the returned study abroad students on how they felt abroad.

Module 10: Course Evaluation

The aim of this module is to have an overall evaluation of the study abroad program. To achieve this aim, each student is asked to review the initial paper they wrote concerning their expectations from the course, and then write about the extent to which their expectations have been met. In addition, students are asked to write a reflection paper of the program. This curriculum has been piloted as an elective course with two course credits during the fall semester of the 2014-2015 academic year. It was attended by 28 prospective teacher candidates, which were most of the prospective study abroad candidates in the Teacher Education department of the University. The instruction was provided by the author of this chapter. The assignments were graded and contributed towards the student performance. Each module was developed to enhance understanding of the content.

FINDINGS AND DISCUSSION

The curriculum described above was piloted for a period of ten weeks, with two hours of weekly instruction. Participants were a group of prospective study abroad teacher candidates in the third year of the 'Teacher Education Program' at Çukurova University, a Turkish state university. The teacher candidates' evaluation of the program was obtained by conducting focus group interviews with them. The interview findings indicated that teacher candidates developed an overall understanding of the culture of the country that they were planning to visit. Subsequently, they increased their awareness of the study abroad program, and gained real and hands-on experience by engaging in problem-solving scenarios. The candidates agreed that scenarios were particularly beneficial in fostering their problem-solving skills. Integrating former students' study abroad experiences back into the curriculum once they returned home was also welcomed and was greatly appreciated by the study abroad candidates, as it gave them real-life experiences and useful and practical strategies that they could apply in their future academic studies.

A number of lessons have been learned during the process of piloting the curriculum tailored to teacher preparation. As the instructor, the first lesson I learned is the critical role of including scenarios similar to those that students are likely to encounter in their study abroad destination. Designing such scenarios significantly minimized the barriers that typically separate the classroom from the real world. By bringing real-world scenarios into the classroom, students' critical thinking was promoted, contributing to their problem-solving ability.

The next important lesson I learned is including interviews and round table discussions into the pro- gram, which made learning more interactive and communicative. The panelists touched on the logistical issues related to study abroad experiences and on a variety of lessons learned during their sojourns. Another lesson I learned is that in a program such as this one, the designers need to expose prospective candidates to information from multiple sources. In our design, we used video, reading texts, and problem scenarios, all of which enabled learners to gather information from multiple sources. This enriched the content of the program and increased learners' motivation. The final lesson I learned is inviting former study abroad students, which made the program experiential, allowing for critical reflection.

IMPLICATIONS AND CONCLUSION

This chapter has described the enhanced innovative *Study Abroad Curriculum* for the prospective study abroad teacher candidates in an English language teacher education program in Turkey. The curriculum is based upon the outcome of an interview, which was conducted with the returned teacher candidates and/or practicing teachers of English from a study abroad program. The aim of the interviews was to identify the challenges experienced by those sojourners and to give insights into the designing of a new curriculum. The most innovative aspect of the new curriculum is that it incorporates problem scenarios, which the prospective study abroad candidates are likely to encounter in their destinations, giving them experiential hands-on practice. It is expected that the curriculum will enhance teacher educators' awareness of the contribution(s) study abroad makes to create global citizens and well-educated teacher candidates, and increase teacher educators' knowledge about the learning needs of prospective study abroad student teachers.

Development of an Enhanced Study Abroad Curriculum in Teacher Education

Some recommendations in the planning and implementation of new programs should be considered in order to effectively improve the experiences for student teachers preparing to teach and/or study abroad. The main recommendation deriving from the present study relates to the planning phase of the program. In planning a study abroad program for teacher preparation, a preparation phase is important. The curriculum should be founded on the basis of the findings from needs analysis with past study abroad students with substantial experience in study abroad, as in the present program.

An increase in efforts to globalize and internationalize Turkish institutions of teacher education increases the need to infuse, integrate and implement pre-study abroad programs if the country is to develop teachers with the aspiration of becoming global citizens. *Are the prospective study abroad candidates equipped with the knowledge, skills, and dispositions required to cope with the challenges awaiting them in a foreign country?* This is the fundamental question that is faced by educators who prepare future teachers. Providing study abroad teacher candidates with preparation experience is the key ingredient if Turkey desires its future teachers to be culturally and globally literate to meet the challenges of the study abroad experience.

This is the first pre-study abroad preparation initiative embedded into an existing curriculum in Turkey. As such, it is expected that this chapter will offer insights into the use of study abroad curriculum in teacher education programs in Turkey and similar contexts. Following this initial design and piloting of the curriculum of the pre-study abroad program, the next step would be to embed it into the current teacher education curriculum. This chapter focused on preservice teacher education; however, it offers implications for the integration of this across the disciplines and in interdisciplinary settings, and will also be of interest to those working in university offices of international education, such as study abroad directors and program specialists.

REFERENCES

Anderson, P. H., Lawton, L., Rexeisen, R. J., & Hubbard, A. C. (2006). Short-term study abroad and intercultural sensitivity. *International Journal of Intercultural Relations, 30*(4), 457-469. doi: .ijintrel.2005.10.004 doi:10.1016/j

Asaoka, T., & Jun Yano. (2009). The contribution of 'study abroad' programs to Japanese internationalization. *Journal of Studies in International Education, 13*(2), 174–188. doi:10.1177/1028315308330848

Brewer, E., & Cunningham, K. (Eds.). (2009). *Integrating study abroad into the undergraduate curriculum: Theory and practice across the disciplines.* Sterling, VA: Stylus Books.

Button, L., Green, B., Tengnah, C., Johansson, I., & Baker, C. (2005). The impact of international placement on nurses' personal and professional lives: Literature review. *Journal of Advanced Nursing, 50*(3), 315–324. doi:10.1111/j.1365-2648.2005.03395.x PMID:15811111

Davies, I., & Pike, G. (2009). Global citizenship education: Challenges and possibilities. In R. Lewin (Ed.), *The handbook of practice and research in study abroad: Higher education and the quest for global citizenship* (pp. 49–60). New York, NY: Routledge.

DeKeyser, R. (1991). Foreign language development during a semester abroad. In B. F. Freed (Ed.), *Foreign language acquisition research and the classroom* (pp. 104–119). Lexington, MA: DC Heath & Company.

Douglas, C., & Jones-Rikkers, C. (2001). Study abroad programmes and American students' world-mindedness. *Journal of Teaching in International Business, 13*(1), 55–65. doi:10.1300/J066v13n01_04

Doyle, S., Gendall, P., Meyer, L. H., Hoek, J., Tait, C., McKenzie, L., & Loorparg, A. (2010). An investigation of factors associated with student participation in study abroad. *Journal of Studies in International Education, 14*(5), 471–490. doi:10.1177/1028315309336032

Dwyer, M. M. (2004a). The impact of study abroad program duration. *The Interdisciplinary Journal of Study Abroad, 10*, 151–163.

Dwyer, M. M. (2004b). Charting the impact of studying abroad. *International Educator, 13*(1), 14–20.

Erasmus. (2015). *Study in Turkey.* Retrieved from http://www.studyinturkey.com/content/sub/exchange_programs.aspx

Fulbright. (2014). *Fulbright program history.* Retrieved from http://us.fulbrightonline.org/about_programhistory.html

Ingram, M. (2005). Recasting the foreign language requirement through study abroad: A cultural immersion program in Avignon. *Foreign Language Annals, 38*(2), 211-222. doi: .tb02486.x doi:10.1111/j.1944-9720.2005

Isabelli-Garcia, C., Bown, J., Plews, J. L., & Dewey, D. P. (2018). Language learning and study abroad. *Language Teaching, 51*(4), 439–484. doi:10.1017/S026144481800023X

King, R., & Raghuram, P. (2013). International student migration: Mapping the field and new research agendas. *Population Space and Place, 19*(2), 127–137. doi:10.1002/psp.1746

Kırkgöz, Y. (2016). Integrating study abroad curriculum in teacher education. In J. A. Rhodes & T. M. Milby (Eds.), *Advancing teacher education and curriculum development through study abroad programs* (pp. 177–197). Hershey, PA: IGI Global. doi:10.4018/978-1-4666-9672-3.ch010

Kurumu, Y. Ö. (YOK). (2019). *Bologna process: Ankara*. Retrieved from https://uluslararasi.yok.gov.tr/en/internationalisation/bologna

Lassegard, J. P. (2013). Student perspectives on international education: An examination into the decline of Japanese studying abroad. *Asia Pacific Journal of Education, 33*(4), 365-379. doi: 91.2013.807774 doi:10.1080/021887

Linder, S., & McGaha, J. (2013). Building on successes: Reflections from two approaches to study abroad for undergraduate. *The Educational FORUM and Graduate Students, 77*, 379–389.

Marriott, H. E. (1993). Acquiring sociolinguistic competence: Australian secondary students in Japan. *Journal of Asian Pacific Communication, 4*(4), 167–192.

OECD. (2011). *Education at a glance 2011: Highlights*. OECD Publishing. doi:10.1787/ eag_highlights-2011-

Skelly, J. M. (2009). Fostering engagement: The role of international education in the development of global civil society. In R. Lewin (Ed.), *The handbook of practice and research in study abroad: Higher education and the quest for global citizenship* (pp. 21–32). New York, NY: Routledge.

Sutton, R., & Rubin, D. L. (2001). The GLOSSARI project. *Frontiers: The Interdisciplinary Journal of Study Abroad, 10*, 65–82.

Taguchi, N., & Collentine, J. (2018). Language learning in a study abroad context: Research agenda. *Language Teaching, 51*(4), 553–566. doi:10.1017/S0261444818000265

Tange, H. (2005). In a cultural no man's land or, how long does culture shock last? *Journal of Intercultural Communication, 10*, 1–1.

Williams, T. R. (2005). Exploring the impact of study abroad on students' intercultural communication skills: Adaptability and sensitivity. *Journal of Studies in International Education, 9*(4), 356–371. doi:10.1177/1028315305277681

Appendix

Figure 1.

Figure 2.

Appendix

Figure 3.

Figure 4.

Appendix

Figure 5.

Figure 6.

Figure 7.

Figure 8.

Appendix

Figure 9.

Figure 10.

Figure 11.

Glossary

Academic Credit: A defined measure of academic accomplishment that is used to determine a student's progress toward a degree, a certificate, or other formal academic recognition. In the US, credit is most commonly counted as credit hours (or credits or units at some institutions) that are assigned to each course. Some institutions count courses rather than credit.

Accreditation: A process of reviewing a school's programs and academics to ensure that quality programs are delivered and meet established standards. The accreditation process, conducted by external reviewers, may include reviews of a school's mission, faculty qualifications, curricula, institutional self-evaluations, peer reviews, committee reviews, and suggestions for improvement. External reviewers and processes are determined through evaluation by recognized agencies (in the US) or the Ministry of Education (in many other countries).

Acculturation: Modification of a person's cultural identity due to adoption of and/or adaption to traits of other cultures. That is, the adjustment of an individual to a foreign culture. Applies to the process of acquiring a second culture, which is added to and mixed with the individual's first culture.

Acculturative Stress: A negative psychological reaction to the experiences of acculturation, often characterized by anxiety, depression, and a variety of psychosomatic problems.

Acute Care IHEs: Experiences that are completed primarily within a hospital setting. These programs range in duration and participants will often participate in hands-on care under the guidance of preceptors.

Advanced Pharmacy Practice Experiences (APPEs): Concentrated hands-on active learning opportunities where students are supervised by practicing pharmacists.

Glossary

Affiliated: These programs are administered by other 'host' institutions/organizations and approved by the 'home' institution. Students will receive support and services, and credits will be posted as resident credit. Students will also work directly with the affiliate.

Agent: An individual who is paid for their services to assist a foreign student in navigating through the application process and being admitted into a higher education institution.

Ambulatory Care IHEs: Experiences that are completed in clinics or community health settings. These programs consist primarily of shadowing opportunities or observerships under the direction of preceptors.

Competency: The cluster of skills, abilities, habits, character traits, and knowledge a person must have in order to perform effectively within a certain environment. Competencies are demonstrated through behaviors and can be developed though training and individual effort.

Contact Zone: The social spaces where disparate cultures meet, clash, and grapple with each other. The term invokes the spatial and temporal co-presence of subjects previously separated for geographic and historical reasons, and which now intersect.

Cultural Confusion: Disorientation and discomfort that an individual may experience when entering an unfamiliar cultural environment.

Cultural Frame of Reference: Network of values, norms, views, concepts etc. on the basis of which an individual perceives and interprets data, events or ideas, and on the basis of which actions are effectuated.

Cultural Immersion: A sojourner's engagement with and interaction in a host culture, with the goal of extensive involvement with host culture members.

Cultural Script: Representations of cultural norms which are widely held in a given society and which are reflected in language e.g., a sequence of expressions and behaviors in certain academic situations like lectures.

Culture: A set of discernible assumptions, attitudes, conceptualizations, and values possessed by members of a specific group that is considered important enough to be actively transmitted to the next generation through socialization and communication involving key symbols, narratives and stories, and a recalled past.

Glossary

Culture in Context: The aspects of culture that are immediately related to preservice teachers' school environments.

Culture of Learning: The norms, values and expectations of teachers and learners that influence classroom relationships and activities in a particular cultural setting.

Culture Shock/Transition Shock: The anxiety and feelings e.g., surprise, disorientation, confusion etc., one feels when coming into contact with an entirely different social environment, such as a different country. An uncomfortable feeling experienced by travelers to new countries whose culture, customs, and landscape are totally foreign from their own that usually passes after a few days. If left unchecked, severe culture shock may turn into depression. Upon returning home from an intense immersion, some travelers also suffer 'reverse' culture shock as they feel no one can understand or relate to what they have just experienced.

Emotional Resilience: The ability to quickly recover when situations go badly. Level of emotional resilience depends upon how good you feel about yourself, which will then determine the ease with which you recover when situations go wrong.

Empathy: The recognition and understanding of the states of mind of others, including beliefs, desires, and particularly emotions, without injecting one's own. The concept is often characterized as the ability to 'put oneself into another's shoes' or to identify with the feelings of the other person on that person's terms. Empathy relies on the ability to set aside temporarily one's own perception of the world and assume an alternative perspective.

Erasmus (European Community Action Scheme for the Mobility of University Students): A program of the Socrates II educational initiative of the European Commission that offers university students from more than 30 European countries the opportunity to study at other European institutions with which their institutions have established direct partnerships. Founded in 1987, it was incorporated into the broader Socrates educational program in 1995 and then into the new Socrates II program in 1999. University credits are transferred as universally recognized ECTS credits. Students, who are required to have completed their 1st Year of study, pay *home* university fees and not those of the *host* institution; most students receive financial grants from the Erasmus program to offset part of their expenses. Sojourns range from 3-12 months. Over 2,000 universities participate in this program.

Glossary

Erasmus+ Student Exchange: An exchange program that enables university students to study for part of their degree in another European HEI within the framework of the Erasmus+ Exchange program. For example, under the Erasmus+ exchange program, a Turkish student in a teacher education program can study in an EU member country for the period or one or two academic semesters provided he/she meets the requirements.

Field Study: Most time is spent living and working outdoors. Coursework often has a specific theme or topic and often involves activities such as data collection. Typically, students have little traditional classroom time, with the emphasis on experiential assignments.

Flexibility/Openness: The willingness to be receptive and enjoy the opportunity of being exposed to different ways of thinking and behavior of another culture.

Fulbright Foreign Language Teaching Assistant (FLTA): A program offered by the Fulbright Program in which the participant spends one year at an accredited institute of HE in the US. FLTAs are expected to teach a foreign language and they can also take some university courses. A Turkish native speaking English language teacher FLTA in the US would be expected to teach Turkish as a foreign language in an American institute of HE, organized by Fulbright.

Global Citizenship: The conscious recognition and response to the inter-connectedness, inter-dependence, and inter-reliance of all peoples of the world community, irrespective of their physical location or their ethnic, cultural, or national affiliation. It is predicated on a sense of beneficence, mutual responsibility, and a reciprocal duty of care towards the wellbeing of all others and for the commonly held world within which we live.

Globalization: The ongoing world-wide trend towards increased economic, financial, and trade integration across national boundaries. Globalization: (a) recognizes the need for a relaxation of exclusively nation-centered and self-serving policies and perspectives; (b) responds to a reconsideration of a world economy that is increasingly interconnected and interdependent; and (c) promotes the unimpeded flow of labor, goods, and services in ways that enhance the growth and development of the global community without unduly harming individual members of that community.

234

Glossary

Higher Education Institution (HEI): An entity established or recognized by the federal or a state/territory government to issue qualifications in the higher education sector. It may be a university, self-accrediting institution or non-self-accrediting institution.

Homestay: Private housing hosted by a local family that often includes a private or shared bedroom, meals, and laundry. Homestay experiences usually provide the greatest immersion in the host language and culture, giving students first-hand experience with family life in the host culture and the opportunity to use the host language in an informal setting. In many cases, the host family welcomes the student as a member of the family and provides a support network.

Homestay Visit: A short-term homestay e.g., weekend, for a student who is otherwise in another type of housing such as a residence hall or an apartment. In this context it is considered a strategy for cultural enrichment rather than a type of accommodation.

Intensive English Program (IEP): These programs provide nonnative English speakers with the skills, fluency, and confidence to communicate effectively. Full-time IEPs typically provide 15 or more hours of class instruction weekly.

Intercultural Communicative Competence: The ability to communicate effectively and appropriately in an L2 in intercultural situations.

International: Between or among nations or encompassing several nations. In addition, in the US the term is commonly used to refer to students, faculty, and visitors who are on temporary visas to be in the US.

International Education: (1) A field involved in facilitating and supporting the migration of students and scholars across geopolitical borders. Professionals involved in this field may be employees of educational institutions, government agencies, or independent program and service providers. This may include, but is not limited to (on US campuses), support for matriculating and exchange students from countries outside the US, instruction in English as a second language (L2), international student recruitment, assessment of non-US HE credentials, student services for postgraduate research students and fellows, facilitation of education

Glossary

abroad for US students, and (outside the US) support and services for visiting US students. And, (2) The knowledge and skills resulting from conducting a portion of one's education in another country. As a more general term, this definition applies to international activity that occurs at any level of education i.e., K-12, undergraduate or postgraduate.

International Educational Exchange: The migration of students (secondary, undergraduate, postgraduate) and scholars between educational institutions in different countries. A narrower usage of the term 'exchange' refers to reciprocal agreements that allow students, faculty or staff to spend a specified period of time at institutional partners of their home institutions.

International Exchange Office: An office that is affiliated with universities that are involved in international exchange programs. Among its numerous functions are establishing academic cooperation with colleges and universities abroad and giving the necessary assistance to outgoing students and academic staff in their selection, placement, and registration at the partner institutions.

International Experience: Any opportunity, credit-bearing or non-credit-bearing, undertaken by a student outside his or her home country.

International Program: (1) any university/college activity, credit-bearing or non-credit-bearing, with an international dimension e.g., non-credit-bearing study tour, credit-bearing study abroad program; (2) an education abroad program; and (3) an administrative and/or academic unit responsible for global efforts e.g., Office of International Programs.

Internationalization at Home: Efforts to internationalize a university's home campus so that its students are exposed to international learning without leaving the home campus.

Internationalizing the Curriculum: A movement to incorporate international content throughout an educational institution's curriculum.

Internship Abroad: A work abroad placement, usually connoting working with professionals, with a primary purpose that is educational. Essentially synonymous with the terms Practicum and Practical Training (the latter term also describes a

236

Glossary

status for international students pursuing an internship in the US). An internship program may be offered for the experience in its own right, or it may be combined with coursework and offered within the context of a study abroad program for academic credit. An internship may be paid or unpaid.

L2 Socialization: The process by which novices in an unfamiliar linguistic and cultural context gain intercultural communicative competence by acquiring linguistic conventions, sociopragmatic norms, cultural scripts, and other behaviors that are associated with the new culture.

Language Confusion: The challenge of understanding and communicating in an L2 in an unfamiliar environment, and confusion about the norms of behavior in a new cultural setting.

Learning Environment: Refers to: (1) the physical setting in which a learner or community of learners carry out their work, including all the tools, documents and other artefacts to be found in that setting; (2) the physical setting, but also the social/cultural setting for such work.

Liminality: A transitory period in which individuals sense that they are neither subject to the social or cultural rules of the previous state, nor to the rules of the future state. It is a 'neither here nor there' or a 'betwixt and between' phase, often associated with ritual or locational displacement. Liminality is a state of fluidity and ambiguity, and it often prompts a critical re-evaluation of behavior, status, and identity. It is also known as a threshold state (Latin, *limen* = threshold).

Medical Mission IHEs: Experiences completed in a foreign location by a group of medical professionals to provide medical care to individuals of an indigent population.

Multicultural/Multiculturalism: A term often used to describe societies (especially nations) that have many distinct groups, usually as a result of immigration or forced migration. Multiculturalism is the belief that a 'cultural mosaic' of various ethnic groups adds value to a society.

Non-Degree Student: A student who is enrolled in classes but has not been admitted to the institution in a degree-seeking status. Degree-granting institutions that permit students from other institutions to participate in their study abroad programs typically choose to place visiting students in non-degree status. Students on reciprocal student exchange programs are also usually considered non-degree students at their host institutions.

Glossary

Non-Governmental Organizations (NGOs): Typically, non-profit groups dedicated to specific issues. While many are community-based, national and international NGOs are common. NGOs serve many purposes from empowering those in need to providing services.

Nonaffiliated Program: Any program abroad that lacks the 'home' institution's affiliation/approval. Faculty have not reviewed the quality of these programs and credit is not guaranteed. Students have the responsibility to ensure safety, quality, and credit on these programs.

Operand Resources: The tangible assets that are factors of production, such as raw materials or machinery. In a goods-centered logic, the operand resources are considered the primary source of a firm's competitive advantage. In an educational context, this refers to a university's economic resources, research facilities, location, or industry contacts.

Otherness: The quality and/or state of being different, of belonging to an out-group.

Pedagogy: The art and science of teaching, and not in its narrower sense of teaching the 'young'. Its common usage is now sufficiently broad that there is no need to import the word 'andragogy', a term which has only limited currency in the mainstreams of HE practice.

Perceptual Acuity: The interpersonal sensitivity to accurately perceive, empathize with and respond properly to different cultural thoughts and feelings.

Personal Autonomy: The ability to maintain your personal identity and values and be respectful when exposed to different cultural values.

Preceptor: A fully trained licensed practitioner within their discipline e.g., medicine, nursing, pharmacy etc., that serves as a student mentor and whom evaluates students' competency on certain clinical aspects while training with them.

Professionalization: The process of developing professionalism as a foreign language teacher, involving self-concept, methodological tools, routines and other teaching-related aspects.

Glossary

Pull Factors: Conditions that operate in the receiving 'host' country to make that country desirable as a place to live and study, and include for example: (a) advanced research conditions; (b) better employment opportunities and career prospects; (c) higher quality education; (d) scholarships; and (e) superiority of the social and economic environment.

Push Factors: Conditions that operate within a source 'home' country to initiate a student's decision to study overseas and include for example: (a) a lack of HE opportunities; (b) government policies; (c) poor quality local educational facilities; (d) scholarships favorable to mobility; (e) the low-level of internationalization of education; and (f) the perceived and actual comparative advantage of the value of a foreign degree in the job markets both home and abroad.

Qualification: The formal certification issued by the relevant approval body that confirms an individual has achieved either all the units of competency or the subject or course or module learning outcomes required of the qualification.

Reflection: A consideration or analysis of a topic or experience that has an academic basis but is also personal in nature. This is a common pedagogical method for courses on study abroad programs that examine cross-cultural issues. Through reflection, participants are asked to examine a cultural issue or practice in the host country and analyze it through their personal lens. Generally, reflection is done through a journal or other piece of writing, also called reflective writing.

Reflective Practitioner: A concept that highlights a reflective attitude with practicing teachers in order to enhance their professionalism.

Research Abroad: An activity abroad that typically pairs a study abroad student or students with on-site faculty and/or other local experts to pursue a specific topic or research question. Such research typically results in the writing of an academic paper or article, whether to fulfill requirements for academic credit.

Research Degree: They include the Doctor of Philosophy, Professional Doctorates and Masters (Honors). Research students work independently on discipline-based topics, becoming an expert in their area of interest.

Rites of Passage: A socially constructed and recognized ritual that marks the transition of an individual from one social status to another in the course of his or her life. The transition is usually marked by three distinct and progressive periods:

Glossary

(a) separation or 'dissociation' from the existing social roles and status; (b) a liminal phase in which there is no imposition of a defined social role or structure; and (c) the reintegration or 'aggregation' of the individual with his or her new social status into the group.

Service-Dominant Logic (SDL): A new paradigm of marketing thinking that emerged over a decade ago. SDL provides a new lens for understanding value creation and exchange. The introduction of SDL is based on seminal work by Stephen Vargo and Robert Lusch who developed 11 foundational premises (FP), which have recently been restated in five axioms. One key premise is that value is always co-created by multiple actors, including the beneficiary (FP6). Furthermore, all actors are resource integrators (FP9). In education, students co-create their own value through integrating their operant resources i.e., skills, knowledge, with the resources of the university and staff.

Service-Learning: A type of pedagogy that incorporates community service with instruction. This teaching approach fosters learning through critical reflection and meaningful engagement with communities.

Service-Learning Abroad/Community-Engaged Learning: A specially designed experience combining reflection with structured participation in a community-based project to achieve specified learning outcomes as part of a study abroad program. The learning is given structure through the principles of experiential education to develop an integrated approach to understanding the relationship among theory, practice, ideals, values, and community. (Nb. Although it is sometimes written as two separate words, service-learning professionals tend to prefer the hyphenated version in order to emphasize the link between the components of service and formal learning).

Stereotype: The application of information (both positive and negative) that one believes about a country or culture group to every individual in that country or culture. Stereotypes are often used in a negative or prejudicial sense and are frequently used to justify discriminatory behaviors. Stereotypes are seen by many as undesirable beliefs which can be altered through education and/or familiarization.

Study Abroad: A program that enables students to attend a school or a program outside their country of residence and receive academic course credit related to their university major. In most cases, two universities have an arrangement which allows them to exchange students so that these students can learn about a foreign culture and broaden their horizons. The program usually grants credit for courses

Glossary

taken at the foreign institution and some also arrange for a work-study or internship agreement. In a typical program, a student can spend a semester studying abroad, but there are also programs that allow participants to stay multiple semesters or up to a year. Some study abroad programs are designed solely for and attending a foreign university, while others emphasize internships or volunteer experiences. that enhances professionalization and global citizenship through increased opportunities for intercultural and experiential learning.

Study Abroad Experience: An example of outbound student mobility in which learners, enrolled in HE programs, spend part of their degree program in formal credit-bearing learning programs, study exchanges, or work placements in countries of which they are not nationals. Within the US educational system, study abroad is predominantly a short-term experience, with the large majority lasting for less than eight weeks.

Subculture: A racial, ethnic, regional, economic, or social community exhibiting characteristic patterns of behavior sufficient to distinguish it from others within a larger culture or society; in other words a culture within a culture (for example, there are gay and lesbian subcultures, youth subcultures, religious subcultures). There is some controversy over the distinction between subculture and culture. As a result, culture and subculture are often used as synonyms.

Teaching Placement/Practicum Abroad: A period spent in a target language school by preservice teachers as part of their teacher education course.

Third-Party Providers: Organizations who facilitate international programs for universities and groups. A third-party provider has contacts and staff in other locations that make housing and meal accommodations, liaise between clinical/service sites, and handle recreational activities and excursions for travelling students. In clinical programs they can establish relationships with local interpreters and preceptors.

Unit Information: Provides approved information in summary form to a prospective student about what the student would expect to learn from studying in the unit. The outline provides information about the formal status of the unit in the curriculum, including credit points, unit level, prerequisites for study, and mode of study. Unit outlines provide information about the approved assessment requirements for the unit.

Glossary

Value: A key concept in marketing. In a traditional goods-oriented view, it refers to a consumer's overall assessment of the utility of a product based on his/her perceptions of the benefits and costs. Value has been defined as the amount of money that something is worth ('what one gets, is what s/he pays'). However, value goes beyond the monetary nature. Literature suggests that value is a complex and multi-dimensional construct with different meanings i.e., value as symbolic meaning, value as a relativistic preference experience or value-in-use. In HE, students play an active role in creating the value of a university service.

Value-in-Use: A term that originates from SDL. According to the traditional logic, or goods-dominant logic, value is created by the firm and then distributed to the consumer in exchange for money (called 'value-in-exchange'). Based on SDL, organizations no longer solely provide value (e.g., by offering a product). Instead, value is determined uniquely by the beneficiary (e.g., consumer) and emerges during usage (value-in-use).

Voluntourism: A form of tourism in which participants partake in voluntary, often charity-based work.

Willingness to Communicate (WTC): An individual's readiness to enter into discourse at a particular time with a specific person or persons.

Work and Travel: A US program that offers students from other nationalities the experience to stay in the US during the summer months and work along with local Americans. The program gives its participants a study abroad experience, and through working in seasonal jobs at various employers across America, the participants can cover their travel and other expenses. Although participants to the program can work in the US for four months, the maximum length of stay is determined by the US State Department.

Related Readings

To continue IGI Global's long-standing tradition of advancing innovation through emerging research, please find below a compiled list of recommended IGI Global book chapters and journal articles in the areas of study abroad programs, quality assurance, and internationalized curriculum. These related readings will provide additional information and guidance to further enrich your knowledge and assist you with your own research.

Amani, M., & Kim, M. M. (2019). Enhancing Study Abroad Participation and Choices of Destination at Community Colleges. In G. Malveaux & R. Raby (Eds.), *Study Abroad Opportunities for Community College Students and Strategies for Global Learning* (pp. 131–146). Hershey, PA: IGI Global. doi:10.4018/978-1-5225-6252-8.ch009

An, H., Hong, C. E., & Fuentes, D. (2017). The Benefits and Limitations of a Short-Term Study Abroad Program to Prepare Teachers in a Multicultural Society. In H. An (Ed.), *Handbook of Research on Efficacy and Implementation of Study Abroad Programs for P-12 Teachers* (pp. 361–382). Hershey, PA: IGI Global. doi:10.4018/978-1-5225-1057-4.ch020

Andrews-Swann, J. (2018). Cultivating Global Citizens: Classroom Tools to Reduce Cultural Judgment and Foster Intercultural Understanding in Higher Ed. In S. Dikli, B. Etheridge, & R. Rawls (Eds.), Curriculum Internationalization and the Future of Education (pp. 119-133). Hershey, PA: IGI Global. doi:10.4018/978-1-5225-2791-6.ch007

Related Readings

Arden, M., & Piscioneri, M. (2018). The New Colombo Plan: Transforming Australian Higher Education's Outward Mobility Programs? In K. Bista (Ed.), *International Student Mobility and Opportunities for Growth in the Global Marketplace* (pp. 81–99). Hershey, PA: IGI Global. doi:10.4018/978-1-5225-3451-8.ch006

Attah, D. A., Boafo-Arthur, S., & Boafo-Arthur, A. (2018). The Sojourner's Return: Risks and Challenges of the Study Abroad Experience on Re-Entry. In D. Velliaris (Ed.), *Study Abroad Contexts for Enhanced Foreign Language Learning* (pp. 218–255). Hershey, PA: IGI Global. doi:10.4018/978-1-5225-3814-1.ch010

Ayuninjam, F. (2018). Beyond Curriculum Internationalization: Globalization for Intercultural Competence. In S. Dikli, B. Etheridge, & R. Rawls (Eds.), *Curriculum Internationalization and the Future of Education* (pp. 216–231). Hershey, PA: IGI Global. doi:10.4018/978-1-5225-2791-6.ch012

Baer, J. (2019). Opening the Door to Study Abroad From Community Colleges. In G. Malveaux & R. Raby (Eds.), *Study Abroad Opportunities for Community College Students and Strategies for Global Learning* (pp. 22–36). Hershey, PA: IGI Global. doi:10.4018/978-1-5225-6252-8.ch002

Bano, S. (2018). From Brain Drain to Reverse Brain Drain: Implications for South Asia and the United States of America. In K. Bista (Ed.), *International Student Mobility and Opportunities for Growth in the Global Marketplace* (pp. 64–79). Hershey, PA: IGI Global. doi:10.4018/978-1-5225-3451-8.ch005

Baporikar, N. (2018). Study Abroad Management Programs: Strategies for Enhancing Returns. In D. Velliaris (Ed.), *Study Abroad Contexts for Enhanced Foreign Language Learning* (pp. 169–188). Hershey, PA: IGI Global. doi:10.4018/978-1-5225-3814-1.ch008

Bentz, J., Pearson, J. N., & Witt, A. (2017). Study Abroad Australia: Practice and Research. In H. An (Ed.), *Handbook of Research on Efficacy and Implementation of Study Abroad Programs for P-12 Teachers* (pp. 87–110). Hershey, PA: IGI Global. doi:10.4018/978-1-5225-1057-4.ch006

Bentz, J., Pearson, J. N., & Witt, A. (2017). Study Abroad Australia: Practice and Research. In H. An (Ed.), *Handbook of Research on Efficacy and Implementation of Study Abroad Programs for P-12 Teachers* (pp. 87–110). Hershey, PA: IGI Global. doi:10.4018/978-1-5225-1057-4.ch006

Bista, K., Sharma, G., & Gaulee, U. (2018). International Student Mobility: Examining Trends and Tensions. In K. Bista (Ed.), *International Student Mobility and Opportunities for Growth in the Global Marketplace* (pp. 1–14). Hershey, PA: IGI Global. doi:10.4018/978-1-5225-3451-8.ch001

Related Readings

Boindala, P. S., Menon, R., & Lively, A. (2018). How Is Mathematics Humanistic, Culturally Rich, Relevant, and Interesting?: Seeking Answers Through the Redesign of an Undergraduate Mathematics Course. In S. Dikli, B. Etheridge, & R. Rawls (Eds.), *Curriculum Internationalization and the Future of Education* (pp. 155–180). Hershey, PA: IGI Global. doi:10.4018/978-1-5225-2791-6.ch009

Bradley, B. A., & Emerson, A. M. (2017). Learning about Culture and Teaching During a Short-Term Immersion-Based Study Abroad. In H. An (Ed.), *Handbook of Research on Efficacy and Implementation of Study Abroad Programs for P-12 Teachers* (pp. 172–189). Hershey, PA: IGI Global. doi:10.4018/978-1-5225-1057-4.ch010

Bradley, B. A., & Emerson, A. M. (2017). Learning about Culture and Teaching During a Short-Term Immersion-Based Study Abroad. In H. An (Ed.), *Handbook of Research on Efficacy and Implementation of Study Abroad Programs for P-12 Teachers* (pp. 172–189). Hershey, PA: IGI Global. doi:10.4018/978-1-5225-1057-4.ch010

Bücker, J., Bouw, R., & De Beuckelaer, A. (2018). Dealing With Cross-Cultural Issues in Culturally Diverse Classrooms: The Case of Dutch Business Schools. In K. Bista (Ed.), *International Student Mobility and Opportunities for Growth in the Global Marketplace* (pp. 117–133). Hershey, PA: IGI Global. doi:10.4018/978-1-5225-3451-8.ch008

Bulgan, G., & Çiftçi, A. (2018). Career Counseling for International Students: Using the Framework of Social Cognitive Career Theory. In K. Bista (Ed.), *International Student Mobility and Opportunities for Growth in the Global Marketplace* (pp. 203–213). Hershey, PA: IGI Global. doi:10.4018/978-1-5225-3451-8.ch014

Burns, R., Rubin, D., & Tarrant, M. A. (2018). World Language Learning: The Impact of Study Abroad on Student Engagement. In D. Velliaris (Ed.), *Study Abroad Contexts for Enhanced Foreign Language Learning* (pp. 1–22). Hershey, PA: IGI Global. doi:10.4018/978-1-5225-3814-1.ch001

Cartwright, A. M., & Mills, M. T. (2017). Consortium Models: Enhancing Faculty Led Study Abroad Programs for Pre- and In-Service Teachers. In H. An (Ed.), *Handbook of Research on Efficacy and Implementation of Study Abroad Programs for P-12 Teachers* (pp. 71–85). Hershey, PA: IGI Global. doi:10.4018/978-1-5225-1057-4.ch005

Cartwright, A. M., & Mills, M. T. (2017). Consortium Models: Enhancing Faculty Led Study Abroad Programs for Pre- and In-Service Teachers. In H. An (Ed.), *Handbook of Research on Efficacy and Implementation of Study Abroad Programs for P-12 Teachers* (pp. 71–85). Hershey, PA: IGI Global. doi:10.4018/978-1-5225-1057-4.ch005

Cho, H., & Peter, L. (2017). Taking the TESOL Practicum Abroad: Opportunities for Critical Awareness and Community-Building among Preservice Teachers. In H. An (Ed.), *Handbook of Research on Efficacy and Implementation of Study Abroad Programs for P-12 Teachers* (pp. 149–171). Hershey, PA: IGI Global. doi:10.4018/978-1-5225-1057-4.ch009

Cho, H., & Peter, L. (2017). Taking the TESOL Practicum Abroad: Opportunities for Critical Awareness and Community-Building among Preservice Teachers. In H. An (Ed.), *Handbook of Research on Efficacy and Implementation of Study Abroad Programs for P-12 Teachers* (pp. 149–171). Hershey, PA: IGI Global. doi:10.4018/978-1-5225-1057-4.ch009

Courtney, M. G. (2018). Emerging Academic and Social Spaces: Toward a Modern Understanding of International Student Integration in Australasia. *International Journal of Cyber Behavior, Psychology and Learning*, 8(3), 36–47. doi:10.4018/IJCBPL.2018070104

D'Haem, J. M., Feola, D., & Norris-Bauer, N. (2017). University Partnerships: Greater Involvement in International Activities for Teachers. In H. An (Ed.), *Handbook of Research on Efficacy and Implementation of Study Abroad Programs for P-12 Teachers* (pp. 1–12). Hershey, PA: IGI Global. doi:10.4018/978-1-5225-1057-4.ch001

D'Haem, J. M., Feola, D., & Norris-Bauer, N. (2017). University Partnerships: Greater Involvement in International Activities for Teachers. In H. An (Ed.), *Handbook of Research on Efficacy and Implementation of Study Abroad Programs for P-12 Teachers* (pp. 1–12). Hershey, PA: IGI Global. doi:10.4018/978-1-5225-1057-4.ch001

Davis-Maye, D., Yarber-Allen, A., & Jones, T. B. (2017). Feeling Silly and White: The Impact of Participant Characteristics on Study Abroad Experiences. In H. An (Ed.), *Handbook of Research on Efficacy and Implementation of Study Abroad Programs for P-12 Teachers* (pp. 400–414). Hershey, PA: IGI Global. doi:10.4018/978-1-5225-1057-4.ch022

Related Readings

de Wit, R., & Furst, M. B. (2019). Internationalized Courses on Campus: A Complement to Study Abroad That Maximizes International Education Participation in the Community College Context. In G. Malveaux & R. Raby (Eds.), *Study Abroad Opportunities for Community College Students and Strategies for Global Learning* (pp. 213–227). Hershey, PA: IGI Global. doi:10.4018/978-1-5225-6252-8.ch015

Dennis, D. V., Branson, S. M., Flores, B. M., & Papke, A. M. (2017). The Cambridge Schools Experience: Developing Literacy Educators within an International School-University Partnership. In H. An (Ed.), *Handbook of Research on Efficacy and Implementation of Study Abroad Programs for P-12 Teachers* (pp. 256–274). Hershey, PA: IGI Global. doi:10.4018/978-1-5225-1057-4.ch015

Dennis, D. V., Branson, S. M., Flores, B. M., & Papke, A. M. (2017). The Cambridge Schools Experience: Developing Literacy Educators within an International School-University Partnership. In H. An (Ed.), *Handbook of Research on Efficacy and Implementation of Study Abroad Programs for P-12 Teachers* (pp. 256–274). Hershey, PA: IGI Global. doi:10.4018/978-1-5225-1057-4.ch015

Dikli, S., Rawls, R. S., & Etheridge, B. C. (2018). Reflecting on New Faculty Training: Internationalized Learning Essentials. In S. Dikli, B. Etheridge, & R. Rawls (Eds.), *Curriculum Internationalization and the Future of Education* (pp. 203–215). Hershey, PA: IGI Global. doi:10.4018/978-1-5225-2791-6.ch011

Dorrell, D. (2018). Using International Content in an Introductory Human Geography Course. In S. Dikli, B. Etheridge, & R. Rawls (Eds.), *Curriculum Internationalization and the Future of Education* (pp. 55–80). Hershey, PA: IGI Global. doi:10.4018/978-1-5225-2791-6.ch004

Dozier, C. L., & Stephens, S. J. (2017). Becoming Responsive Teachers during a Practicum-Based Study Abroad Experience: Learners Leading to New Perspectives. In H. An (Ed.), *Handbook of Research on Efficacy and Implementation of Study Abroad Programs for P-12 Teachers* (pp. 206–220). Hershey, PA: IGI Global. doi:10.4018/978-1-5225-1057-4.ch012

Dozier, C. L., & Stephens, S. J. (2017). Becoming Responsive Teachers during a Practicum-Based Study Abroad Experience: Learners Leading to New Perspectives. In H. An (Ed.), *Handbook of Research on Efficacy and Implementation of Study Abroad Programs for P-12 Teachers* (pp. 206–220). Hershey, PA: IGI Global. doi:10.4018/978-1-5225-1057-4.ch012

Fell, W. D., & Wright, S. (2019). The Hybrid Model: Providing Options for a Small Community College. In G. Malveaux & R. Raby (Eds.), *Study Abroad Opportunities for Community College Students and Strategies for Global Learning* (pp. 147–157). Hershey, PA: IGI Global. doi:10.4018/978-1-5225-6252-8.ch010

Gambrell, J. A. (2017). Embracing Teaching as Social Activism: Rejecting Colorblindness through Cultural Inclusion during Study Abroad. In H. An (Ed.), *Handbook of Research on Efficacy and Implementation of Study Abroad Programs for P-12 Teachers* (pp. 322–340). Hershey, PA: IGI Global. doi:10.4018/978-1-5225-1057-4.ch018

Gambrell, J. A. (2017). Embracing Teaching as Social Activism: Rejecting Colorblindness through Cultural Inclusion during Study Abroad. In H. An (Ed.), *Handbook of Research on Efficacy and Implementation of Study Abroad Programs for P-12 Teachers* (pp. 322–340). Hershey, PA: IGI Global. doi:10.4018/978-1-5225-1057-4.ch018

Gephart, D. A. (2019). Low-Cost Initiatives for Expanding Study Abroad Opportunities. In G. Malveaux & R. Raby (Eds.), *Study Abroad Opportunities for Community College Students and Strategies for Global Learning* (pp. 158–171). Hershey, PA: IGI Global. doi:10.4018/978-1-5225-6252-8.ch011

Gilley, M. (2018). Internationalizing Music Appreciation. In S. Dikli, B. Etheridge, & R. Rawls (Eds.), *Curriculum Internationalization and the Future of Education* (pp. 100–118). Hershey, PA: IGI Global. doi:10.4018/978-1-5225-2791-6.ch006

Gyurov, B. G., & Schlueter, M. A. (2018). Creating a Vibrant STEM Study Abroad Program With a Cultural Component. In S. Dikli, B. Etheridge, & R. Rawls (Eds.), *Curriculum Internationalization and the Future of Education* (pp. 181–202). Hershey, PA: IGI Global. doi:10.4018/978-1-5225-2791-6.ch010

Han, F., & Wang, Z. (2018). Willingness to Communicate: English Language Learners From China in Australian EAP Programs. In D. Velliaris (Ed.), *Study Abroad Contexts for Enhanced Foreign Language Learning* (pp. 96–119). Hershey, PA: IGI Global. doi:10.4018/978-1-5225-3814-1.ch005

He, Y., & Lundgren, K. (2017). Bridging Local and Global Experiences: A Faculty-Led Study Abroad Program for Teachers. In H. An (Ed.), *Handbook of Research on Efficacy and Implementation of Study Abroad Programs for P-12 Teachers* (pp. 415–429). Hershey, PA: IGI Global. doi:10.4018/978-1-5225-1057-4.ch023

Related Readings

Hitchens, C. W., Clark, P., Kline, A., Mucherah, W., Popplewell, S., & Thomas, K. J. (2017). Studying Abroad to Inform Teaching in a Diverse Society: A Description of International Elementary Education Teaching Experiences at Ball State University. In H. An (Ed.), *Handbook of Research on Efficacy and Implementation of Study Abroad Programs for P-12 Teachers* (pp. 52–70). Hershey, PA: IGI Global. doi:10.4018/978-1-5225-1057-4.ch004

Hitchens, C. W., Clark, P., Kline, A., Mucherah, W., Popplewell, S., & Thomas, K. J. (2017). Studying Abroad to Inform Teaching in a Diverse Society: A Description of International Elementary Education Teaching Experiences at Ball State University. In H. An (Ed.), *Handbook of Research on Efficacy and Implementation of Study Abroad Programs for P-12 Teachers* (pp. 52–70). Hershey, PA: IGI Global. doi:10.4018/978-1-5225-1057-4.ch004

Ho, H. W. (2017). International Students' Perceptions of Services and Supports Provided: A Case Study of a Mid-Sized University in the USA. *International Journal of Technology and Educational Marketing*, 7(1), 1–14. doi:10.4018/IJTEM.2017010101

Hong, C. E., Kopp, S., & Williams, S. (2017). From Cultural Immersion to Professional Growth: Effects of Study Abroad Experiences on Classroom Instruction. In H. An (Ed.), *Handbook of Research on Efficacy and Implementation of Study Abroad Programs for P-12 Teachers* (pp. 383–399). Hershey, PA: IGI Global. doi:10.4018/978-1-5225-1057-4.ch021

Kasun, G. S. (2017). A Decolonizing Study Abroad Program in Mexico for Pre-Service Teachers: Taking on the Cultural Mismatch between Teachers and Students. In H. An (Ed.), *Handbook of Research on Efficacy and Implementation of Study Abroad Programs for P-12 Teachers* (pp. 190–205). Hershey, PA: IGI Global. doi:10.4018/978-1-5225-1057-4.ch011

Kasun, G. S. (2017). A Decolonizing Study Abroad Program in Mexico for Pre-Service Teachers: Taking on the Cultural Mismatch between Teachers and Students. In H. An (Ed.), *Handbook of Research on Efficacy and Implementation of Study Abroad Programs for P-12 Teachers* (pp. 190–205). Hershey, PA: IGI Global. doi:10.4018/978-1-5225-1057-4.ch011

Keller, T. M. (2017). "The World is So Much Bigger": Preservice Teachers' Experiences of Religion in Israel and the Influences on Identity and Teaching. In H. An (Ed.), *Handbook of Research on Efficacy and Implementation of Study Abroad Programs for P-12 Teachers* (pp. 275–294). Hershey, PA: IGI Global. doi:10.4018/978-1-5225-1057-4.ch016

Keller, T. M. (2017). "The World is So Much Bigger": Preservice Teachers' Experiences of Religion in Israel and the Influences on Identity and Teaching. In H. An (Ed.), *Handbook of Research on Efficacy and Implementation of Study Abroad Programs for P-12 Teachers* (pp. 275–294). Hershey, PA: IGI Global. doi:10.4018/978-1-5225-1057-4.ch016

Kong, K. (2018). Learning Chinese: Connections and Comparisons in Study Abroad. In D. Velliaris (Ed.), *Study Abroad Contexts for Enhanced Foreign Language Learning* (pp. 44–69). Hershey, PA: IGI Global. doi:10.4018/978-1-5225-3814-1.ch003

Kreitinger, J., & Corsi, T. F. (2019). Utilizing a National Association to Increase Access to Education Abroad. In G. Malveaux & R. Raby (Eds.), *Study Abroad Opportunities for Community College Students and Strategies for Global Learning* (pp. 255–264). Hershey, PA: IGI Global. doi:10.4018/978-1-5225-6252-8.ch018

Kwok, T. K. (2018). The Bridge to America: A Passageway for International Graduate Students. In K. Bista (Ed.), *International Student Mobility and Opportunities for Growth in the Global Marketplace* (pp. 147–159). Hershey, PA: IGI Global. doi:10.4018/978-1-5225-3451-8.ch010

Lee, S. (2018). Expatriate Cantonese Learners in Hong Kong: Adult L2 Learning, Identity Negotiation, and Social Pressure. In D. Velliaris (Ed.), *Study Abroad Contexts for Enhanced Foreign Language Learning* (pp. 151–168). Hershey, PA: IGI Global. doi:10.4018/978-1-5225-3814-1.ch007

Lewkowicz, M. A., Young, L. D., Budrytė, D., & Boykin, S. A. (2018). Bringing the Study of American Government to Life in a Diverse Classroom: Internationalization and Individualization. In S. Dikli, B. Etheridge, & R. Rawls (Eds.), *Curriculum Internationalization and the Future of Education* (pp. 1–17). Hershey, PA: IGI Global. doi:10.4018/978-1-5225-2791-6.ch001

Li, J. (2018). Open Minds: Study Abroad and Student Global Perspectives. In K. Bista (Ed.), *International Student Mobility and Opportunities for Growth in the Global Marketplace* (pp. 100–116). Hershey, PA: IGI Global. doi:10.4018/978-1-5225-3451-8.ch007

Lindley, T. (2018). Active Learning and the "Teaching" of Migration in Geography: A Critical Reflection on the Twenty-First Century Multicultural College Classroom. In S. Dikli, B. Etheridge, & R. Rawls (Eds.), *Curriculum Internationalization and the Future of Education* (pp. 36–54). Hershey, PA: IGI Global. doi:10.4018/978-1-5225-2791-6.ch003

Related Readings

Liu, M. (2018). Assessing Intercultural Sensitivity and Effectiveness: Adult Learners of Chinese as a L2. In D. Velliaris (Ed.), *Study Abroad Contexts for Enhanced Foreign Language Learning* (pp. 70–95). Hershey, PA: IGI Global. doi:10.4018/978-1-5225-3814-1.ch004

Liu, R. (2018). Transforming a Beginner's Foreign Language Course Into an Internationalized Course: Language Exchange Pal Project. In S. Dikli, B. Etheridge, & R. Rawls (Eds.), *Curriculum Internationalization and the Future of Education* (pp. 134–154). Hershey, PA: IGI Global. doi:10.4018/978-1-5225-2791-6.ch008

Lo, L. (2017). Collective Learning: An Exploration of the Hong Kong and U.S. Special Education Systems. In H. An (Ed.), *Handbook of Research on Efficacy and Implementation of Study Abroad Programs for P-12 Teachers* (pp. 237–255). Hershey, PA: IGI Global. doi:10.4018/978-1-5225-1057-4.ch014

Lo, L. (2017). Collective Learning: An Exploration of the Hong Kong and U.S. Special Education Systems. In H. An (Ed.), *Handbook of Research on Efficacy and Implementation of Study Abroad Programs for P-12 Teachers* (pp. 237–255). Hershey, PA: IGI Global. doi:10.4018/978-1-5225-1057-4.ch014

Lu, G., Tian, M., & Lai, M. H. (2018). Analysis of Factors Influencing Chinese Undergraduate Students' Choice of Foreign Postgraduate Education. In K. Bista (Ed.), *International Student Mobility and Opportunities for Growth in the Global Marketplace* (pp. 215–245). Hershey, PA: IGI Global. doi:10.4018/978-1-5225-3451-8.ch015

Malfatti, G. (2017). Of Chalk and Chai: Teach Abroad Experiences that Enhance Cultural Adaptability of Pre-Service Teachers. In H. An (Ed.), *Handbook of Research on Efficacy and Implementation of Study Abroad Programs for P-12 Teachers* (pp. 341–359). Hershey, PA: IGI Global. doi:10.4018/978-1-5225-1057-4.ch019

Malveaux, G. F. (2019). How to Survive and Thrive as a Community College Consortium: A Case Study of the Maryland Community College International Education Consortium. In G. Malveaux & R. Raby (Eds.), *Study Abroad Opportunities for Community College Students and Strategies for Global Learning* (pp. 265–283). Hershey, PA: IGI Global. doi:10.4018/978-1-5225-6252-8.ch019

Malveaux, G. F., Rhodes, G. M., & Raby, R. L. (2019). Community College Education Abroad Health and Safety Concerns: Standards Needed to Meet the Challenges. In G. Malveaux & R. Raby (Eds.), *Study Abroad Opportunities for Community College Students and Strategies for Global Learning* (pp. 53–71). Hershey, PA: IGI Global. doi:10.4018/978-1-5225-6252-8.ch004

McKee, A. (2019). A Case Study Exploring Ways to Increase Access to Education Abroad for Career and Technical Students With Limited Availability. In G. Malveaux & R. Raby (Eds.), *Study Abroad Opportunities for Community College Students and Strategies for Global Learning* (pp. 242–254). Hershey, PA: IGI Global. doi:10.4018/978-1-5225-6252-8.ch017

Parker, A., Webb, K. E., & Wilson, E. V. (2017). Creating a Studying Abroad Experience for Elementary Teacher Candidates: Considerations, Challenges, and Impact. In H. An (Ed.), *Handbook of Research on Efficacy and Implementation of Study Abroad Programs for P-12 Teachers* (pp. 111–132). Hershey, PA: IGI Global. doi:10.4018/978-1-5225-1057-4.ch007

Parker, A., Webb, K. E., & Wilson, E. V. (2017). Creating a Studying Abroad Experience for Elementary Teacher Candidates: Considerations, Challenges, and Impact. In H. An (Ed.), *Handbook of Research on Efficacy and Implementation of Study Abroad Programs for P-12 Teachers* (pp. 111–132). Hershey, PA: IGI Global. doi:10.4018/978-1-5225-1057-4.ch007

Perry, C. J., Lausch, D. W., & Weatherford, J. (2018). Comparing Academic Concerns of International and Domestic Students. In K. Bista (Ed.), *International Student Mobility and Opportunities for Growth in the Global Marketplace* (pp. 190–202). Hershey, PA: IGI Global. doi:10.4018/978-1-5225-3451-8.ch013

Pinar, A. (2018). Learning Languages Abroad: The Influence of the Length of Stay on Communicative Competence. In D. Velliaris (Ed.), *Study Abroad Contexts for Enhanced Foreign Language Learning* (pp. 23–43). Hershey, PA: IGI Global. doi:10.4018/978-1-5225-3814-1.ch002

Putman, S. M. (2017). Teacher Candidates in International Contexts: Examining the Impact on Beliefs about Teaching Culturally and Linguistically Diverse Learners. In H. An (Ed.), *Handbook of Research on Efficacy and Implementation of Study Abroad Programs for P-12 Teachers* (pp. 295–321). Hershey, PA: IGI Global. doi:10.4018/978-1-5225-1057-4.ch017

Putman, S. M. (2017). Teacher Candidates in International Contexts: Examining the Impact on Beliefs about Teaching Culturally and Linguistically Diverse Learners. In H. An (Ed.), *Handbook of Research on Efficacy and Implementation of Study Abroad Programs for P-12 Teachers* (pp. 295–321). Hershey, PA: IGI Global. doi:10.4018/978-1-5225-1057-4.ch017

Related Readings

Quinones, C. (2018). Process of Transforming Regular Courses Into I-Courses: The Case of Two Political Science Courses at GGC. In S. Dikli, B. Etheridge, & R. Rawls (Eds.), *Curriculum Internationalization and the Future of Education* (pp. 18–35). Hershey, PA: IGI Global. doi:10.4018/978-1-5225-2791-6.ch002

Raby, R. L. (2019). Changing the Conversation: Measures That Contribute to Community College Education Abroad Success. In G. Malveaux & R. Raby (Eds.), *Study Abroad Opportunities for Community College Students and Strategies for Global Learning* (pp. 1–21). Hershey, PA: IGI Global. doi:10.4018/978-1-5225-6252-8.ch001

Rawls, R. S. (2018). Internationalizing a Course on the Cultural and Intellectual History of the Ancient World. In S. Dikli, B. Etheridge, & R. Rawls (Eds.), *Curriculum Internationalization and the Future of Education* (pp. 81–99). Hershey, PA: IGI Global. doi:10.4018/978-1-5225-2791-6.ch005

Roberts, S. L., & Rouech, K. (2017). "Should I Go to Ireland or Mexico?": A Comparison of Two Pre-Student Teaching Study Abroad Programs Offered by the Same Department. In H. An (Ed.), *Handbook of Research on Efficacy and Implementation of Study Abroad Programs for P-12 Teachers* (pp. 34–51). Hershey, PA: IGI Global. doi:10.4018/978-1-5225-1057-4.ch003

Roberts, S. L., & Rouech, K. (2017). "Should I Go to Ireland or Mexico?": A Comparison of Two Pre-Student Teaching Study Abroad Programs Offered by the Same Department. In H. An (Ed.), *Handbook of Research on Efficacy and Implementation of Study Abroad Programs for P-12 Teachers* (pp. 34–51). Hershey, PA: IGI Global. doi:10.4018/978-1-5225-1057-4.ch003

Robertson, J. J. (2019). The Outreach Triad for Successful Study Abroad Programs: Students, Faculty, and the Local Community. In G. Malveaux & R. Raby (Eds.), *Study Abroad Opportunities for Community College Students and Strategies for Global Learning* (pp. 107–119). Hershey, PA: IGI Global. doi:10.4018/978-1-5225-6252-8.ch007

Sableski, M., Arnold, J. M., & White, J. (2017). Developing a Multicultural Cross-Curricular Study Abroad Experience. In H. An (Ed.), *Handbook of Research on Efficacy and Implementation of Study Abroad Programs for P-12 Teachers* (pp. 221–236). Hershey, PA: IGI Global. doi:10.4018/978-1-5225-1057-4.ch013

Sableski, M., Arnold, J. M., & White, J. (2017). Developing a Multicultural Cross-Curricular Study Abroad Experience. In H. An (Ed.), *Handbook of Research on Efficacy and Implementation of Study Abroad Programs for P-12 Teachers* (pp. 221–236). Hershey, PA: IGI Global. doi:10.4018/978-1-5225-1057-4.ch013

Saint-Phard, R. E., & Gregorutti, G. (2018). International Undergraduate Students Coping With Challenges at a Private Faith-Based University. In K. Bista (Ed.), *International Student Mobility and Opportunities for Growth in the Global Marketplace* (pp. 160–173). Hershey, PA: IGI Global. doi:10.4018/978-1-5225-3451-8.ch011

Sansotta, A. M. (2018). Promoting U.S. Community Colleges in Sweden: From the Perspective of Swedish Education Agents. In K. Bista (Ed.), *International Student Mobility and Opportunities for Growth in the Global Marketplace* (pp. 261–278). Hershey, PA: IGI Global. doi:10.4018/978-1-5225-3451-8.ch017

Sengupta, E. (2018). Islamophobia and Mobility of Kurdish Students From Northern Iraq. In K. Bista (Ed.), *International Student Mobility and Opportunities for Growth in the Global Marketplace* (pp. 31–48). Hershey, PA: IGI Global. doi:10.4018/978-1-5225-3451-8.ch003

Silber-Furman, D., & Zagumny, L. (2018). Dare to Hope: A Critical Examination of Culturally and Linguistically Diverse International Students – Graduate Students' Experiences in the Southeastern United States. In K. Bista (Ed.), *International Student Mobility and Opportunities for Growth in the Global Marketplace* (pp. 135–146). Hershey, PA: IGI Global. doi:10.4018/978-1-5225-3451-8.ch009

Smith, C. (2019). Institutionalizing International Education and Embedding Education Abroad Into the Campus Community. In G. Malveaux & R. Raby (Eds.), *Study Abroad Opportunities for Community College Students and Strategies for Global Learning* (pp. 172–183). Hershey, PA: IGI Global. doi:10.4018/978-1-5225-6252-8.ch012

Smith, C., & Hubbard, A. (2019). Good Practices and Program Standards: Considering the Unique Needs of Community Colleges. In G. Malveaux & R. Raby (Eds.), *Study Abroad Opportunities for Community College Students and Strategies for Global Learning* (pp. 37–52). Hershey, PA: IGI Global. doi:10.4018/978-1-5225-6252-8.ch003

Smith, D. J. (2019). Peacebuilding as a Means to Global Citizenry. In G. Malveaux & R. Raby (Eds.), *Study Abroad Opportunities for Community College Students and Strategies for Global Learning* (pp. 200–212). Hershey, PA: IGI Global. doi:10.4018/978-1-5225-6252-8.ch014

Smith, S., & Keng, N. (2017). A Business Writing OIL (Online International Learning): A Finland/UK Case Study. *International Journal of Computer-Assisted Language Learning and Teaching, 7*(4), 33–43. doi:10.4018/IJCALLT.2017100103

Related Readings

Tangpricha, T. G. (2019). Lessons Learned: Building Inclusive Support for Study Abroad Programming at Delaware Technical Community College. In G. Malveaux & R. Raby (Eds.), *Study Abroad Opportunities for Community College Students and Strategies for Global Learning* (pp. 120–130). Hershey, PA: IGI Global. doi:10.4018/978-1-5225-6252-8.ch008

Thomas, M. (2019). Practical Strategies for Rural-Serving Community College Global Programming. In G. Malveaux & R. Raby (Eds.), *Study Abroad Opportunities for Community College Students and Strategies for Global Learning* (pp. 228–241). Hershey, PA: IGI Global. doi:10.4018/978-1-5225-6252-8.ch016

Urdziņa-Deruma, M., & Šelvaha, L. (2018). Crafts and Home Economics Studies Abroad: Student Identified Differences and Suggestions for Teacher Education in Latvia. *International Journal of Smart Education and Urban Society*, *9*(4), 77–89. doi:10.4018/IJSEUS.2018100107

Vaughn, M., & Swanson, K. W. (2018). Fieldwork in Developing Countries: Preparing Pre-Service Teachers. In S. Dikli, B. Etheridge, & R. Rawls (Eds.), *Curriculum Internationalization and the Future of Education* (pp. 273–292). Hershey, PA: IGI Global. doi:10.4018/978-1-5225-2791-6.ch015

Velliaris, D. M. (2018). Across the Four Domains: Pathway Students' Self-Reported Perceptions of English Proficiency. In D. Velliaris (Ed.), *Study Abroad Contexts for Enhanced Foreign Language Learning* (pp. 120–150). Hershey, PA: IGI Global. doi:10.4018/978-1-5225-3814-1.ch006

Viggiano, T. (2019). Thinking Globally About Social Justice. In G. Malveaux & R. Raby (Eds.), *Study Abroad Opportunities for Community College Students and Strategies for Global Learning* (pp. 184–199). Hershey, PA: IGI Global. doi:10.4018/978-1-5225-6252-8.ch013

Virtue, D. C. (2017). Case Study of a Sustained Educator Partnership between the U.S. and Norway. In H. An (Ed.), *Handbook of Research on Efficacy and Implementation of Study Abroad Programs for P-12 Teachers* (pp. 13–33). Hershey, PA: IGI Global. doi:10.4018/978-1-5225-1057-4.ch002

Virtue, D. C. (2017). Case Study of a Sustained Educator Partnership between the U.S. and Norway. In H. An (Ed.), *Handbook of Research on Efficacy and Implementation of Study Abroad Programs for P-12 Teachers* (pp. 13–33). Hershey, PA: IGI Global. doi:10.4018/978-1-5225-1057-4.ch002

Wadhwa, R. (2018). International Student Mobility: Theoretical Context and Empirical Evidence From Literature. In K. Bista (Ed.), *International Student Mobility and Opportunities for Growth in the Global Marketplace* (pp. 15–30). Hershey, PA: IGI Global. doi:10.4018/978-1-5225-3451-8.ch002

Wang, Y. (2018). It Sharpens My Brain: International Teaching Assistants Develop Communicative Competence. In K. Bista (Ed.), *International Student Mobility and Opportunities for Growth in the Global Marketplace* (pp. 174–189). Hershey, PA: IGI Global. doi:10.4018/978-1-5225-3451-8.ch012

Welsch, M. (2018). Interest and Intent in Pursuing Higher Education: Nepali Students' Perceptions on Study Abroad Experiences. In K. Bista (Ed.), *International Student Mobility and Opportunities for Growth in the Global Marketplace* (pp. 246–260). Hershey, PA: IGI Global. doi:10.4018/978-1-5225-3451-8.ch016

Whatley, M. (2019). Clearing the Hurdle: The Relationship Between Institutional Profiles and Community College Study Abroad. In G. Malveaux & R. Raby (Eds.), *Study Abroad Opportunities for Community College Students and Strategies for Global Learning* (pp. 90–106). Hershey, PA: IGI Global. doi:10.4018/978-1-5225-6252-8.ch006

Witt, A., Pino-Yancovic, M., & Neal, B. (2017). Study Abroad for Preservice Teachers: Critical Learning and Teaching in a Diverse Context. In H. An (Ed.), *Handbook of Research on Efficacy and Implementation of Study Abroad Programs for P-12 Teachers* (pp. 133–148). Hershey, PA: IGI Global. doi:10.4018/978-1-5225-1057-4.ch008

Witt, A., Pino-Yancovic, M., & Neal, B. (2017). Study Abroad for Preservice Teachers: Critical Learning and Teaching in a Diverse Context. In H. An (Ed.), *Handbook of Research on Efficacy and Implementation of Study Abroad Programs for P-12 Teachers* (pp. 133–148). Hershey, PA: IGI Global. doi:10.4018/978-1-5225-1057-4.ch008

Wood, D. R. (2019). Study Abroad Outcomes Assessment: A Community College Case Study. In G. Malveaux & R. Raby (Eds.), *Study Abroad Opportunities for Community College Students and Strategies for Global Learning* (pp. 72–89). Hershey, PA: IGI Global. doi:10.4018/978-1-5225-6252-8.ch005

Yang, P. (2018). Experiential Learning Opportunities: Removing Language Barriers and Maximizing Cultural Immersion. In D. Velliaris (Ed.), *Study Abroad Contexts for Enhanced Foreign Language Learning* (pp. 189–217). Hershey, PA: IGI Global. doi:10.4018/978-1-5225-3814-1.ch009

Related Readings

Ye, X., Molitoris, I., & Anderson, D. (2018). Opening the Classroom to the World: A Grounded-Theory Study of Student Perceptions of Integrating Intercultural Competence Into Curriculum. In S. Dikli, B. Etheridge, & R. Rawls (Eds.), *Curriculum Internationalization and the Future of Education* (pp. 251–272). Hershey, PA: IGI Global. doi:10.4018/978-1-5225-2791-6.ch014

Yu, L. (2018). From Teaching Software Engineering Locally and Globally to Devising an Internationalized Computer Science Curriculum. In S. Dikli, B. Etheridge, & R. Rawls (Eds.), *Curriculum Internationalization and the Future of Education* (pp. 293–320). Hershey, PA: IGI Global. doi:10.4018/978-1-5225-2791-6.ch016

Zagalo-Melo, P., Atteberry, C., & Turner, R. (2018). Grounded Globalism: Regional Identity Hypothesis as a Framework for Internationalizing Higher Education Curriculum. In S. Dikli, B. Etheridge, & R. Rawls (Eds.), *Curriculum Internationalization and the Future of Education* (pp. 233–250). Hershey, PA: IGI Global. doi:10.4018/978-1-5225-2791-6.ch013

Zheng, J. (2018). International Student Mobility, Government Policies, and Neoliberal Globalization: Exploring Chinese Graduate Students' Perspectives on Pursuing Higher Education in Canada. In K. Bista (Ed.), *International Student Mobility and Opportunities for Growth in the Global Marketplace* (pp. 49–63). Hershey, PA: IGI Global. doi:10.4018/978-1-5225-3451-8.ch004

About the Contributors

Donna M. Velliaris holds two Graduate Certificates: (1) Australian Studies; and (2) Religious Education, two Graduate Diplomas: (1) Secondary Education; and (2) Language and Literacy Education, as well as three Master's degrees: (1) Educational Sociology; (2) Studies of Asia; and (3) Special Education. In 2010, Dr. Velliaris graduated with a PhD in Education focused on the social/educational ecological development of school-aged transnational students in Tokyo, Japan. Her primary research interests include: human ecology; schools as cultural systems; study abroad; and Third Culture Kids (TCKs). With publication of over 30 book chapters, titles comprise: *Academic reflections: Disciplinary acculturation and the first-year pathway experience in Australia* [Garnet]; *Conceptualizing four ecological influences on contemporary 'Third Culture Kids'* [Palgrave Macmillan]; *Culturally responsive pathway pedagogues: Respecting the intricacies of student diversity in the classroom* [IGI Global]; *Metaphors for transnational students: A moving experience* [Cambridge Scholars]; and *The other side of the student story: Listening to the voice of the parent* [Sense]. This is Dr Velliaris' fifth edited book with IGI Global, following the titles: *Handbook of research on study abroad programs and outbound mobility* (2016); *Handbook of research on academic misconduct in higher education* (2016); *Study abroad contexts for enhanced foreign language learning* (2017); and *Prevention and detection of academic misconduct in higher education* (2019).

* * *

Renier Coetzee is a Senior Lecturer at the School of Pharmacy at the University of the Western Cape in Cape Town, South Africa. He holds a Graduate Degree (BPharm) and a Master's Degree (MPharm) from North West University in Potchefstroom, South Africa and a PharmD degree from Rhodes University in Grahamstown, South Africa. He serves as clinical facilitator for exchange programs with various US universities, allowing students and faculty an opportunity to visit

About the Contributors

health care institutions in South Africa. Dr Coetzee is a member of the South African National Department of Health's Standard Treatment Guideline and Essential Medicines List Committee and various local health department committees. He has a keen interest in rational medicine use, quality improvement and health outcomes in vulnerable populations, as well as antimicrobial stewardship. As a practicing clinical pharmacist, he collaborates nationally and internationally to advance the practice of clinical pharmacy in South Africa.

Jane Jackson (PhD, U of Toronto) is Professor in the English Department at the Chinese University of Hong Kong, where she teaches courses in applied linguistics/intercultural communication. Her research centers on education abroad, intercultural communication, language and identity, and eLearning. Recent Routledge books include: *Online intercultural education and study abroad: Theory into practice* (2019); *Interculturality in international education* (2018); *Intercultural interventions in study abroad* (2018, co-edited with Susan Oguro); *Introducing language and intercultural communication* (2014); and *The Routledge handbook of language and intercultural communication* (2012). She has also authored: *Intercultural journeys: From study to residence abroad* (Palgrave MacMillan, 2010); and *Language, identity, and study abroad: Sociocultural perspectives* (Equinox, 2008).

Yasemin Kırkgöz is a Professor in the English Language Teaching Department of Çukurova University, Turkey. Her main research interests include English for Academic and Specific Purposes, English-medium instruction in higher education, Problem-Based Learning (PBL), language policy, curriculum renewal and innovation management, pre-service and in-service teacher education, and study abroad programs. She has published in a number of international journals including *Teaching and Teacher Education, Educational Policy, Teaching in Higher Education* and *Current Issues in Language Planning*. She received the 2013 IATEFL award for her work on Initiating and Managing the Process of Curriculum Innovation from the IATEFL's Leadership and Management Special Interest Group. She is the co-editor of the book *Key issues in English for specific purposes in higher education* published by Springer in 2018.

Beth Nardella is an Associate Professor of Exercise Physiology in the Department of Human Performance and Applied Exercise Science housed in the West Virginia University School of Medicine's Professional Programs. She earned her Master's degree in English from West Virginia University in 2004 after finishing a Master's of Fine Arts from the University of North Carolina at Chapel Hill. Dr Nardella also

About the Contributors

serves as the Academic Coordinator for Amizade, a non-profit organization based in Pittsburgh, Pennsylvania. She has travelled with students to Jamaica, Trinidad, and Brazil on multiple faculty-led programs in addition to facilitating numerous international experiences for faculty and students engaged in global service learning at West Virginia University.

Douglas Slain is a Professor and Infectious Diseases Clinical Specialist at West Virginia University (WVU) and at WVU Healthcare Hospital. He received his BS Pharmacy degree and his Doctor of Pharmacy degree from Duquesne University. He completed a residency and fellowship in Infectious Diseases Pharmacotherapy at the Medical College of Virginia-Virginia Commonwealth University. Dr Slain serves as a consultant on antibiotic stewardship and on developing education and training programs related to clinical pharmacy, and has participated in consultant and exchange programs in Asia, South America, and Europe. Dr Slain serves as the WVU School of Pharmacy Global Affairs Liaison and is a member of the WVU Health Sciences Center Global Engagement Steering Committee. He is serving as a school representative for the US-Thai Consortium for the Advancement of Pharmacy Education in Thailand and was a recent recipient of a Fulbright Specialist Scholarship which supported a project in India.

David Starr-Glass is a mentor with the International Education (Prague) at SUNY Empire State College. He teaches a range of business and cross-culture courses online and is also a dissertation supervisor for undergraduate dissertations in business and economics. Over the last 20-years, he has published more than 100 book chapters and peer-reviewed articles. David has earned Master's degrees in business administration, occupational psychology, and online education. When not in Prague, he lives in Jerusalem and teaches economics and business-related courses at several local colleges.

Sven Tuzovic is Senior Lecturer of Marketing at the QUT Business School. Prior to joining QUT, Dr Tuzovic was Associate Professor at the Business School of Pacific Lutheran University, Tacoma WA, in the US. He was a Visiting Professor at Griffith University, Murray State University, and the University of New Orleans. He holds a Doctoral Degree in Marketing from the University of Basel in Switzerland, a Master's Degree from the Catholic University of Eichstaett-Ingolstadt in Germany, and a BBA from Georgia Southern University. His research has been published in several academic journals including the *Journal of Service Management* and *Journal of Services Marketing*, and in international conference proceedings. Dr Tuzovic is currently Associate Editor of the *Journal of Services Marketing*.

260

About the Contributors

Karin Vogt is a professor for Teaching as a Foreign Language at the University of Education Heidelberg, Germany. Her research interests include intercultural learning, teaching practicums abroad, vocationally oriented language learning, classroom-based language assessment, the Common European Framework of Reference for Languages and media and telecollaboration in the foreign language classroom.

Jon P. Wietholter is a Clinical Associate Professor at West Virginia University School of Pharmacy (WVUSOP), an Adjunct Associate Professor at West Virginia University School of Medicine (WVUSOM), and an Internal Medicine Clinical Pharmacist at WVU Medicine Ruby Memorial Hospital in Morgantown, WV, where he collaborates with the West Virginia University Internal Medicine department. He earned his Doctor of Pharmacy degree from the University of Pittsburgh in 2007 and completed a PGY-1 pharmacy practice residency at Pitt County Memorial Hospital in Greenville, NC. Additionally, Dr Wietholter developed and coordinates an international 'Advanced Pharmacy Practice Experience' (APPE) in South Africa completed by 4th Year WVUSOP students. His practice interests cover a broad range of topics within the world of internal medicine, with a specific interest in healthcare in underserved populations such as South Africa.

Index

A

acculturation 80-82, 90, 104-106, 169, 173
acute care 115-116, 118-119
ambulatory care 118-120

C

cultural capital 33, 37-38, 48
cultural competence 133
cultural sensitivity 111-112, 114, 134
culture confusion 81-82, 96
Cultures of Learning 81, 84
curriculum 64, 67, 91, 122, 144-145, 151, 198-200, 204, 207, 210-213, 216, 219-221

E

education abroad 6, 10, 16, 26-28, 30, 35, 88
Erasmus + 203-204
experiential learning 60-61, 122, 145, 180, 210-211

F

focus group 59, 62-63, 71, 143, 153-156, 164, 167, 183, 219

G

global citizenship 113, 118, 125, 144-145, 147, 150, 199
global engagement 113-114, 124
global health 112-115, 125, 128

I

intercultural awareness 31-33, 38, 40, 43, 47-49, 149, 155, 183
intercultural competence 32, 35, 40, 48, 57-58, 61, 88-89, 144, 147-151, 155-156, 165, 174, 180, 182-183, 200
intercultural competency 32-33, 39
international exchange programs 1, 84, 104-105, 200
internationalization 4, 9, 31, 33, 58, 80, 104-105, 199, 201

L

Language Teaching 151, 201
liminality 31, 33, 40-41, 43, 45-47, 49
linguistic competence 83

N

needs analysis 182, 204, 221
non-governmental organizations 113

O

operant resources 60, 67-68, 72

P

problem scenarios 198, 218-220
professionalization 145, 152, 157, 159, 164, 177-180, 182-183

Index

R

resource integration 57, 63, 65, 67

S

second language socialization 80
service-dominant logic 57, 59
service-learning 61, 113, 118, 199
study abroad 1-3, 7-10, 16, 19, 26, 31-38,
40-41, 43, 45, 47-49, 57-73, 80-81,
83-84, 86, 88-91, 94, 96, 104-107, 112,
144-153, 155, 170, 178-183, 198-206,
210-216, 218-221
study abroad duration 33

T

teacher education 151, 154, 198, 204, 215,
219-221
teaching practicums 143-144, 150-153,
155, 176, 178-183

Purchase Print, E-Book, or Print + E-Book

IGI Global's reference books can now be purchased from three unique pricing formats:
Print Only, E-Book Only, or Print + E-Book.
Shipping fees may apply.

www.igi-global.com

Recommended Reference Books

ISBN: 978-1-5225-9348-5
© 2019; 454 pp.
List Price: $255

ISBN: 978-1-5225-7763-8
© 2019; 253 pp.
List Price: $175

ISBN: 978-1-5225-7531-3
© 2019; 324 pp.
List Price: $185

ISBN: 978-1-5225-7802-4
© 2019; 423 pp.
List Price: $195

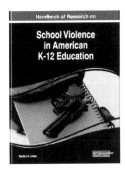

ISBN: 978-1-5225-6246-7
© 2019; 610 pp.
List Price: $275

ISBN: 978-1-5225-2998-9
© 2018; 352 pp.
List Price: $195

Looking for free content, product updates, news, and special offers?
Join IGI Global's mailing list today and start enjoying exclusive perks sent only to IGI Global members.
Add your name to the list at **www.igi-global.com/newsletters**.

Publisher of Peer-Reviewed, Timely, and Innovative Academic Research

IGI Global
DISSEMINATOR of KNOWLEDGE

www.igi-global.com | Sign up at www.igi-global.com/newsletters | facebook.com/igiglobal | twitter.com/igiglobal

Ensure Quality Research is Introduced to the Academic Community

Become an IGI Global Reviewer for Authored Book Projects

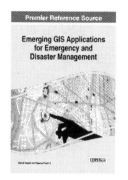 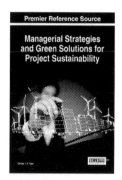  

The overall success of an authored book project is dependent on quality and timely reviews.

In this competitive age of scholarly publishing, constructive and timely feedback significantly expedites the turnaround time of manuscripts from submission to acceptance, allowing the publication and discovery of forward-thinking research at a much more expeditious rate. Several IGI Global authored book projects are currently seeking highly-qualified experts in the field to fill vacancies on their respective editorial review boards:

Applications and Inquiries may be sent to:
development@igi-global.com

Applicants must have a doctorate (or an equivalent degree) as well as publishing and reviewing experience. Reviewers are asked to complete the open-ended evaluation questions with as much detail as possible in a timely, collegial, and constructive manner. All reviewers' tenures run for one-year terms on the editorial review boards and are expected to complete at least three reviews per term. Upon successful completion of this term, reviewers can be considered for an additional term.

If you have a colleague that may be interested in this opportunity, we encourage you to share this information with them.

IGI Global Proudly Partners With eContent Pro International

Receive a 25% Discount on all Editorial Services

Editorial Services

IGI Global expects all final manuscripts submitted for publication to be in their final form. This means they must be reviewed, revised, and professionally copy edited prior to their final submission. Not only does this support with accelerating the publication process, but it also ensures that the highest quality scholarly work can be disseminated.

English Language Copy Editing

Let eContent Pro International's expert copy editors perform edits on your manuscript to resolve spelling, punctuaion, grammar, syntax, flow, formatting issues and more.

Scientific and Scholarly Editing

Allow colleagues in your research area to examine the content of your manuscript and provide you with valuable feedback and suggestions before submission.

Figure, Table, Chart & Equation Conversions

Do you have poor quality figures? Do you need visual elements in your manuscript created or converted? A design expert can help!

Translation

Need your documjent translated into English? eContent Pro International's expert translators are fluent in English and more than 40 different languages.

Hear What Your Colleagues are Saying About Editorial Services Supported by IGI Global

"The service was very fast, very thorough, and very helpful in ensuring our chapter meets the criteria and requirements of the book's editors. I was quite impressed and happy with your service."

– Prof. Tom Brinthaupt,
Middle Tennessee State University, USA

"I found the work actually spectacular. The editing, formatting, and other checks were very thorough. The turnaround time was great as well. I will definitely use eContent Pro in the future."

– Nickanor Amwata, Lecturer,
University of Kurdistan Hawler, Iraq

"I was impressed that it was done timely, and wherever the content was not clear for the reader, the paper was improved with better readability for the audience."

– Prof. James Chilembwe,
Mzuzu University, Malawi

Email: customerservice@econtentpro.com   www.igi-global.com/editorial-service-partners

www.igi-global.com

Celebrating Over 30 Years of Scholarly Knowledge Creation & Dissemination

InfoSci-Books

A Database of Over 5,300+ Reference Books Containing Over 100,000+ Chapters Focusing on Emerging Research

GAIN ACCESS TO **THOUSANDS** OF REFERENCE BOOKS AT **A FRACTION** OF THEIR INDIVIDUAL LIST **PRICE**.

InfoSci®-Books Database

The **InfoSci®-Books** database is a collection of over 5,300+ IGI Global single and multi-volume reference books, handbooks of research, and encyclopedias, encompassing groundbreaking research from prominent experts worldwide that span over 350+ topics in 11 core subject areas including business, computer science, education, science and engineering, social sciences and more.

Open Access Fee Waiver (Offset Model) Initiative

For any library that invests in IGI Global's InfoSci-Journals and/or InfoSci-Books databases, IGI Global will match the library's investment with a fund of equal value to go toward **subsidizing the OA article processing charges (APCs) for their students, faculty, and staff** at that institution when their work is submitted and accepted under OA into an IGI Global journal.*

INFOSCI® PLATFORM FEATURES

- No DRM
- No Set-Up or Maintenance Fees
- A Guarantee of No More Than a 5% Annual Increase
- Full-Text HTML and PDF Viewing Options
- Downloadable MARC Records
- Unlimited Simultaneous Access
- COUNTER 5 Compliant Reports
- Formatted Citations With Ability to Export to RefWorks and EasyBib
- No Embargo of Content (Research is Available Months in Advance of the Print Release)

*The fund will be offered on an annual basis and expire at the end of the subscription period. The fund would renew as the subscription is renewed for each year thereafter. The open access fees will be waived after the student, faculty, or staff's paper has been vetted and accepted into an IGI Global journal and the fund can only be used toward publishing OA in an IGI Global journal. Libraries in developing countries will have the match on their investment doubled.

To Learn More or To Purchase This Database:
www.igi-global.com/infosci-books

eresources@igi-global.com • Toll Free: 1-866-342-6657 ext. 100 • Phone: 717-533-8845 x100

www.igi-global.com